THE STREETS OF LAREDO

American Wests
Sponsored by the Center for the Study of the American
West at West Texas A&M University

Alex Hunt, General Editor

THE STREETS
of LAREDO

Texas Modernity and
Its Discontents

José E. Limón

Foreword by Alex Hunt

Texas A&M University Press
College Station

First edition

On the cover: *Young but Not Afraid,* by Eric Bowman. Used by permission.

♾ This paper meets the requirements of ANSI/NISO Z39.48-1992 (Permanence of Paper). Binding materials have been chosen for durability.

Library of Congress Cataloging-in-Publication Data

Library of Congress Control Number: 2024945730
Identifiers: LCCN: 2024945730 | ISBN 9781648432705 (cloth) |
ISBN 9781648432712 (ebook)
LC record available at https://lccn.loc.gov/2024945730

Cover design by Noah Van Soest

In Memoriam
Juan Gómez-Quiñones
(1940–2020)

It begins somewhere in Texas and winds through
California.
—From his poetry collection, *Fifth and Grande Vista*
(1973)

and

Rolando Hinojosa
(1929–2022)

And home, home to Texas, our Texas,
That slice of hell, heaven,
Purgatory and land of our fathers.
—From his long poem, *Korean Love Songs* (1978)

Contents

Series Editor's Foreword, by Alex Hunt ix

Preface xiii

Introduction 1

1 Songs and Sites 24

2 Song and Signification 56

3 Modernity's Song 76

4 Siren Song. 124

Coda. 165

Notes. 167

Works Cited. 185

Index 201

Series Editor's Foreword

Alex Hunt

You may not be from Texas, but, as Lyle Lovett proclaims, "Texas wants you anyway." This song ran through my mind often even as I read José Limón's book about another Texas song, "The Streets of Laredo," which naturally dominated my internal radio's bandwidth. Limón's book does a fine job in helping us understand the peculiar interest that Texas holds for many non-Texans the world over (to say nothing of Texans themselves), as if the Lone Star State has a sort of gravitational pull that draws the unwary into its powerful orbit.

The same could be said of the American West more generally. The American West, which we inevitably encounter as an amalgam of physical geography and imaginary or generic realm, remains powerful in the American, and indeed the global, imagination. If the West is a frontier associated with violence, injustice, and exploitation, it can also be a place of negotiation, regeneration, and justice. The West continues to be a space of encounter, wherein some traditional ideas of the past are challenged by problems that face us in our present. This encounter is what Limón, in this book, considers as the cowboy's lament against "modernity and its discontents."

It is an old and well-recognized convention of the western genre that the cowboy rides away. Having made the world safe for civilization, the hero cannot be confined by that civilization, defined by the law, the church, the schoolhouse, and the domestic sphere of women that civilization enables and empowers. Similarly, as Limón shows us, "The Streets of Laredo" communicates the cowboy's "discontent" with or "dissent" from modernity. The cowboy's engagement with modernity, which is to say capitalist development of land and labor on the frontier, takes the familiar shape of the pleasures of "town"—the appeal of purchasing new clothing and gear along with morally fraught activities of gambling, drinking, and prostitution.

This moral peril, the idea that someone has "done wrong," goes all the way back to the earliest versions of "The Streets of Laredo," which have absolutely nothing to do with cowboys or Laredo. Certainly a great part of the appeal of Limón's book is his tracing the movement and evolution of "The Streets of Laredo" from its Anglo-Irish origins, its transformations through Spanish and Mexican and US history, its coming "home" to Laredo, Texas, and its rise to prominence among western folklorists. Along the way, Limón shows us how the tensions between Texas history and global modernity resonate with our negotiations of familiar scholarly binaries of local and global, traditional and modern, romantic and real. And through this analysis, Limón finds something authentic—though this is not his word—in "The Streets of Laredo" despite the many unknowns of the song's historical development.

In exploring such tensions, Limón's book hits the bullseye in my own ideal of Western American Studies at its best. The field of Western American Studies is not as prominent as I wish it were, though I could quickly point to many great scholars, books, and essays from previous eras and in our current moment that exemplify what is to me Western American Studies. But Jose Limón's latest effort, while of course important to many other areas of critical discourse, for me embodies Western American Studies and in turn my hopes for the Texas A&M University Press "American Wests" series. Limón takes the American West seriously as an actual place as well as an imaginative space. But for Limón, this space is further complicated by its emergence from local, regional, national, transnational, and globalized forces, all of which produce its unique "western" quality. Moreover, this western space is further charged with issues of identity, including race/ethnicity/nationality, gender/sexuality, class/capital/exploitation, along with associated issues of social and environmental justice. The American West is a space of both power and critique.

Importantly, in Limón's work there remains after the critique and the moral accounting sympathy and perhaps love—even for the problematical vaquero/cowboy who rides beyond the margins of Limón's hometown of Laredo. It is more difficult to dismiss this as nostalgia when we see the cowboy not as agent of imperialism but one of resistance. We are used to imagining the cowboy as the tool of expansion riding the western frontier of wilderness; we are much less inclined to imagine the cowboy as an agent of resistance riding the eastern frontier of industry, aware that the very forces that enable his way of life ensure its imminent demise. Like Gus McCrae in Larry McMurtry's *Lonesome Dove*, Limón's cowboy is deeply ambivalent about whether he's been on the right side of history. For Limón, this is what *The Streets of Laredo* is finally all about.

A significant "turn" late in Limón's book, focused on McMurtry's fiction, comes in relation to the historically male gendering of the cowboy hero. By means of a brilliant new reading of McMurtry's *Streets of Laredo*, Limón in the end shows us the elevation of the woman out west, even the prostitute implicated in the demise of the young cowboy who has "done wrong," who becomes the hero who saves the day. This hero, furthermore, need not ride away from the gates of town in the end, suggesting the many possibilities of the more constructive ends of modernity.

In one of my favorite discussions in the book, Limón speaks of the cowboy as having, despite all the problematic associations, something worthy of our attention and admiration, still. In a special category of modern labor, the cowboy is craftsman—highly skilled and creative in his work. Limón argues that the cowboy, because of his (literal, horseback) elevation, skill, and association with freedom, is in the best sense a laboring figure who has uniquely commanded respect and thus embodied the dignity of labor.

In my personal and intellectual enthusiasm for Limón's work, speaking of craftsmanship, I hope it will not seem facile to suggest, in conclusion, that what distinguishes Limón's book as a skilled and highly crafted piece of Western American scholarship is its dexterous multidisciplinary approach. Limón's is a skilled craft elevated through a long career of research, teaching, writing, and thinking, that can bring together history, literature, folklore, music; along with ideas from postcolonial, feminist, Mexican-American/Chicano Studies, Marxist, and other critical discourses. Collectively, these elements form, from "The Streets of Laredo," José Limón's *The Streets of Laredo*. What's in a song? Find out, and enjoy.

Preface

It seems to me that the imagery of book covers is usually bypassed and unremarked by readers who, of course, want to get to the reading. Indeed, I also suspect these covers are often overlooked by the authors themselves in the development of their narratives. I find this unfortunate, because they are literally one's first encounter with the book, and often, they are in themselves works of art—or should be—and, if well done, should illuminate what is therein, perhaps even offer the foundational premise of the story. So, let me take this opportunity to address the one that graces this book, this study of the cowboy ballad, "The Streets of Laredo." I chose my own cover with the enthusiastic approval of Texas A&M University Press and the editor of this series. I first came upon Eric Bowman's painting, *Young but Not Afraid*, at the Autry Museum of the American West in Los Angeles, while I was there viewing an exhibit of Mexican American activist photography of the 1960s. While at first glance, this conjunction between a cowboy and Mexican Americans would seem purely fortuitous, I now think it not because it brought together two of my personal and social commitments, both rooted in the same history albeit with distinct trajectories. One also has to ask why the Autry could host both. As my introduction will spell out in greater detail, I am a Mexican American from southern Texas with an ancestral linkage to *vaqueros* (ethnic Mexican cowboys); the latter, of course, forerunners and teachers of the Anglo-American Texas cowboy.[1] Such a cowboy is represented by Bowman's painting, but a close examination might also reveal that he could be a young *vaquero* as well, possibly biracial, since there is a long history of such interethnic relationships in the American West.

Since the late 1950s, I have primarily addressed the sociocultural condition of ethnic Mexicans in the United States in different ways, principally academic. I have also always been and will always be a Texan, even today with residence in California. Any Texan of any duration will understand this persistent and sometime insistent Texas identity, not merely as a regional placeholder in answer to "where are you from?"—but a commitment that can be articulated in various ways, deep and shallow, conscious and unconscious, for better and worse. The Texas cowboy with his latent Mexican identity has always been one symbolic locus of my Texas identity—not the "cowboys" of western films nor of the Saturday night *Travoltian* sort, all hat, sequined shirts, tight jeans and no cattle, but rather ordinary working cowboys much as represented by Bowman without any discernible idealizing fanfare and with that steady look across the open range and into a future he can barely discern. For me, but I suspect of others as well, this ordinary working cowboy—working with his horse—is always imaginable as a quiet, socially efficient and socially integrated being whose hard labor on the open ranges that were once Texas carried its own intrinsic redemption, a feeling now transferred to us in our need. We'll get to "The Streets of Laredo" momentarily, but, for now, when I first viewed Bowman's work, I easily imagined that his subject could have been one of the cowboys in this ballad, and I immediately decided that he would be on the cover even as this book was just in its beginning stages. I am most grateful to Eric Bowman for his kind permission.

The beginnings of this book actually occurred in graduate school as a short class discussion paper circa the early 1970s, but it then went into abeyance as other priorities emerged, especially my growing specialization in Mexican American Studies.[2] There it remained, until I received a notification and an invitation from the *Western Literature Association* in 2018, more precisely from Professor Emily Lutenski of St. Louis University, representing the WLA. I was informed that I had been selected to receive the WLA's Distinguished Achievement Award for that year and was invited to attend the annual conference to receive such, but I was also asked to deliver a major lecture suitable for the association and the occasion. I suppose I could have prepared a topic based on my Mexican American Studies scholarship, not at all inappropriate given that most of this population does indeed continue to reside in the American West as they have since 1598. And, in the recent past, the WLA and its journal, *Western American Literature*, have been more than hospitable to such a topic. However, I wanted to do something that would have a broader appeal to the WLA membership, and also something new for me, while perhaps still retaining my commitments to Mexican America.

I finally recalled that early graduate student paper I had done on the cowboy ballad, "The Streets of Laredo," about Anglo cowboys but with its supposed setting in a very Mexican American Laredo, Texas, and its implicit evocation of *vaqueros*. Almost needless to say, since it was a short paper, written in that ancient time before electronic documents, I no longer had that essay, so, for the WLA, I retrieved what I could from memory and fashioned the rest from new research and secondary reading. It helped immeasurably that I had read and taught Larry McMurtry's novel, *Streets of Laredo*, and thus the various pieces started falling into place to produce that lecture for WLA with the simple title "The Streets of Laredo." It has since expanded into the present book, but I continue to be most grateful to Emily Lutenski and the WLA for making possible its beginning.

The lecture was well received, at least to judge from the Q&A, but more so from the very kind informal comments offered to me afterward throughout the conference. As it happened, one conference attendee, Professor Alex Hunt of West Texas A&M University in Canyon, Texas, was sufficiently impressed that as Director of WTAMU's Center for the Study of the American West (CSAW), he then invited me to present "The Streets of Laredo" as CSAW's annual Gary L. Nall Distinguished Lecture on that campus in October 2019. I did revise and expand it for that occasion in a manner appropriate to that West Texas setting famous for its Palo Duro Canyon, and it became "From the Streets of Laredo to the Palo Duro Canyon and Other Texas Stories." My wife and I were there for the lecture, but a freak West Texas snowstorm—much as could also come upon cowboys on the open range in the nineteenth century—descended upon Canyon, and it had to be canceled due to unsafe driving conditions for the attendees. Then, along came COVID, making rescheduling untenable. I was finally able to present the lecture, but only in a YouTube video format (Limón 2020). Shortly thereafter, by serendipity, Texas A&M University Press named Alex as the new editor of their book series, "American Wests," and, in return for his kindness and generous interest in the project, I offered my developing book manuscript for the series. After its completion and the appropriate reviews, the book was accepted and now here we are. I thank my two reviewers—one anonymous—for their very helpful commentaries but especially Professor Cordelia Barrera from Texas Tech University who identified herself. But again, I cannot thank Alex Hunt and TAMU Press enough for this opportunity, and I thank him even more for introducing me to such a hospitable social and academic environment at WTAMU and for his friendship as well as that of his wife, Professor Bonnie Roos, and other colleagues at WTAMU. I also thank Sherry Howard Salois for her very competent and generous copyediting, and Helen Wheeler for her very professional editorial management of the project.

The only major drawback to my retirement in Long Beach, California, has been a relative inaccessibility to a major academic library. This problem was then compounded by COVID when, at my age, I could no longer make occasional and very long trips to UCLA or even to Austin where I have borrowing and research privileges at my former academic home, the University of Texas. Later, however, I also taught at the University of Notre Dame and served as Director of its Institute for Latino Studies where, of course, I also continue to have borrowing privileges at its wonderful Hesburgh Library. The staff at the Institute, principally Idalia Maldonado and Maribel Rodríguez, responded to my dire need by arranging mail delivery of Hesburgh books to my Long Beach home as needed. I am most grateful to Laly and Mari. I can truly say that this book would not have been possible without them. I also thank the current ILS Director, Luis Fraga.

As we shall soon see in greater detail, as a ballad, "The Streets of Laredo" has an Anglo-Irish ancestry that ostensibly made its way to the American West in the nineteenth century via an Irish-origin population now migrating internally, primarily from the eastern United States. One such person was William McKenna, who came west and found work on the new railroads into the west, those that would also make the Texas cattle drives profitable and therefore possible with cowboy labor. However, in comparison to most of his Anglo-Irish brethren, William did something a bit unusual. It is often forgotten that those same railroad companies were also connecting their westering tracks with lines south into Mexico in the 1870s, supported by the new and autocratic Mexican government of Porfirio Díaz. William also helped to build those connecting lines into Mexico, but once he was done railroading, he chose to remain in Mexico, married a Mexican woman, and raised a Mexican family who, of course, carried his name, "McKenna." He changed his first name to "Guillermo" (Spanish equivalent for William) and surely learned Spanish, but it would seem he did not pass on any English to his family who by that time were spelling the family name "Maquena," pronouncing it ma-keh-na.

Porfirio Diaz's autocracy then set in motion the Mexican Revolution of 1910, and like thousands of other Mexicans, William's children and grandchildren—*los Maquena*—now Mexicans in every respect, left a war-torn and starving Mexico for the United States on the same railroads that William had helped build, but this time going north. Passing through El Paso, many of them then headed to California—for *los Maquena*, specifically Wilmington, California—to work in the fish canneries and the docks of that port city, or in whatever work there was to be had. Eventually, one of them, William's grandson, José Luz McKenna, helped build Liberty ships for World War II and later joined the Teamsters when he went to work for a construction company. If only for purposes of citizenship paperwork, the family recovered their name as "McKenna," but, of course, they were also learning English in US schools. Through the present, they have raised generations of their extended family, producing a large assortment of college graduates with professional service as public administrators, K-12 teachers, attorneys, Special Forces military, and firefighters. These also included José Luz's and his wife Concepción's three daughters, now in retirement. Amelia, with an MA from UCLA, became an associate superintendent with the Los Angeles school district and now presides as the family matriarch. The other two women earned PhDs in comparative literature at UCLA. Irene served as professor of English and Mexican American Studies at Cal State-Domínguez Hills, while Teresa became professor of English and American Studies at the University of Southern California and chair of their English department and then later my wife. In addition to bringing me into this wonderful and supportive family, Teresa has, of course, read every line of the manuscript for this book, and I am much indebted to her for that, but also for her always stimulating conversation and her wide-ranging literacy across the Western canon but also Native American and Mexican American literature. She has now added cowboy balladry. But above all, I have had her immeasurable and enduring love to sustain me in the later years of my life and to afford me the time for the writing of this book. *Mi compañera de primera.* As I write, our daughter, Renata, is completing her PhD in American history at the Graduate Center, City University of New York. Yes, she is aware of the job market, but she loves the field and is an unrepentant intellectual. Her love and support also contributed to the writing of this book, for which she also provided critical commentary.

This book came to fruition at the end of a long academic career spelled out in more detail in the introduction that follows. During that career, I became increasingly aware of what I see as an unwelcome divergence between the general, well-educated public and most academic writing in the humanities and social sciences. It is my hope that this book and its prose will have a broader appeal to a well-educated, culturally literate audience interested in these matters, encompassing but not restricted to the world of academia.

Finally, I dedicate this book in memoriam to two of the foremost Mexican American intellectuals I have ever known: the late Juan Gómez-Quiñones and Rolando Hinojosa, both important contributors to the study of the American

West. In an older language, they were both men of letters. Born and raised in East LA, Juan served as a distinguished professor of history at UCLA and was only too well known for his magnificent research and writing on Mexican American labor history and politics but also for his essays and poetry. Juan spent a postdoctoral year at the University of Texas at Austin, a momentous time where he inspired Texas labor historians such as Emilio Zamora and Victor Nelson-Cisneros. Emilio is presently the George W. Littlefield Professor of American History at the University of Texas at Austin, a prolific Texas A&M University Press author, and my good friend. Victor, my dear best friend, died recently after a distinguished career as associate dean of Colorado College. While in Austin, Juan also published the book of poetry cited in my dedication. For his part, Rolando Hinojosa was born and raised in the Lower Rio Grande Valley of South Texas. After a University of Illinois at Urbana PhD, he went on to serve as the Ellen Clayton Garwood Professor of English at the University of Texas at Austin. He will always be remembered for his *Klail City Death Trip* series, his novelistic saga of Mexicans in Texas from the eighteenth century to the present. Rolando was also a combat veteran of the Korean War, and the saga also includes his long poem, *Korean Love Songs*, also cited for this dedication. Both men were also my very close friends, and I think of them almost every day. I think they would both be pleased with this book.

THE STREETS OF LAREDO

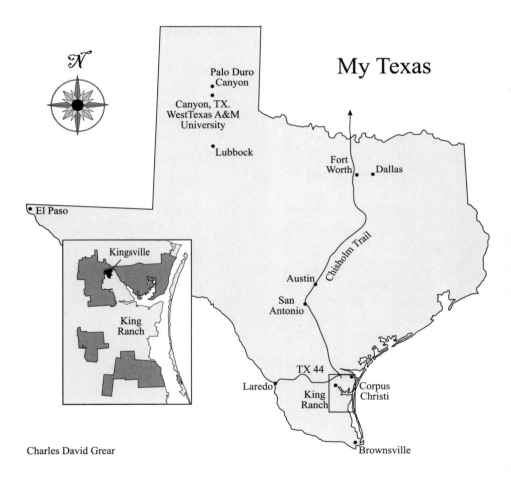

My Texas

Palo Duro Canyon

Canyon, TX.
WestTexas A&M
University

Lubbock

Fort Worth

Dallas

Chisholm Trail

El Paso

Kingsville

King Ranch

Austin

San Antonio

TX 44

Laredo

King Ranch

Corpus Christi

Brownsville

Charles David Grear

Introduction

"The Streets of Laredo," also known as "The Cowboy's Lament," is "the most famous of American cowboy ballads," or so said Wayland Hand, an eminent UCLA folklorist, in 1958 (200). Five years later, Américo Paredes, another folklorist and a native Texan, also spoke of this ballad's "fame" (1963, 236). Like Hand, Paredes would also achieve eminence—he, at the University of Texas at Austin (Limón 2012, 72–99). Both scholars seemed to mean that the ballad was famous in its own time and place in the later-nineteenth-century United States and then into the early twentieth, when it was first collected by folklorists, amateur and professional, but its fame had been continuous throughout their own time and to the present day. Ostensibly set in the then small "border town" of Laredo, Texas, this nineteenth-century song spawned many sung renditions by well-known popular artists into our own time. It has also deeply influenced films, modern poetry, a short story collection, three novels, a television series, memoirs, and pop-rock music. In a more recent instance, the Coen brothers used it in their 2018 film, *The Ballad of Buster Scruggs*, because, they said, it is "familiar to almost everyone" (Coen and Coen, 2018b).

Professors Hand and Paredes spoke of its fame, and the Coen brothers speak of the "familiar," but none of them tried to explain this fame and familiarity, nor has anyone else asked why this should be the case. What is it about this ballad—its imagery, narrative style, tonality, and tempo, but also its historical contexts—that should make for such fame and familiarity from the later nineteenth century into the present? This is the general question I shall try to address in this book. With such a familiarity, by now perhaps some of you may be itching to stream the song on YouTube or such. Those closer to my age, and in a fit of nostalgia, may even be hunting for those old Burl Ives, Joan Baez, Marty Robbins, or Johnny Cash LPs in the garage. Let me save you the trouble. Here are the lyrics as arranged by John A. Lomax and his son, Alan.

"The Streets of Laredo"

As I walked out in the streets of Laredo,
As I walked out in Laredo one day,
I spied a dear cowboy wrapped up in white linen,
Wrapped up in white linen as cold as the clay.

"I see by your outfit that you are a cowboy"—
These words he did say as I boldly stepped by.
"Come sit down beside me and hear my sad story:
I'm shot in the breast and I know I must die.

"It was once in the saddle I used to go dashing,
It was once in the saddle I used to be gay;
First to the dram-house, then to the card-house:
Got shot in the breast, I am dying to-day.

"Oh, beat the drum slowly and play the fife lowly, in the o-riginal
Play the dead march as you carry me along;
Take me to the green valley, there lay the sod o'er me,
For I'm a young cowboy, and I know I've done wrong.

"Get six jolly cowboys to carry my coffin;
Get six pretty maidens to bear up my pall;
Put bunches of roses all over my coffin,
Put roses to deaden the clods as they fall.

"Then swing your rope slowly and rattle your spurs lowly,
And give me a wild whoop as you carry me along;
And in the grave throw me and roll the sod o'er me
For I'm a young cowboy and I know I've done wrong.

"Go bring me a cup, a cup of cool water,
To cool my parched lips," the cowboy then said;

Before I returned his soul had departed,
And gone to the round-up—the cowboy was dead.

We beat the drum slowly and played the fife lowly,
And bitterly wept as we bore him along;
For we all loved our comrade, so brave, young, and handsome,
We all loved our comrade although he'd done wrong.
(1947, 264–265)

And this is the accompanying musical score (fig. 1) by Charles and Ruth Seeger, Pete's parents.

Lomax and Lomax offered this important example, but there are very many different versions varying principally in the arrangement and/or selective use of stanzas although the overall lyrics do not change much (1947). As with the stanzaic arrangement, the usually lento tempo can also have several variations, as can the rhythm and accompanying instrumentation, although the guitar is always central. This condensed 1947 version seems to be the more accepted standard version, and I will return to it in detail before too long. But, it is based on a much longer version of this ballad, initially collected and published in 1910 by the elder Lomax, John Avery, a Texan whom we will meet later in greater detail. Both this longer version and Lomax Sr. himself had their moment of fame and familiarity.

An introduction to a book should serve at least two purposes. It should certainly tell you what you might expect to find in the book, i.e., its contents and its argument. I have already said something about my central subject—this ballad and its interpretation—or lack thereof, an absence which I propose to remedy. To this end, I will center this ballad in Texas where it is thought that it first appeared, where it seemed to have its greatest saliency among Texas anglophone cowboys, and where it was first collected. From this probable Texas base, many versions of it would appear nationally and even internationally, probably owing initially to the Texas cowboy's migratory influence throughout the American West; and later, of course, to the general diffusion of American folksong through assorted means. The ballad's appearance, saliency, and collection may also speak to the distinctive, if not unique, role of Texas in the development of modernity, the central socioeconomic but also cultural process in world history since at least the eighteenth century. To the substantial degree that we can trace this ballad to cowboys in the nineteenth century, as a developing thesis I argue that "The Streets of Laredo" may have articulated a dissenting perspective toward such a modernity in Texas, but

The Streets of Laredo

Words and melody adapted and arranged by
John A. and Alan Lomax

Piano arrangement by
Charles and Ruth Seeger

Figure 1. *Source:* Lomax and Lomax (1947, 264).

perhaps other places as well, a discontent with modernity with a response keyed on their horse culture and on this ballad.

The ballad's likely origin as "The Streets of Laredo" in the nineteenth century, however, was mediated in the twentieth when the ballad garnered the greatest attention and did so principally from two prominent Texas literary intellectuals: the aforementioned John Avery Lomax (1867–1947) and the late Larry McMurtry (1935–2021). To a substantial degree, then, this book is also about these two formidable Texas writers. In their respective treatments of this ballad, we find a continuing negotiation with modernity that nineteenth-century Texas cowboys may have experienced and articulated through "The Streets of Laredo," but was also carried into the twentieth by these two writers who, as Texas literary intellectuals, were especially sensitive to an intensified modernity in their native Texas. They were not and have not been alone in this regard. Thus, my interpretive effort will be largely confined to Texas—already a very large sociocultural space—although further and broader studies may also be warranted.

An introduction may also offer something of a broader rationale, a more encompassing and perhaps more personal reason for the book's existence, as it were, especially if that project represents a departure from past work. This book is such, and I hope that what follows will prove interesting to my readers, especially those familiar with my past work, although it may also be inherently interesting in itself as a kind of brief essay on Texas history. My trajectory toward this ballad and therefore this book has been at once a personal, social, and academic voyage, a career that now paradoxically is coming to a close with "The Streets of Laredo." I say "paradoxically," because, given the twentieth-century Texas history that I inherited and lived through, it would seem unusual to now be writing this book—unusual that is, in its ethnic subject, the Texas anglophone cowboy and this ballad. However, this interest has been in abeyance for some time and harkens back to southern Texas, the formative context for the emergence of "The Streets of Laredo" and of my own life and career.

FROM THE STREETS OF LAREDO...

To begin with—and in the interests of full disclosure—I was born in Laredo, Texas, in 1944 and largely raised there as a member of a predominantly ethnic Mexican-origin community that made up most of the then small city's population and still does even as the city has now grown greatly. While we were, in effect, "Mexican Americans," such ethnic labels were rarely deployed. In everyday life, if any such a reference was even required, we were simply *mexicanos* (Mexicans). Since Mexico was just across the river, when socially necessary, we might politely say we were *mexicanos de aquí* (Mexicans, but from "here"). However, the English term, "Mexican," was almost never heard, nor even "Mexico." We would simply say "*el otro lado*" (the other side) and Mexican citizens of Nuevo Laredo just across the Rio Grande would say the same thing about the United States. (Indeed, for a good part of my childhood, I thought that the name of this town across the river was *Elotrolado* with all five syllables phonetically run together as one word).

Nevertheless, we mexicanos de aquí, were American citizens as well, mostly native-born. After all, did we not celebrate George Washington's Birthday every February in a citywide festival lasting a week (Peña 2020; Cantú 2023)?[1] And, we were for the most part fluent in an everyday American culture, including the English language. Nevertheless, Laredo was a town where Spanish was the first language. A formal, if slightly accented, English was reserved for official sites and occasions—school, the legal system, news media, etc., although at times even these included some Spanish.[2] There were few Anglo-Americans in town, or *americanos*, as we called them, although they also often learned to speak Spanish, or at least their children did.[3]

At that time, for a lower-middle-class Mexican American family like ours, trying to ascend to middle-class status or better, Laredo was the most comfortable of spaces in comparison to other Texas places. As mexicanos de aquí and the dominant demographic—and unlike most of the rest of Texas—we were also very well-accustomed to having successful Laredo Mexican Americans in the law, banking, accountancy, medicine, education, public service, and the export-import business, the latter two focused principally at the International Bridge into Mexico. There were also several small-business entrepreneurs like my mom and dad with their small grocery store. Had we remained in Laredo, I have little doubt that I would have returned to Laredo into one of these occupations after college. Although we were decidedly lower middle class, there was no question that I was going to college, probably at St. Mary's University in San Antonio or St. Edward's University in Austin, not surprisingly, since we were all mostly Roman Catholic, and many of us attended Laredo's Catholic schools. The correlated expectation was that I would marry a girl-next-door, she very likely a graduate of Our Lady of the Lake or Incarnate Word, both women's colleges also in San Antonio, with the likely career as a teacher in Laredo.[4] Norma Elia Cantú, professor at Trinity University in San Antonio, immediate past President of the

American Folklore Society, and my cogenerational colleague and friend, is also a native of Laredo. Her recent ethnographic novel, *Cabañuelas*, well captures our shared Laredo at that time (2019).

Our shared sense of Laredo could be taken as bordering on the idyllic, so I must also note that the city has a history of machine politics and seemingly intractable poverty, especially after the Mexican Revolution of 1910. Fernando Piñón, also a native Laredoan from this generation, and a former editor of its principal newspaper, is an astute critical observer of this other Laredo. In yet another example of our ballad's influence, the title of Piñón's book, written in San Antonio, is *Searching for America in the Streets of Laredo*, although I would have used the preposition "from" rather than "in." While growing up amidst such poverty, he nevertheless also evinces a sense of Laredo as a special mexicano enclave in which he derived great benefit from a first-rate Catholic education. It was only when he left Laredo to live elsewhere in Texas that he "knew that outside my own world I was not truly welcomed in the Anglo American society that surrounded me" (2015, 34–88). Thus, it would be for me as well.

... TO THE BODY OF CHRIST

Given the total cultural but also economic circumstances that constituted Laredo, it is thus very likely I would not be writing this book, nor had the career I had, if we had remained in Laredo, the ostensible site for our ballad. When I was about ten in the mid-1950s, my father failed in his small grocery business, and, too proud to ask anyone in our small town for a job, he moved the family to Corpus Christi on the Texas Gulf Coast and spent the rest of his working life with HEB.[5] This move of some 150 miles across upper southern Texas would also change everything in my life and eventually take me from the streets of Laredo to "The Streets of Laredo." As we moved along Texas State Highway 44 in the big truck that my dad had borrowed, I could not know at the time that we were also traversing a significant part of Texas historical geography that would resurface for me in the story of this ballad.[6]

Very unlike Laredo, Corpus Christi and most of the rest of Texas at that time, was sharply divided between largely Catholic Mexicans and largely Protestant Anglo-Americans with the latter always and everywhere visibly in power and purveyors of a quite discernible racism.[7] Inevitably, a few Anglo kids (Jewish) in school were friendly enough, if only in slightly forced conversation, usually over school matters, always looking over our shoulders at our respective ethnic brethren as all such contacts were viewed with great suspicion.[8] It can easily be said that in Corpus Christi and most of Texas, Mexican Americans existed as an Other to Anglos.

For readers unfamiliar with the term, "the Other" has been used by philosophers and psychologists to name that which is not the putative human rational self, such as the Freudian unconscious. In analyzing the process of world colonization beginning in the sixteenth century from Europe outward, social scientists and cultural critics expanded the term to name the manner in which dominant social groups may view and treat their subordinates in a given social system. In such an arrangement, the term builds on but is not the same as social structural disparities such as in income and education. Rather, it refers more centrally to the dominant's view of subordinates as culturally different but inferior in matters such as intelligence, etiquette, language, labor, kinship practices, and general world view. To render peoples as differently inferior is to engage in Othering. However, being from Laredo and not at all accustomed to such "Othering," in Corpus Christi, I had the strange experience of actually Othering the Anglo; of thinking of them as somehow culturally inferior to me, at least in matters of etiquette (they were boorish), food (their endless mashed potatoes), language (in comparison to their unintelligible "Texas" drawl, my own Catholic school English was ever so much clearer and more precise), and I was fluent in Spanish as well. And, when it came to sexuality, my mom had a lot to say about Anglo girls. Even having now become a member of the lower working class in Corpus Christi, living in public housing, did not relieve me of a certain presumptuous Laredo sensibility. Let's call it counter-Othering, while clearly recognizing that all Othering often indulges in considerable stereotyping.

Yet even back in my Laredo childhood, I had already met a different kind of "Anglo": the cowboy on the silver screen, *a la* John Wayne, on Saturday afternoons at the Tivoli theatre much as did another little boy, Fernando Piñón (2015, 46). They afforded us our principal sense of "Anglos" that we admired, and such a filmic influence continued in Corpus Christi as well, albeit viewed from the back of the theater where mexicanos sat.[9] But, as it happened, by the unintended consequences of geography, there were also real cowboys in my teenage life. I had known of *vaqueros* (mexicano cowboys) working the Mexican American-owned ranches just outside Laredo.[10] But, in Corpus, one could occasionally see Anglo cowboys on Saturdays, or some semblance thereof, quite discernible in faux Stetsons, boots, and jeans.[11] There they were, not on the streets of Laredo, but on Chaparral Street, then the downtown shopping area in Corpus before the malls arrived.[12] I was told that they were from the famous King Ranch just south of Corpus, in town shopping on a Saturday off. Later in the evening, I heard they would make their way up to north Chaparral to a small collection of bars with country-and-western music on their jukeboxes. Although some seemed not much older than me, and I never talked to one, they seemed nice enough, and perhaps this was so because they worked alongside vaqueros, also at the King Ranch.

Vaqueros on the King Ranch were often called *kineños*.[13] With a great reputation for their cowboy skills, they were otherwise ordinary Mexican American citizens, although the best known of them, Lauro Cavazos, went on to earn a PhD and served as US Secretary of Education and President of Texas Tech University, his alma mater (Cavazos 2008).[14] The kineños also came into Corpus, but they seemed to prefer spending their Saturdays on Leopard Street in the traditional mexicano shopping zone punctuated with *cantinas* and *conjunto* music. Now, with hindsight, it is quite possible that people in Corpus may have been confusing kineños with stoop labor cotton pickers, plentiful in the surrounding Coastal Bend cotton growing area, especially in the summers, who also came into town on Saturdays. In Texas, cotton often overlapped with ranching. More likely it was a mix, with far more of the latter, encapsulating yet another cross-cultural theme in Texas history: the stoop laborer—white, black, or Mexican—versus his counterpart on horseback, but also the great Texas agricultural duality of cash crop farming versus cattle ranching, both of which will also concern us in these pages.

"Western" films and real-world cowboys thus first introduced me to my present concern, but music was decisive. For, indeed, it was in that moment of adolescence circa 1960 that I first heard "The Streets of Laredo" by Marty Robbins. Robbins, of course, became better known for the very popular, "El Paso," of that same moment. "El Paso" dealt with Anglo-mexicano, or more specifically, Anglo-*mexicana* romantic relationships, as the young cowboy in "El Paso" dies in the arms of his mexicana lover. Such inter-racial relationships were frowned upon in real world Corpus Christi (by both sides), although later, I would discover that this ethnic *nexus-sexus* had a much longer history in Texas, and that Marty Robbins may have been right on target; Anglo cowboys had taken up with Mexican women from the beginning (Limón 1998, 124–127). While "El Paso," with its "Mexican" sound, played an interesting role in Texas ethnic relations, I was actually much more taken with the Robbins rendition of "The Streets of Laredo" from that same period. At that adolescent moment in my life and in racist Corpus, I probably nevertheless identified with the dying young Anglo cowboy.

FOLLOWING THE CHISHOLM TRAIL
AND THE LONGHORNS

With all of this in my background, I eventually made my way to the University of Texas at Austin, transferring as a junior undergraduate in 1964 after two years at Del Mar, the local community college for which I will always be grateful. I did not then realize that in my trip up to Austin, I was essentially tracking the Old Chisholm Trail for cattle drives from the Corpus Christi area through Austin, Fort Worth, and then up to Kansas. My upcoming studies were first and foremost on my mind. I am convinced that my decision to first major in philosophy and English and then take up an MA in English, in addition to their intrinsic merits, were to some degree conditioned by my experience in Anglo-dominated Corpus Christi, as if to demonstrate that I could be a kind of universally transcendent "Anglo" in superior command of "their" culture as well as mine, although, of course, that academic culture really wasn't "theirs," at least not for most of them.[15] In effect, I would also be continuing my "Othering" of Anglos even more so than I already had based only on my Laredo cultural capital. Indeed, my original plan was to return to Corpus to teach high school English, possibly becoming the first Mexican American to do so in Corpus, and thus an implicit continuation of my "Othering."

This path, this peculiar kind of hubris, then took another direction. Anticipating my MA and encouraged by my "Anglo" professors, usually not native Texans, I began to apply for PhD programs in English (and received some acceptances) in the Ivy Leagues and other high-ranking places.[16] Then serendipity struck. In 1967, in the second year of my MA program at UT and as part of my departmental support, I was seemingly randomly assigned as a teaching assistant to one Professor Américo Paredes whom, in a large department, I had never heard of before. He taught folklore and American literature, and I had been spending my time in the thickets of Victorian literature and the Renaissance, undoubtedly also part of my racially tactical hubris. I had taken one undergraduate survey class in American literature which caught his attention, since he was scheduled to teach it that semester. But much more so, he told me later, he noticed my Spanish surname on the list of applicants and went no further down the list. An always present consciousness of ethnicity in Texas has thus made its way even into the halls of high academia.

ACADEMIC MEXICANOS

It did not take long to come under the Paredes spell. He was from my native South Texas (Brownsville), and, obviously, an already well-respected tenured member of the department. More obviously yet and with greater personal relevance, he was a *Mexican American* in an *English* department at the *University of Texas–Austin* in *1967*. Then, a perhaps even greater realization emerged. He had garnered such a status working in a field that I had never heard of before that he called "the folklore of Greater Mexico." I had grown up with such folklore—*lloronas, corridos, curanderos* and all; I just did not know that it could be the subject of academic work of the highest scholarly and intellectual quality, as I became familiar with his writings. I soon followed his lead by enrolling in the UT PhD program in folklore studies under his direction.[17]

Paredes's scholarship was particularly evident in his first book, *With His Pistol in His Hand: A Border Ballad and Its Hero* (1958), that he loaned to me because I was a poor graduate student and the library copy was perpetually checked out.[18] I did not realize at the time that this classic book would also lead to the present study of Anglo-Texan balladry. In 1901, the eponymous hero of the Mexican American ballad of Gregorio Cortez—the subject of the book— lived out an adversarial confrontation with Anglo lawmen, especially the hated Texas Rangers, in the very South Texas terrain that I knew and now even included the Austin area where his adventure actually began. A sheriff came to arrest him and his brother for horse thievery. The charge was false, compounded by a misunderstanding of language, but nevertheless the sheriff shot and killed Cortez's brother and in turn Cortez killed the sheriff "with his pistol in his hand." Knowing he would face certain lynching, he then fled for the Mexican border roughly following today's I-35 into South Texas, skillfully outriding and outshooting racist lawmen as he made for the border on a little mare. And, as if the book had been written just for me, Cortez actually reached safety in none other than *Laredo* before voluntarily giving himself up to save his wife and children who had been imprisoned precisely to force him to give up. After considerable litigation, he was finally set free. How could I and others not help but wish to be identified with this hero? According to folk legend, mexicanos in South Texas would say of him, "he was not too dark and not too fair, not too thin and not too fat, not too short and not too tall, and he looked just a little bit like me" (Paredes 1958, 34).[19] Even to this day, I cannot travel from Austin to South Texas without noting the places that Cortez rode through.

I have critically revisited this fundamental book many times (Limón 1981; 1991; 1992, 61–80; 1993; 2012, 72–89). Now and paradoxically, perhaps, I enlist *With His Pistol in His Hand* to my present purpose in taking up the Texas anglophone cowboy and "The Streets of Laredo." For, even as I was in rapt admiration of Paredes's Cortez, this Texas mexicano hero wrought so skillfully by my mentor, one could not help but notice Cortez's cultural proximity to the Texas anglophone cowboy of fact and fiction, an identity by way of the vaquero often missed in the very many commentaries on Paredes's book. As legend had it, "he was a vaquero, and a better one there has not ever been from Laredo to the mouth [of the Rio Grande][;] . . . no man knew a good horse better than Gregorio Cortez[,] . . . the best vaquero and range man that there ever was" (1958, 34–35). Folk legend also ascribes to Cortez a certain moral attitude that we also associate with the ideal cowboy.

> Gregorio Cortez was not of your noisy, hell-raising type. That was not his way. He always spoke low, and he was always polite, whoever he was speaking to. And when he spoke to men older than himself he took off his hat and held it over his heart. A man who never raised his voice to parent or elder brother, and never disobeyed. That was Gregorio Cortez, and that was the way men were in this country along the river. That was the way they were before these modern times came, and God went away. (35–36)

It is probably for these reasons that, according to Paredes, "not all people who came to Cortez's aid were of Mexican descent." A "curious ambivalence developed in the Anglo-American attitude toward him[;] . . . many people found it hard not to admire the courage, skill, and endurance of the hunted man" including undoubtedly his right to defend himself against injustice "with his pistol in his hand" (89). It would seem that their admiration for Cortez was conditioned by their admiration for the ideal Texas cowboy who surely would have done the same as Cortez in such circumstances. Thus, when it came to Mexicans in Texas, while Paredes placed the moral onus largely on the Anglo Texas Rangers and their interpreters such as Walter Prescott Webb, he also took great care to remind us that Cortez and mexicanos had considerable support within the Anglo-Texan community. Paredes also adds that "some very prominent Anglo-Texans were to come to the aid of Cortez, among them the Hon. F.C. Weinert, who was Texas secretary of state at the time . . . the lawyer who worked the hardest to get Cortez justice in the courts was R.B. Abernathy of Gonzales, the county where the . . . gunbattle took place and . . . in which prejudice against Cortez was the strongest" (89–90). Later, after being unjustly convicted and serving time in Huntsville, and with the recommendation of the warden who thought him a model prisoner, Cortez would be pardoned by Texas Governor O. B. Colquitt in 1913, who had to endure considerable vituperation from some Anglo-Texans (97–98). Paradoxically enough, it appears to be the case that in 1901, with the fading of the classical cattle drive cowboy, Gregorio Cortez on horseback may have momentarily replaced him at least symbolically for an Anglo-Texan public. Together with its strident criticism of Anglo-Texan racialized domination, *With His Pistol in His Hand* also recognized a political cultural diversity among Anglo-Texans, and I have also taken this lesson from my mentor.[20]

But this recognition extends to balladry as well, for this, after all, is my central subject. Paredes' book is, of course, focused on the native Texas mexicano balladry surrounding Gregorio Cortez and other similar mexicano heroes as well, or what he calls, the heroic ballad or *corrido* that expresses this critical relationship. But he then offers this observation about the other side. "In the conflict along the Rio Grande, the English-speaking Texan . . . disappoints us in a folkloristic sense. He produces no border balladry" (15). Paredes was mostly right. For him balladry usually emerges from the underdogs in social conflict who ultimately must give way to superior forces even though the good fight has been waged. In a wonderful comparison, he reminds us that "it was the Scot, usually on the losing side, who produced the most stirring of the British border ballads. On the Rio Grande it was only the losers in the conflict, the Border Mexicans, who produced ballads" (244). That is, it would seem that those who triumph in a conflictive social encounter do not need such a balladry which turns out to be a compensatory expressive instrument.

However, it is a fundamental premise of this study that the Anglo cowboy did face a truly formidable adversary—not Mexican nor Indian—but rather modernity, a faceless but far more powerful adversary, and to this end, he developed a different kind of balladry of social conflict such as "The Streets of Laredo" in a struggle he was bound to lose but in which he wages the good fight by way of this ballad, thereby initiating its fame. As it happens, Cortez also struggled against modernity by way of the railroad and mass communications. As Paredes notes, "the greatest handicap that Cortez faced . . . was the Corpus Christi to Laredo railroad. Special trains moved up and down the tracks, bearing men, horses, and dogs which kept in touch with other searching parties by telephone and telegraph" (74). This is part of the same modernity that Anglo-Texan cowboys also encountered. Such a modernity was a larger force and not as clearly delineated nor unambiguous as the Anglo-Texan was for the Mexican in Texas. It is not surprising that the resulting Anglo-Texan balladry such as "The Streets of Laredo" would be more allusive and indirect, an expression of discontent rather than a full-blown opposition. It therefore may not be the case that the Anglo-Texan "disappoints" because he produced "no border balladry" as Paredes says, but rather that it was balladry in a different register and not that of the "heroic." Hence, also, my argumentation may, at times, be more tentative and somewhat introspective in comparison to that of *With His Pistol in His Hand*. Nevertheless, the latter remains the major influence and model for this work. Indeed, a reviewer of this manuscript has graciously suggested that it may possibly be seen as "a companion piece to the classic *With His Pistol in His Hand*" (Barrera 2023, 3). I would be pleased and proud if that were the case, and I thank her, but I am not wholly persuaded. That is a very high bar!

THE NEW WESTERN HISTORY

Beyond this account of my own personal yet social history and the centrality of *With His Pistol in His Hand* to this study, I also want to take account of more recent scholarly issues, principally broached by the New Western history that Patricia Limerick and others initiated now some thirty odd years ago although the issues continue in the present day (Limerick et. al 1991; Aron 2016). Put perhaps too simply, Limerick and others lent great emphasis to the problematic aspects of the development of the American West in terms of racial, ethnic, and gendered oppression, environmental degradation, and the exploitation of labor in a capitalist-driven development. This development was seen as driven by a white male supremacy that had received a too uncritical understanding in a previous and now "old" American Western history (Armitage 1989; Malone 1989; Aron 2016). Surprisingly, this new history did not pay much focused, explicit attention to the cowboy in the nineteenth-century American West, for the most part subsuming and blurring him into the larger white imperial project of hegemony. In the most encompassing of the New Western histories, for example, the cowboy is briefly mentioned several times but not discussed as a distinct category (R. White 1991).[21]

Before too long, this New Western critique also flowed over into literary studies and continues to the present day and substantially questions the New Western History. I refer principally to *The New Western History: The Territory Ahead*, consisting mostly of literary critics who offered a range of critiques of the New Western perspective (Robinson 1997a; 1997b). I offer the following as a summary of these critical perspectives.

1. The New Western historians have not lent much attention to the literary including the popular literary.
2. Thinking that they alone have discovered the degraded character of the West, the New Western historians have ignored the plentiful dissidence, doubt, dissolution and despair in the kinds of traditional texts and sources that inform the Old Western historians including their personal careers.
3. Preferring tragedy as a mode of employment, the New Western historians would do well to pay more attention to Irony as a better way to apprehend Western discourses.
4. In their insistent portrayal of the repression of women and racial groups in the West, the New Western historians tend to ignore them as active agents in their own lives.

It is within these critiques in Robinson's volume that I wish to lodge my discussion of this song and its expressive legacy, eve as I note the absence of folklore especially cowboy balladry in their work.[22]

Yet one must also note the relative absence of folklore, especially the cowboy ballad in this work. One such study does bring up the folk balladry of cowboys (Tatum 1997). Stephen Tatum chastises the New Western history for wholly ignoring or demonizing the more imaginative, which is to say literary, representations of the cowboy in the nineteenth century. Such historians, quite specifically Limerick, viewed these usually romanticized representations as so much ideological masking of a white capitalist oppression. In response, Tatum argues for an examination of cowboy popular culture so as to understand that such cultural items and formations are not univocal, speaking only the hegemony of the dominant culture but are, rather, sites of negotiation and contradiction. As examples, he offers first, E. C. (Teddy Blue) Abbott's well-known 1939 memoir of his nineteenth-century cowboy days, followed by an extended discussion of Zane Grey's *Riders of the Purple Sage*, both intended to illustrate what he and the New Western historians mean by "popular" culture, which appears to be mass-mediated

productions including printed materials, films, television, etc., "for popular consumption by the masses desiring leisure time entertainment" (157). But this demarcation would seem not to include far more face-to-face orally transmitted and
relatively autochthonous cultural acts that we habitually have called folklore such
as our ballad. As a specific example of the "problem of the popular" in the New
Western history, Tatum does offer an anecdote from Abbott in which he and some
friends have a jocular discussion about "The Streets of Laredo," but the emphasis
is clearly on the anecdote itself rather than on the ballad (184). (We will return to
this instance of our ballad later in this book.) Thus, I seek to address a general
absence in the current scholarship which is any focused scholarly discussion of
the cowboy's vernacular creativity, especially his singing and even more so his singing of "The Streets of Laredo," this most famous of his ballads. We do find two
notable exceptions in another of Tatum's work but also that of Blake Allmendinger,
and these will be taken up in my more focused interpretive discussion of our ballad (Allmendinger 1992; Tatum 1994). While there has been a relative paucity of
attention to cowboy balladry in New Western literary studies, we are not at all
surprised given its focus on written texts such as the dime novel.

As will soon become more evident, this study is fundamentally focused on
folklore both as subject and discipline. Apart from several popular and general
collections of cowboy songs, we note a general absence of such analytical folkloristic work after the mid-twentieth century, especially on this particular ballad and
its folkloristic history. This absence is especially marked because, as we have
already seen, two major folklorists—Hand and Paredes—thought it worthy of
their attention in the 1950s and '60s we shall soon meet several others from that
same period.[23]

Finally, in this "review of the literature," let me also note another body of work
to stress what this book is *not* about, especially for readers wholly new to the subject. I do not offer a detailed accounting of the cattle industry nor of the full
spectrum of cowboy culture and labor practices such as the ubiquitous work on
"branding." These themes have been dealt with elsewhere and extensively, mostly
in popular histories, although I recommend David Dary's prodigious scholarship
(1989; 1995).[24] Allmendinger's study of cowboy "work culture" is less readable but
theoretically more engaging and will be recalled later (1992). For my part, I focus
only on the early modernization of the cattle drives—and on the subdued, residual romanticism of the cowboy on his horse on the open range and therefore this
ballad. Within this literature, however, my indebtedness to Jacqueline Moore's historical study of Texas cowboys will be evident everywhere. In the most helpful

fashion, she summarizes a great deal of historical scholarship on the cowboy that I try to distill here (2010).

As the reader will soon see, my personal and academic history taken together have also led me to a kind of interdisciplinary scholarly vision and ranging interests that I hope my various readers might find either eclectic, synoptic, or wide-ranging, but hopefully not that of a dilettante. Put another way, my interest in the Texas cowboy and "The Streets of Laredo" might be seen as a kind of palimpsest, or a stimulus for exploring other sometimes hidden layers of my native Texas and its history, society, and culture, including the preceding account of my personal history in relation to Texas, while also reaching out to global concepts such as Romanticism and cultural sites such as Haiti in a continuing and enlarging recognition of the Texas cowboy and his place in global culture. I can only hope that these seeming excursions will be tolerated and perhaps even welcomed by my readers in the certainty that I will always return to Texas and "The Streets of Laredo."

CHAPTER SUMMARIES

Chapter 1, "Songs and Sites," first offers an account and analysis of two ballad traditions and several sociocultural sites and formations that directly influenced the emergence of "The Streets of Laredo." I open with a review of the song's provenance from its putative origins in eighteenth-century Ireland from a pair of ballads about young people who die from sexually transmitted disease after socially illicit encounters. These two ballads are, respectively, "The Unfortunate Rake" and "The Bad Girl's Lament." This balladry then made its way into the nineteenth-century American West following two distinctive streams of Irish immigration into the United States wherein these Anglo-Irish songs were likely transformed into "The Streets of Laredo" in Texas, which then leads us into a review of Texas history and the material basis for this ballad's emergence.

Texas combined three unique correlated sociocultural factors that contributed significantly to our ballad. For this reason and because the readers of these pages may simply be wholly unfamiliar with this history, I offer my assessment of these factors with a detail that may perhaps seem excessive to some. Especially for those not well-versed in a complicated Texas history, I saw this as an opportunity to bring different aspects of this history together in an innovative way, that, although inspired by the cowboy and his ballad, nevertheless constitute their own distinctive contribution. The first of these is the state's origins as a colony of Spain and then Mexico which then led to their shared but sequential colonization of Texas that centered on ranching and gave rise to the vaquero. The Mexican phase of this colonization included the importation of colonists directly from Ireland, who then, in close contact with Mexican ranching in all probability account for the first anglophone cowboys in Texas and possibly an alternative origin point for our ballad in the United States. Secondly, after an almost ten-year period of independence, Texas was finally annexed to an expanding United States in 1845, followed by the rest of the US Southwest in 1848. Thirdly, after becoming a state, Texas then joined the Confederacy in 1861 with two significant outcomes for the state given its location at the geographical margins of the Old South: first, Texas did not experience the severe social dislocations in the Old South as a result of the Union victory, and therefore, second, Texas indeed took advantage of this sociogeographical privilege by quickly and fully embracing what I shall be calling *agricultural modernity* even as the Civil War was underway.

Agricultural modernity came to Texas in three significant cultural geographical arenas and two commodities: cotton and cattle. In general, that story is only too well established. Here, however, I want to specify two economic/cultural regions and activities. While cotton was very important in an eastern Texas contiguous to the Old South, here I briefly discuss the Civil War and contraband Southern cotton that directly affected Laredo, the supposed setting for our song. Of greater significance was the expansion of agricultural modernity in another direction, one centered on ranching and the long cattle drives from coastal South Texas to eastern markets via the Midwest from about the 1860s to the 1880s, the very length of these drives and the time they took determined by the sheer size of the state from its northern to its southern border with Mexico. Finally, such agricultural modernity also contributed to a nonagricultural form that also contributed to our ballad—small scale urbanization—by way of the towns established along the cattle trails: San Antonio, Waco, Austin, and Fort Worth—and, of course, also at the end of the cattle trails in railhead towns such as Abilene, Kansas.

As an integral part of the cattle drives, the Texas cowboy played a key role within this fundamentally economic transaction, but much more as a conscript rather than a willing volunteer within this enveloping modernity. David Scott furnishes this idea of a "conscript to modernity" based on his work on Haiti (2004). Following Scott and other anthropologists and my own training in cultural anthropology, I could not resist the temptation to place the cowboy in a comparative relationship to other sociocultural groups also caught up within such a worldwide modern hegemony. Such groups sometimes articulated a culture of dissent to such modernity that nevertheless had to give way to this inexorable process as it did with the cowboy. As with my detailed accounts of Texas history, my cross-cultural rendering may also seem excessive to some, but again, I was concerned to expand our usual nation- and region-bound understanding of the cowboy.

Chapter 2, "Song and Signification," is devoted to an extended and interpretive account of the Texas cowboy's emerging culture of dissent and its articulation in our song. I argue that the Texas cowboy may be seen in an ambivalent posture toward modernity even though it provided him with a livelihood. Paradoxically, this cowboy encounter created a certain cultural discontent with that very modernity, at least among some of them, a discontent based on a dissident cultural residue with a distanced linkage to what has been called Romanticism, as once again, I seek to expand our conventional understanding of the cowboy. Within a hard and challenging labor process, he nevertheless may have developed a culture of what I call a late and low-level residual Romanticism keyed to his particular sense of masculinity and focused fundamentally on his horsemanship, a distinctive cowboy culture paradoxically centered on his necessary and most fundamental instrument of labor—his horse—and what that might have meant to him in terms of his labor. Too much generalization has been offered in the past about a cowboy "philosophy" (Frantz 1967). Put another way, I am not interested in his fundamental "character" or "lifestyle," much less his dress, but much more on the probable attitude toward himself and his world as a working man "once in the saddle," as the ballad says.

As a correlated expression of this residual Romanticism, the cowboy also composed and sang ballads and other kinds of songs although which, when, where and how remain a subject of some debate. The 1947 Lomax and Lomax text that I offered at the beginning of this introduction was *not* collected directly in what would have been a classical primal field, that is, in this case, among cowboys driving cattle to Kansas and other places such as Montana in the later nineteenth century. We have no such primal text. Nevertheless, in the interests of an earlier rather than later articulation of my primary thesis, and, in close conjunction with the immediately foregoing commentary on agricultural modernity and residual Romanticism, at the close of this chapter, I offer a contingent and heuristic interpretation of the ballad using this 1947 text.

In this chapter, I propose that in its imagery and lento tempo, "The Streets of Laredo," reflects and reinforces the cowboy's romantic ambivalence. It offers a critical focus on the town as a site of a threatening modernity. In partaking of this modernity by way of gambling and liquor, sometimes with exuberance, the cowboy nevertheless knows he "has done wrong," and his response is the quiet, Romantic evocation of the cowboy's horseman's culture by way of the song's key stanzas. The cowboy's Romantic discontent with modernity and his worried song were not at all misplaced because, indeed, modernity will eventually bring to an end to the cattle drives and the horseback culture of the cowboy. However, my interpretation is keyed to the 1947 Lomax and Lomax ballad, and I am therefore obligated to demonstrate at least some probable linkage to its nineteenth-century origins within cowboy country, so that the reader can now have a more persuasive sense of the textual and historical basis for such an interpretation.

Chapter 3, "Modernity's Song," thus tracks the retrieval and recognition of the ballad mostly in the twentieth century in the context of the emerging reflective awareness of cowboy songs beginning in the late nineteenth century. It is offered in two parts. The first focuses on the discipline of folklore studies. While it is intended primarily for an audience of professional folklorists, a well-educated lay audience may find it of considerable interest as well. The second part takes up the ballad's influence primarily in the twentieth century by way of later recordings/performances, film, and the American novel.

I begin Part I recalling popular nineteenth-century "cowboy" writers such as Owen Wister who, although not working cowboys, became interested in the cowboy's life as a subject, writers mostly of pulp fiction which is to say, the dime novel. Wister will figure in my discussion, but I am primarily interested in the poets who also took up the topic of cowboys, including cowboys themselves, such as N. Howard "Jack" Thorp and Frank Maynard, both of whom dealt with "The Streets of Laredo." All such writing was itself already a probable symptom of modernity and its impending victory over the cowboy—an effort to salvage this culture in written fashion. This same modernity was also responsible for the more intellectual endeavors that we have come to call folklore studies as such intellectuals—amateur and professional—sought to retrieve, salvage, and occasionally mimic traditional cultures against the oncoming changes wrought by modernity, and the cowboy and his songs were no exception.

We have already noted the interest of professional folklorists like Hand and Paredes, but they did not actually collect the song. That distinction first fell to John Avery Lomax, a Texan who participated in and helped shape the nascent academic folklore studies of his moment. He first collected, fashioned, and published the ballad in 1910 for a wide audience, both popular and academic, although he, in turn, had been preceded by "collectors" of a different kind, namely the two aforementioned nineteenth-century cowboy poets and Wister, the novelist, who had published versions of the song at least in some fashion. In this juncture between Lomax and these writerly predecessors, a compositional and collecting controversy ensued between Lomax and the aforementioned Thorp. We will also witness Lomax's unorthodox method of collecting and editing in which the term "collecting" did not necessarily mean a face-to-face recording of the ballad between a field worker and a performer as became more customary later as professional folklore studies emerged. Rather, Lomax edited these songs into a new textual existence by soliciting and receiving versions and/or parts of this ballad—along with many other songs—principally through the US mails and mostly from correspondents in Texas, in effect becoming a cocreator of the ballad but not without substantial criticism from academic folklorists. Against such criticism, I enlist the assistance of one of the great modern folklorists, another esteemed teacher at the University of Texas at Austin, Roger D. Abrahams.

Thus, I argue that the 1947 version noted at the beginning of this introduction and the basis for my earlier interpretation is the textual result of an editing process that (1) drew on native nineteenth-century Texas versions of the ballad; (2) was largely shaped by Lomax, a folklorist but also a native rural Texan closely identified with cowboys; and, who (3) together with his son, Alan, then distilled what may be called the ballad's "emotional core," which is fundamentally the 1947 text with which I began.

Part II continues with the Lomaxes but as public intellectuals, and here too Abrahams continues to ratify my argument. They were primarily responsible for bringing our ballad to far greater national and international consciousness through their very popular books. These themselves became texts that, in league with other literary formations such as high modernism and the Southern Agrarians, became part of a growing discontent with modernity. In Texas, this now-accelerated twentieth-century modernity fueled by oil also produced the discontent of an emerging cadre of Texas intellectuals and writers such as Lomax's fellow Texan and UT-Austin colleague, the also famous J. Frank Dobie who, as it happens, also recognized our ballad. The ballad then received a further impetus through the folk music revival of the 1950s and '60s, including renditions of our song by very well-known performers such as Burl Ives and Joan Baez. It also had some limited influence on the cowboy "western" films that were becoming so popular, especially after World War II.

The remainder of this chapter then tracks the ballad into the later twentieth century and the early twenty-first. If the ballad had a critical signification for the cowboy, it continued to do so for others, not cowboys, in the twentieth century and into our own time, and perhaps even more so as modernity's journey became even more complicated and challenging. In an even greater entwinement with modernity, the ballad then emerged into full national and international conscious-ness when it crossed over from "folk" into "country-western" music and then into "pop," especially by way of the very popular renditions by Marty Robbins and Johnny Cash in the early 1960s. It was within this popular culture, especially in its pop musical expression, that I—and very many of us—first learned the song.

Beyond this public scholarship and largely musical performances, the ballad also inspired poems and novels. Musicians simply performed the song, albeit with stylistic innovations, and while that is obviously important, the treatment of the ballad in literature is of greater ideological significance. Oddly enough, the bal-lad's primary influence on poetry occurred abroad, in Great Britain, a discussion I will take up elsewhere. Here I am principally concerned with fictional narratives in the United States, which by definition offer an extended narration and devel-opment of an argument, or at least an attitude or perspective. Two such narrative appropriations of our ballad occurred in settings other than Texas, but because I wanted to keep this book tightly focused on this social laboratory called Texas, I have largely reserved treatment of such narratives for another time and place. How-ever, in this chapter, I do offer at least some brief commentary on two of these authors, both American, if only because Texas, even in its distinctiveness, is still, after all, an American place. But one major American writer, a Texan, more than merits—he demands—our extended attention in a book devoted to this ballad and Texas history.

Chapter 4, "Siren Song," turns to the work of the late Larry McMurtry for whom "The Streets of Laredo" has been like a siren song in his Odyssean writing epic through Texas and the American West. Like the cowboys he admired so much, it is as if McMurtry continues their discontent with modernity, albeit with fiction and essays that transferred this discontent to the first two-thirds of the twentieth century but focused on Texas, that continuing social laboratory for this global process. The cowboy's lament will turn into McMurtry's as well. As a final and only partially symbolic solution to this vexation, his later fiction and essays eventually will also have the added benefit of bringing us back, at least fictively, to nineteenth-century Texas where this story began, and where he narratively returns to the cowboy's conversation with modernity but also historically concludes it. My principal texts are the Pulitzer Prize-winning novel *Lonesome Dove* (1985) and its sequel *Streets of Laredo* (1993), but also two unpublished 1972 screenplays that McMurtry wrote with Peter Bogdonavich that anticipate these two novels in which the Texas cowboy fictionally emerges as a conscript of modernity (1972a; 1972b).

The presence of our ballad in much of McMurtry's work has received almost no scholarly critical attention, especially surprising for the novel *Streets of Laredo*, where we also witness a paradoxical use of the ballad. Paradoxically, for such a male-centered cowboy culture, *Streets of Laredo* offers a metaphorical and revisionary use of the song that comes to terms with modernity in the interests of an emerging women's late-nineteenth-century emancipation. This paradoxical use of our ballad reflects McMurtry's own moment at the markedly feminist end of the twentieth century, a concern for women already evident in of all McMurtry's work before *Lonesome Dove*. Hence, in his work, this ballad which sustained the cowboy is now given over to a *she* who stood at the margins of his existence in recognition that it had to come to an end. Nevertheless, this feminist recognition is always tempered by a sense of loss—the loss of a special cowboy way of life that momentarily marked a certain limit to an always expanding and encroaching modernity that will haunt McMurtry and our Texas well into our own time. I close this chapter with an epilogue, "Se Le Acabó la Canción" (Now His/Her Song Is Over) as an homage to the late Larry McMurtry, the cowboy's and this ballad's most critical partisan. To this end, I turn to his last two collections of essays that speak of the cowboy through his own parents' difficult marriage and their passing. At the center of these final essays in his life, we find our ballad, "The Streets of Laredo," bringing final closure to our interpretive story of this ballad. I close with some interpretive remarks—a coda—on this study and contemporary Texas in terms of its history and "The Streets of Laredo."

Songs and Sites

As a ballad, "The Streets of Laredo" has an ancestry that began in the late-eighteenth-century British Isles, and from there, moved to its mid-nineteenth-century American appearance. In that semi-mythic place called Texas, versions of the ballad likely emerged within certain cultural geographical and material socioeconomic sites. In this chapter, I take up the ballad's ancestral provenance and its movement to Texas while discussing certain formative sites in Texas as an explanatory background for the ballad's eventual emergence but also in their own right. Because they bear directly on the song and the American cowboy, its collective composers and first performers, I will discuss these Texas sites in some detail since one can imagine many readers—including native Texans—who are unfamiliar with this complicated Texas history . . . those Six Flags, you know. But, speaking of Six Flags, events in Texas may also be seen in relation to global affairs, and these will also be addressed in this chapter and the next, at least tangentially. These include the cowboy's comparability to other societies encountering modernity which may also not be familiar to many. For such readers and others as well, I hope these contextual renderings stimulated by this ballad will prove interesting and educational in themselves and not considered digressive or overly detailed. For even when, at brief moments, it might seem I have abandoned our song, it threads through all these discussions and will be addressed fully in following chapters.[1]

FOLKLORIC ANTECEDENTS

For the most part, the extant scholarship on this ballad has focused on its geneal-ogy. According to most folklore scholars, our song's ancestry appears in the form of two ballads from Ireland circa the turn of the eighteenth into the nineteenth century, although this origin is now in some dispute, as we shall see later (Barry 1911, 1912; Lodewick 1955; Hand 1955, 1958; Goldstein; 1959; 1960; Breen 2016). The first has traditionally been called

"The Unfortunate Rake"

As I was a-walking down by St. James' Hospital,
I was a-walking down by there one day,
What should I spy but one of my comrades
All wrapped up in flannel though warm was the day.
I asked him what ailed him, I asked him what failed him,
I asked him the cause of all his complaint.
"It's all on account of some handsome young woman,
'Tis she that has caused me to weep and lament.
"And had she but told me before she disordered me,
Had she but told me of it entire,
I might have got pills and salts of white mercury,
But now I'm cut down in the height of my prime.
"Get six young soldiers to carry my coffin,
Six young girls to sing me a song,
And each of them carry a bunch of green laurel
So they don't smell me as they bear me along.
"Don't muffle your drums and play your fifes merrily,
Play a quick march as you carry me along,
And fire your bright muskets all over my coffin,
Saying: There goes an unfortunate lad to his home."
(Goldstein 1960, 1).

We know little else contextually about this ballad, nor much else about another companion precursor:

"The Bad Girl's Lament"

As I walked down to St. James Hospital,
St. James Hospital early one day,

l spied my only fairest daughter
Wrapped up in white linen as cold as the clay.
CHORUS:
So beat your drums and play the fife lowly,
And play the dead march as you carry me along;
Take me to the churchyard and lay the sod over me,
I am a young maid, and I know I've done wrong.
Once in the street I used to look handsome;
Once in the street I used to dress gay;
First to the ale house, then to the dance hall
Then to the poor house and now to my grave.
(CHORUS)
Send for the preacher to pray o'er my body,
Send for the doctor to heal up my wounds,
Send for the young man I first fell in love with,
That I might see him before I pass on.
(CHORUS)
Let six pretty maidens with a bunch of red roses,
Six pretty maidens to sing me a song,
Six pretty maidens with a bunch of red roses
To lay on my coffin as they carry me along.
(Goldstein 1960, 1)

In both cases, the ballads lament dying young persons. In the presumably older variant (hereafter, "Rake") the young men are sometimes soldiers or sailors, while in the later female version (hereafter "Bad Girl"), they are simply identified as young maids. Both male and female variants typically end with a funeral march assisted by various numbers of young men or women, although six seems to be preferred, and with fifes and drums playing respectively, lowly and slowly (Hand 1955, 1958; Goldstein 1960, 1). Although we have precious little other information about these two songs, we can at least minimally note the socially marginalized protagonists—soldiers, probably conscripted, and not officers, and a young woman, probably a prostitute—both of whom meet their deaths of venereal disease; he, certainly, as witness his neglect of the folk cure, "pills and salts of white mercury." For its part, "Bad Girl" speaks about a "doctor to heal up my wounds" clearly suggesting violence, possibly rape. However, Kenneth S. Goldstein makes an interesting gender point, to wit that the female variant of "the ballad has been reported with greater frequency than any other," as if to suggest a greater sense of crisis for women, resulting in increased prostitution as English industrialization and intensifying urbanization were underway (1960, 1). In both cases, we also seem to be witnessing an emerging urbanizing social fluidity of ale houses and poor houses, hospitals and presumably medical personnel consistent with the approximate time of their composition. From this beginning point, these ballads made their way to the rest of Great Britain and eventually to the United States, propelled by the engines of an emerging modernity but already in discontent with that modernity. As Nestor Rodríguez recently reminded us,

> In Ireland, large-scale rural emigration to Britain was partly a consequence of the subordinating core-periphery order in the world-system. Losing the industrial war to Britain early, Ireland became increasingly incorporated into the British-dominated world-system through the commercialization of its heavily agricultural economy. Rural labor in Ireland became redundant as large landowners enclosed their lands for agricultural commercial development. Dispossessed from their farming subsistence, poor Irish workers emigrated abroad for economic survival by the hundreds of thousands. In Britain and in other regions such as the United States, poor Irish migrants usually took undesirable jobs. (2023, 136)

TOWARD "THE STREETS OF LAREDO"

Kerby A. Miller has provided the most comprehensive and analytical account of the complicated history of Irish emigration to North America, an emigration that undoubtedly brought these two ballads to the United States (1985). Both ballads gave way to a new form in the United States, a process first noted by Phillips Barry (1911, 1912). Wayland Hand and Kenneth S. Goldstein pursue this transformation further. Speaking only of "Rake," Hand says, "the song apparently came to the new country by way of the northerly sea route, and, like a number of other songs that arrived in the New England states, it then went on to the south and the west, where it turned into a cowboy song" (1955, 151).[2] With the opening of the West, especially after the Civil War, both of these older forms were known and sung in this new territory (Goldstein 1960). But, very importantly, says Goldstein, soon "they were crowded out of the picture by the popularity of a western revision of the male rake theme" (1960, 1). Goldstein continues, "we can only guess that some frontiersman brought a version of either the older 'Rake' ballad, or its sister mutation, 'The Bad Girl's Lament,' to the West where it was readily adapted to the frontier situation" (2). In saying "guess," Goldstein is suggesting a certain paucity of hard data and a predominance of circumstantial evidence and creative conjecture in all these assessments, including mine. The emerging discipline of folklore was not in a position to assess the cowboy empirically until he was almost gone. Nevertheless, what Goldstein means by the "frontier situation" is that in the later nineteenth century, we can detect a cowboy, a male figure, and a song in which he is no longer a victim of a sexual encounter gone bad, but rather "meets his violent end as a result of drinking and gambling which lead to an argument over cheating at cards, and his eventual death from 'lead poisoning'" (2). Hand is a bit more specific about the cowboys. The song's transformation, he says, "could hardly have occurred before the Civil War, when for the first time, there were great herds of cattle and the occupation of cowboy first came into being" (Hand 1955, 151). Thus, we have the appearance of the American variants that will come to be known as "The Cowboy's Lament" and eventually our song, "The Streets of Laredo" (hereafter "Lament" and "Streets").

With this review before us, however, we must now consider a very recent and major intervention that revises the foregoing in minor and major keys. In his recent Katherine Briggs Memorial Lecture to The Folklore Society, Richard Jenkins convincingly demonstrates that the name, "The Unfortunate Rake," habitually given to the primal Anglo-Irish ancestor for our ballad, is a mistake, one begun by Phillips Barry badly misusing the work of an early Irish folklorist, P. W. Joyce, who "did not use the name in the book on which Barry draws" (2019, 116). In a further "egregious mistake," Barry's "original error" has been compounded over time to the present day among all the folklorists noted (118). Jenkins offers compelling archival evidence that it should instead be called "The Unfortunate Lad" (117–19). I will nevertheless continue to use "Rake" wherever I cite its use by others while recognizing that it has now been discredited, and I will now also speak of "Lad" where that is appropriate. However, "Rake" and "Lad" are much the same ballad, including shared membership in the "tune family," to which the Irish, British, and North American "Rake" variants and "Laredo" all belong" (116). Hence, I think of this as a critical revision, but textually only in a minor key as the song remains largely the same. The major key, however, is that in arguing thus against "Rake" and for "Lad," Jenkins also effectively undercuts the presumed exclusively Irish origins of this balladry primarily evidenced by Joyce (1909). Instead, Jenkins locates it in a broader "British-Irish" background of several nineteenth-century broadside ballads with the title "The Unfortunate Lad" published by H. P. Such of London (117).[3] Thus, he concludes, "the conventional wisdom about the Irish roots of this group of songs in the shape of 'The Unfortunate Rake' must be approached with considerable scepticism" (119).

After Jenkins, we now have a more complicated ancestry for "Lad," and presumably "Bad Girl," and therefore "Streets." However, the first two may be of geographical, although not necessarily of *cultural* English origins. Jenkins implies that "Lad" was collected, or even authored, primarily in England, not Ireland, but there is also the distinct possibility that it could have been collected and/or authored from within the Irish internal migration to England's industrializing cities which, of course, was prolonged and substantial, and, it must be noted, drew more heavily from Ireland's Catholic southern and eastern areas (G. Davis 1991). We are left only with the certainty that this balladry is very broadly Anglo-Irish in origin and that it came to North America in the eighteenth and/or nineteenth centuries to then make its way west, carried by an anglophone migration.

Under Barry's influence, Hand thought of it as an Irish balladry, but if we now grant its probable mixed origins, we can now better see one major implication in his observation that after arriving on the East Coast, the song "then went on to the south and the west, where it turned into a cowboy song" (1955, 151). When he says "the south *and* the west [emphasis mine]," Hand is likely signaling that there were historically two major moments in Irish immigration—one beginning in the eighteenth century, substantially from northern and Protestant Ireland, which came first to the "New England states" and then on to the American South by way of Appalachia, inhabitants of which are sometimes called the Scots-Irish; and a later second movement: the post-Irish famine immigrants in the 1840s, primarily Catholic, who settled chiefly in the urbanizing North.[4] Nevertheless, members of both groups eventually also headed west, especially in the nineteenth century, but they also tended to bifurcate geographically and occupationally. The earlier Scots-Irish were agriculturalists principally tied to southern cotton, and, as we shall see, their most significant westward migration was into Texas beginning in the 1820s. The later northern, largely Catholic, Irish were strongly oriented toward cities such as Butte, Montana, and nonagricultural occupations such as railroads, mining, and slaughterhouses (Emmons 2010, 210–216).

As noted earlier, Hand said that the cowboy ballad, "Lament"/"Streets" "could hardly have occurred before the Civil War, when for the first time there were great herds of cattle and the occupation of cowboy first came into being" (1955, 3). He is then even more specific as to where "great herds of cattle and the occupation of cowboy first came into being," noting that the song is clearly connected with the small town of Laredo, Texas, on the Mexican border, "an excellent choice as it lies at the beginning of the famous Chisholm trail just south of San Antonio" (1955, 4). While we will significantly qualify this observation in our later discussion of Laredo and South Texas, we can say with some certainty that the transformation of the Anglo-Irish ballad tradition into "Lament"/"Streets" probably occurred in Texas, given the very name of "Laredo," and clearly among cowboys. And, if these internally migrating Irish carried with them "Lad" and/or "Bad Girl," as Goldstein suggests, it would seem likely that it was the southern cultural trajectory—that is, through the Appalachian South into Texas—that provided the initial basis for its cowboy transformation. At least it would seem that way at first and even at second glance. However, we must also take into account yet a third competing and relatively unknown Irish social formation, also Catholic like that northern urban group from the 1840s but with a very separate chronological and settlement trajectory. In their respective studies of Irish emigration to North America, neither Miller, David M. Emmons (2010), nor Patrick Griffin (2006) mention this latter formation, but I am deeply indebted to British historian, Graham Davis, for this relatively overlooked and alternative possibility (2002).

As it happens, both the Scots-Irish movement into Texas and this alternative Catholic Irish narrative were set in motion by the Republic of Mexico, heir to the Spanish in Texas who had also established the town of Laredo. In this next section, and before returning to our song, I will chart and interweave all of these stories—Mexico, the Scots-Irish, and the Catholic Irish—but also Laredo itself, with some emphasis on their transition into a period of modernity after the Civil War. It is a complicated story of overlapping geographies, societies, and politics involving these three principal colonizing actors (fig. 2).

THE TEXAS COLONIAL THREE-STEP

Laredo, the ballad's ostensible setting, was founded in 1755 by the Spanish as part of their relatively late northward expansion after the initial conquest of indigenous Mexico in 1521 and earlier more limited efforts northward such as the founding of the small province of Santa Fe, New Mexico, in 1598. In addition to other incursions into much of what is now the American Southwest, this later expansion occupied primarily what is now southern Texas from the Rio Grande to the Nueces River and the pueblo of San Antonio with a lessening presence across the Nueces into eastern and northern Texas. While I do not show it here, this South Texas settlement also extended southward across the Rio Grande into northern

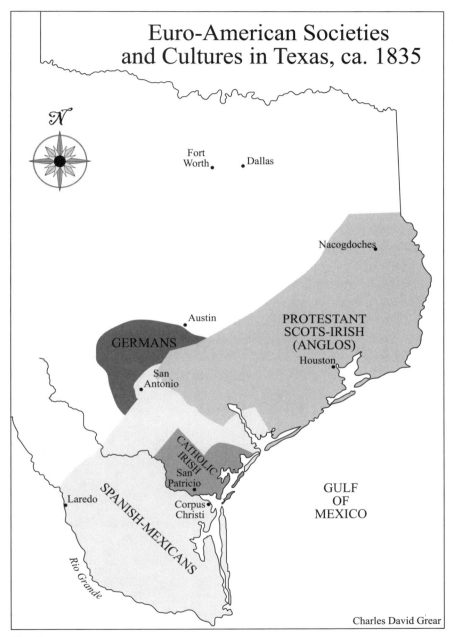

Figure 2

Mexico, but for our purposes, we emphasize South Texas. These settlers were predominantly Catholic and, after some two hundred years since the Spanish arrival in New Spain they were primarily mestizos, "racial mixtures of Spanish and Mexican Indian blood" (R. Campbell 2003, 114). They were also predominantly sheep herders and cattle ranchers, although Laredo served as an administrative and distribution center for local livestock from large ranches to the north and southeast of the town (A. Alonzo 1998, 67–94). Yet, Laredo was also developing into a trading nexus for all manner of other goods between the interior of New Spain/Mexico up to San Antonio and beyond to other Spanish territory, French Louisiana, and the new United States (Adams 2008, 32–34). By the early nineteenth century, "Laredo became the crossroads of the first wave of what we have come to know today as commercial globalization" (45). We shall hear more on Laredo later.

After a protracted war of independence from Spain, the newly-founded Republic of Mexico of 1821 inherited what is now the American Southwest but also Texas, including Laredo and this larger South Texas settlement now numbering "several thousand," hereafter *Tejanos*, or "Texans" in Spanish (R. Campbell 2003, 114).[5] In the mid-1820s, the new Republic of Mexico faced an expansive United States after the Louisiana Purchase. Mexico's eastern and northern Texas provinces became the closest "open" territory bordering the expanding United States. Mexico tried to establish settlements of its own citizens in this more northern area as well, but it "had no more success than Spain in persuading settlers to move to the northern frontier" (114).

As is only too well-known, Mexico then turned to the regulated admission and settlement of Anglo-Americans into northern and eastern Texas principally from the southern United States from 1825 to 1830 and led by colonial managers or *empresarios* such as Stephen F. Austin. They were mostly of Scots-Irish heritage (Barber 2010, 31–32). These folks were given land grants along the Colorado and Brazos Rivers with the provisos that they would become citizens of Mexico, therefore presumably learning the Spanish language, becoming Catholics, and eventually giving up slavery, which Mexico had discouraged and later outlawed (R. Campbell 2003, 110–113). It did not take long for these white, southern, mostly Protestant slaveholders to chafe under these conditions (131–33). The Mexican authorities were soon "convinced of the dangers posed by the presence of American colonists in Texas and more aware of the expansionist plans of the United States" even as illegal white southern immigrants also continued to enter this territory as squatters (G. Davis 2002, 28). By 1835, these southern-based "Anglos," as they came to be called, outnumbered the South Texas ethnic Mexican population now identifying as *Tejanos* (Campbell 2003: 113–14).

In 1830, as tensions were increasing, Mexico decided to put an end to further immigration from the United States and to prohibit slavery in Texas. Yet, still needing more immigrants for the area's further economic development and to offset the southern Anglo "illegals," Mexico tried another tactic which was to recruit European immigrants, "establishing a certain number of foreign families on an equal basis with the Mexican families" already in the area (G. Davis 2002, 30). By "European," the Mexican government clearly had in mind Catholic Europe, and within this demarcation,

> the Irish . . . were identified as the most desirable of settlers. They were regarded as loyal Catholics, having suffered persecutions in defense of their faith. They possessed outstanding moral virtues and were known to be highly industrious.

And, there was a fascinating political calculation as well. The Irish

> . . . were thought to be not too friendly to England or to the United States, so that in the case of war, Mexico could rely on brave soldiers, famous in previous centuries for their military valor in fighting for imperial Spain to defend its borders. (32)[6]

For this complicated task, Mexico appointed four empresarios—James Hewston, James Power, John McMullen, and James McGloin. They were all native-born Irishmen, "who had left their native country as young men" and made their way, not yet to Texas as such, but to the Mexican cities of Saltillo and Matamoros, where they became successful businessmen, Mexican citizens, fluent in Spanish, married Mexican women, and became "familiar with Mexican ways" (G. Davis 2002, 72–76). They were successful in recruiting Irish colonists, some recently arrived in places like New York, more of them directly from Ireland, numbering some two hundred family units (79). They came principally from the Tipperary and Wexford areas of Ireland (166). Mexico and the Irish empresarios established two primary settlements along the Gulf Coast proximate both to the earlier established southern Anglo-American colonies just to the north and west and to the Mexican community just to the south. One of these was called Refugio after a nearby Mexican settlement and its Catholic Church, *Nuestra Señora del*

Refugio (Our Lady of Refuge), and the other was called *San Patricio de Hibernia* (St. Patrick) for obvious reasons. These were immediately north of present-day Corpus Christi. The Irish were thus settled amongst the older South Texas Spanish-Mexican ranching settlements that had been there since 1749 but also now with additional Tejanos as part of Refugio and San Patricio (82–90). According to Graham Davis, the two Catholic peoples had amicable relationships, including sharing the established Mexican churches, some intermarriage, and learning each other's language (106–53).

Meanwhile during this period from 1830 to 1836, many more largely white southerners entered eastern and northern Texas and continued their southern-bred engagement in cotton agriculture based on slavery, although most did not do so as plantation owners (R. Campbell 2003, 207). The "great majority" of such Anglos were, in Randolph B. Campbell's apt phrase, "plain folk" and "most were farmers" who "owned a relatively small share of land and other forms of property"; few were slave owners. There was also a "bottom rung" of "poor whites" who did not own land and worked for others "on a rent or share agreement" (217–18).

By contrast, the Irish in San Patricio and Refugio had developed a very different mode of economic subsistence based on their continuing amicable relationship to Tejanos. At first, they farmed in the new colony, much as they had done in Ireland, but soon, they also learned cattle ranching from their Tejano neighbors and began to dedicate their land holdings to this purpose. According to Graham Davis, "a cultural transfer was evident in the relations between Tejano families . . . and their Irish neighbors, who inherited and acquired the Hispanic ranching tradition" (2002, 195).[7] And, "what deserves greater recognition is the presence of Catholic Irish settlers who were taught the rudiments of Hispanic ranching culture, *vaquero* know-how, by their co-religionists and their fellow settlers" (204). From the Spanish word for cow, *vaca*, "*vaqueros*" were Tejano cowboys. Thus, alongside and learning from vaqueros, Irish-Texan cowboys emerged in this area beginning in the late 1830s, and at first they were almost exclusively of Irish heritage.[8] Indeed, as late as 1860, it is estimated that in this general area, "at least a third of large-scale cattle raisers . . . were Irish" (213). Presumably, some large part of the remaining two-thirds were still ethnic Mexican Tejanos.

Chief among these Irish ranchers, we find one Thomas O'Connor, who at age seventeen, was recruited from County Wexford in Ireland by his uncle, the aforementioned empresario James Power, to come make his fortune in Texas, which he amply did. He arguably became the first of the later legendary Texas cattle barons such as Richard King of the fabled King Ranch (himself Irish) and the West

Texan, Charles Goodnight. Following the example of Tejano ranchers, O'Connor and others drove their cattle to the Texas port of Indianola for shipment through the Gulf of Mexico to Caribbean sites such as Cuba and, of course, the United States (G. Davis 2002, 208–10). At the time of his retirement, O'Connor's land holdings were essentially congruent with the original Irish settlements and more.

Even as the Irish colonization project was underway, the rapidly expanding and restive Scots-Irish, or Anglo, settlements to the north continued in their displeasure with Mexican rule. It soon led to led to the well-known political conflicts of the Texas independence movement and war of 1835–36 through which these dominating Anglos created Texas, first as a republic, followed by annexation into the United States, leading to the US–Mexico War of 1846–47, and final incorporation into the United States in 1848. Too distant from the Anglo center of rebellion, Laredo maintained at least nominal loyalties to the central Mexican government not to mention that, not surprisingly, it also became "the primary marshaling point and crossing for troops, supplies, and livestock for the armies moving north from Mexico" to suppress the Anglo rebellion initially at the Alamo in San Antonio (Adams 2008, 54). One is sure that John A. Adams meant to say "internal" Mexico, for the national identity of southern Texas as a whole, including Laredo, would not really be settled until 1848.

The Texas War for Independence and the US–Mexico War waged against the Republic of Mexico put both Tejanos and the Irish in a serious dilemma. Some members of both groups had supported the independence movement, while others remained loyal to a Mexico that had brought them to Texas with land grants in the first place (R. Campbell 2003, 133). Thus, many Tejanos actually fought *alongside* Anglos for a shared Texas independence and an imagined bilingual, bicultural republic. All this was soon forgotten as all Tejanos were all seen as complicit with Mexico. This perception of Tejanos-as-traitors—like Issei/Nisei Japanese in the United States at the beginning of World War II—were then compounded by racist and anti-Catholic Anglo attitudes carried over from the slave-holding Old South, for Tejanos were, after all, Catholic and a mixed, not-white race, or, "half-breeds" in the idiom of the day, attitudes also resulting, no doubt, from the genocidal Indian wars in the South before the Civil War (De León 1983).

The rapidly growing Anglo population expanded its enclave especially after the establishment of the Republic of Texas. This already politically, religiously, and racially conditioned expansion had a more fundamental economic intent: the acquisition of ranching land, even if owned by Tejanos, especially those within or bordering on the Anglo settlements. In the areas closest to the primary Anglo enclaves, between the Nueces and San Antonio Rivers and upriver to San Antonio, "*Tejano* landholders found themselves threatened with violence and at times actually physically assaulted because they stood in the way of ambitious Anglos," Campbell continues, and, under such pressure, Tejanos lost their lands such that "more than a million acres changed hands, largely from Mexican to Anglo, between 1837 and 1842" (2003, 191). In recounting his own family's history in Mexican Texas in an interview with Rámon Saldívar, Américo Paredes tells us that his great-grandfather, Leonardo Paredes Ybarra, "had a ranch south of the Nueces . . . but he was forced to give it up after 1848" (Saldívar 2006, 68). This always-expanding Anglo demographic enclave would eventually extend to and almost wholly dominate the entire state, although a Tejano enclave would persist in deep southern Texas closer to the Rio Grande and centered on Laredo to which we will return in a moment (Arreola 2002, 64–68).

In this developing hostility between Tejanos and the southern Scot-Irish, some of the Catholic Texas Irish were themselves adversely affected by the Anglo newcomers as both "the Irish and Mexican settlers of San Patricio and Refugio suffered a disproportionate loss of property, and many were forced to abandon their land" as if the old fights in Ireland between Irish and those "Anglos" had been transferred to Texas (G. Davis 2002, 239). While their Catholic faith may have played some role in this adversity, some of the Irish more likely suffered because of "the close personal ties between Mexican and Irish neighbors" that had "survived the clash of loyalties of combatants in the war of 1835–36" and presumably that of 1846–47. And Graham Davis adds, "the threats to their respective land grants" happened because at least some of the Irish had wished to honor the generosity of the Republic of Mexico with their loyalty during the wars (236). Moreover, such tension may also have been aggravated by the anti-Catholic/Irish sentiment in the US in the 1840s and '50s. The numbers of Irish in Texas also increased by migrants from an unlikely quarter, the post-famine northern Catholics referenced earlier, some of whom also eventually headed for Texas.

> the increasing numbers of the Irish-born within Texas borders may also have raised concerns. Spurred by the lingering effects of the potato famine and the continued availability of inexpensive land that made the tribulations of city life in the Northeast and Midwest seem especially onerous, in 1860 some 3,450 Texans claimed Ireland as their place of birth—an increase of 143 percent over the decade. (Barber 2010, 79)

Yet, for all of their differences, the Texas Catholic Irish did share a language and racial phenotype with the Scots-Irish. Under the pressures noted, and always a relatively much smaller population, over time, the Catholic Irish gradually assimilated and separated themselves from Tejanos. By 1857, even their Catholicism was no longer socially shared as the Irish began to develop their own parishes with priests from Ireland (Barber 2010, 80). Over time, the US Bureau of the Census reported the number of self-identified Irish in Texas from 1850 to 1900 as "inconsequential" (Emmons 2010, 214).

Within this complicated Texas three-step colonial process—Tejanos, Anglos, and Catholic Irish—we return to our song and its primary social base, the Texas cowboy.

TRADITIONAL BALLADS AND EMERGING COWBOYS

During the period 1826 to about 1860 and within this social context, we can now see two possible pathways for our balladry but also for the emergence of its sustaining social base—the Texas cowboy—the conjunction that would eventually yield "The Streets of Laredo." Was it the Scots-Irish from the American South entering Texas in 1826, or the later Irish colony established by Mexico, or perhaps a confluence of both? First, is there any evidence that either group had the song tradition in their cultural repertoire? Cecil J. Sharp, the foremost collector and scholar of the Scots-Irish folk song in the Appalachian South does not report this balladry except, oddly enough, one version of "Lament," something of an irony because it appears to be the Texas cowboy song that originated in Texas and then made its way *back* into the South by the time Sharp was collecting in the early 1900s (1932, 164). Yet, another later collection of southern folksongs does not contain "Rake," "Lad," nor "Bad Girl." As with Sharp's, it also includes a version of "Lament" dealing with the dying cowboy, which makes it clear that it is again a product of a reverse movement from the West to the Old South rather than the other way (Cox 1925, 242–46). Finally, in her study of British ballads in Texas, Mabel Major (1932) clearly notes the Scots-Irish origins of this balladry, but she did not find "Rake," "Lad," nor "Bad Girl" in Texas. In short, the record is not at all helpful in determining whether or not the newly arriving Scots-Irish/Anglos knew "Rake," "Lad," and/or "Bad Girl," although they may have learned them later from some unknown quarter. Even with this paucity of evidence, we cannot absolutely rule out that the Scots-Irish folk song tradition of "Lad" and "Bad Girl" was carried into Texas by these white southerners and then transformed into "Streets" once the requisite anglophone cowboys appeared in largely appropriated ranch land. But there is also another intervening issue that makes this supposition at least questionable: namely, how did these southern, primarily cotton-agriculturalist Anglos learn to become cowboys so as to then fashion the song?

It has generally been said that the Texas anglophone cowboy came into being by learning the practices of cattle ranching from Tejanos in a relatively benign fashion. As Américo Paredes noted, "cattle and horses as well as land were Mexican to begin with; and when the Anglo took them over, he also adopted many of the techniques developed by the *ranchero* for the handling of stock" (1978, 71). Although heretical for some Anglo-Texans, the Tejano-origin thesis has prevailed over time such that the leading historian of Texas acknowledges this influence (R. Campbell 2003, 210, 296).[9] However, this learning relationship—this adoption, to paraphrase Paredes—seems assumed rather than demonstrated. Left unexplained is how this could happen between two peoples generally so hostile to each other at that moment. We are asked to imagine these Anglos just watching Tejanos at their work, or perhaps, like good students, asking them ranching questions in their "fluent" Spanish, perhaps just before they shot them, lynched them, or just cheated them out of their land holdings. And why would Tejanos want to be so helpful to these white, Protestant, racist interlopers? Even in the most benign reading, why would you want to help the competition, especially a competition with such a different culture? It is as if we are asked to assume accommodating, very polite Tejano gentlemen wishing to be of the utmost service to this new people who were aggressively encroaching on their ancestral land and demeaning their culture, race, and religion.

By contrast, as Graham Davis has clearly shown us, the Irish colony had fully and amicably availed itself of such a ranching culture from their neighbor Tejanos. Rather than a binary contact between Tejanos and "Anglos," as Paredes and others suggest, it is more likely that the assimilating Irish may have functioned as a go-between, as cultural mediators, passing on their Tejano-acquired skills to the new Anglo arrivals flowing aggressively out of Austin's colonies. But did the Texas Irish know "Rake," "Lad," and "Bad Girl"? Did they then also pass on these songs in their ancestral form to their incoming southern Anglo-Irish brethren? As with all frontier peoples, Irish subsistence and survival in 1830s Texas demanded much time and labor, but there was also time and space for entertainment, including on the then short cattle drives. Davis also tells us that these Irish also brought their rich traditions of folklore, music, and dancing to the new colony although he does not describe these (2002, 189). Unfortunately, no one in the 1830s thought to record the folkloric traditions of the Texas Irish before they assimilated into Anglo-Texan culture. While the evidence is quite circumstantial, the chronologically proximate appearance of "Bad Girl," "Rake," and "Lad" in the Anglo-Irish folkloric canon in the early nineteenth century argues for their likely introduction into Texas by the Catholic Irish at this moment of settlement in the 1830s. We must remember that this ballad tradition may not have been Irish in origin as Jenkins (2019) has reminded us, but by the 1830s, it is not at all impossible for the Texas Catholic Irish to have acquired it in the British Isles before their departure from Ireland and arrival in Texas.

This historical conjunction of Irish folklore and cowboys of Catholic Irish ancestry in Texas based on their cultural proximity to Tejanos seems to me to provide a more plausible initial sociocultural base for the later song. While the Scots-Irish Protestants cannot be completely ruled out as autonomous creators of cowboy and song, the contextual evidence would seem to favor the Catholic Irish in Texas. Along with their Tejano ranching skills, they may have also passed on "Lad," "Bad Girl," and possibly already some version of "Streets" to their distant cultural cousins, the Scots-Irish. (Later, I shall point to another piece of circumstantial evidence concerning "Bad Girl" at a more appropriate moment.)

We especially note that all of this could have happened before the Civil War between 1834 and 1861, and thus, we must now call into question Wayland Hand's claim that our song "could hardly have occurred before the Civil War, when for the first time there were great herds of cattle and the occupation of cowboy first came into being" (1955, 3). Yet, perhaps Hand is somewhat correct in that both anglophone cowboys and our ballad did not come into *full* prominence until circa the Civil War and after. That is, the full saliency of the song and its textual details seem to require a much more developed cowboy culture and a larger theatre of cattle drives and modernity that soon appeared once an Anglo-American hegemony was established.

THE PEACE STRUCTURE

This larger theatre emerged from an emergent sociocultural configuration developing after southern Texas definitively became part of the United States in 1848. By the late 1850s, the East Texas Anglo settlements noted earlier were aggressively expanding into southern Texas south of the Nueces almost to the Rio Grande, establishing ranches but within certain limitations and much less violence. The largest of these would become the King Ranch (Graham 2002).[10] Nevertheless, Tejanos continued to exercise considerable land tenure and a concomitant socio-cultural presence but only within a far more restricted area now much more con-fined to the border area adjoining Mexico. In 1860, Tejano ranchers continued to outnumber Anglos by ten to one in Cameron and Hidalgo counties, respectively represented by the towns of Brownsville and McAllen (A. Alonzo 1998, 215). Even in Nueces County around Corpus Christi, "fully 33% of the landholders who claimed livestock in 1860 were Tejanos," although this figure also tells us that already 67% were not (190). Under these circumstances, the two landed groups— Anglos and Tejanos—seemed to reach "an accommodation that proved reasonably satisfactory to both as South Texas became part of the United States" (R. Campbell 2003, 193). Or, in the apt phrase of historian, David Montejano, a "peace structure" largely prevailed (1987, 34).

Campbell's use of the phrase "reasonably satisfactory" and Montejano's "peace structure" are probably quite appropriate to describe what was nevertheless an ambivalent relationship undoubtedly still deeply affected by race, religion, and the historical memory of the wars, official and unofficial. Yet, while Tejanos had some land and ensuing political power in comparison to the regions north of the Nueces River, over time, even this would also be somewhat eroded by highly questionable Anglo economic practices (Montejano 1987, 59–74). Even within the "peace struc-ture," Anglos, now including the assimilating and disappearing Catholic Irish, were still culturally apart and were economically dominant such that even into the late nineteenth century, "Mexican and Anglo relations . . . were inconsistent and con-tradictory" and "the general direction pointed to the formation . . . where ethnic or national prejudice provided a basis for separation and control" (82).

On the eve of the Civil War, we are then left to visualize two very different societies occupying the South Texas space between the Nueces and the Rio Grande and all the way to the Gulf of Mexico. However, we must also now lend more nuance to this observation by noting that the Tejano enclave itself contained two distinct sociocultural spheres: one, the aforementioned Tejano ranching areas and two, the town of Laredo. As we shall see, as a trade nexus, Laredo itself was poised to enter a developing American capitalist modernity, while to the east, toward the Gulf Coast, the King Ranch and other Anglo-owned ranches, were also poised to fully enter it as well. From 1861 through the end of the century, these respective new and very distinctive relationships to such a modernity eventually brought forth both cowboys in significant numbers and also our song that is so marked by Laredo.

Both seem to me so intertwined with this new sociocultural development that it merits some extended attention as does a particular cowboy reaction to it.

AGRICULTURAL MODERNITY

Anthony Giddens and Christopher Pierson have noted that "the emergence of modernity is first of all the creation of . . . a capitalist economic order" (1998, 96). And, in *A Singular Modernity*, Fredric Jameson argues for such a modernity as a "break" within a larger narrative of the broader Euro-American West—a "narrative effect" with a particular economic character (2013, 145). For him, "technological development lends itself irresistibly to subsumption under the empty form of the break: it offers itself as content for the formal beginning as do few other types of historical material." Thus, "the narrative concept of modernity, the implantation of the first industrial machines come together with a well-nigh gravitational impact, and therefore seem indissoluble, even in our own historiographically far more self-conscious era" (145). For the United States, such "technology" and "industrial machines" that seem "indissoluble" with modernity are usually narrativized as the post-Civil War capitalist industrialization in the North and Midwest. This is much the same process or narrative effect popularly known as "The Gilded Age" that Alan Trachtenberg also referred to as "the incorporation of America" (1982). Yet at that post-Civil War moment and even before, the narrative slot of modernity usually occupied by "industry" and "technology" should also more than afford a place for agriculture, now better understood as "agribusiness," in the developing Midwest but also in the South, which had already established itself as a source for the cotton mills of an incipient technologically driven modernity in the United States but also England. That is, while agriculture at that moment seems to stand apart from modernity, it is obvious that what usually counts as American modernity—the industrialization of the Great Lakes area and the Northeast—was inextricably linked to and deeply influenced the agricultural sectors of the United States so as to make the latter essential to, if not centrally definitive of, the modern process.

Between 1861 and 1890, agricultural modernity exerted this kind of influence in southern Texas in two new distinct places: Laredo, Texas, and then what came to be called the "brush country" east of Laredo to the Gulf Coast and centered on the King Ranch where the cattle kingdom would emerge. A new kind of "content" for Jameson's "narrative break" thus appeared in two parts of South Texas, both of which figure into our song. The ostensible setting for our song—Laredo, Texas—became a paradoxical site for agricultural modernity because it was not "agricultural" in the way one would conventionally imagine. Let's revisit this site first and then from there move to the other form of agricultural modernity, the cattle kingdom in South Texas, east of Laredo, within which, in all probability, our song fully emerged.

THE GRIDDED STREETS OF LAREDO

The expanding Anglo population that came to dominate most of southern Texas by 1861 largely did not influence Laredo and its immediate surrounding area for perhaps a seventy-five-mile circumference around the town, NE by SE. The Laredo area and certainly the city itself experienced this relative immunity, far more than the rest of South Texas. Why was Laredo different? Perhaps it was the greater distance from the area of initial Anglo and racist settlement in eastern Texas; the larger presence of hostile indigenous peoples around Laredo; or, even the arid climate and intense, sometimes year-round, heat. Most likely, the most significant factor was that the Laredo city council, led by Mayor Florencio Villarreal, after 1848, immediately and successfully petitioned the new Texas state government to recognize and validate the original Spanish land grants in the Laredo area, keeping such land in the hands of their Tejano heirs and no longer available to Anglo appropriation (Adams 2008, 74–77). On this complicated basis, Laredo maintained a decisive historically Spanish, then Mexican and Tejano, demography and cultural identity to the present day which is not to say that some new immigrants did not come to the town.

Earlier we noted Montejano's Anglo/Tejano "peace structure," but he also notes that Laredo, Texas, "represented the peace structure at its best" as "the wealth and power of the landed elites were generally left undisturbed," and "considerable intermarriage bound the old and new elites" (1987, 36). Indeed, the old Tejano elites were joined by new elites in Laredo, but in a manner quite different from the rest of South Texas. In Laredo, what Montejano calls the "new elites" were first of all relatively few in total number. While they included some southern heritage Anglos, Laredo did not experience large-scale, southern "plain folk" immigrants since it was not really an available ranching or cash crop area, Mayor Villarreal having attended to that issue. In fact, these few new elites were not principally ranchers but rather businessmen attracted by Laredo's developing identity as a commercial export-import site. Laredo was also different in that that the few southerner émigrés among them were also joined by yet another kind of elite: continental Europeans and some even from the Middle East, attracted not by agriculture but by Laredo's emerging reputation as a commercial trading nexus with Mexico. Thus, a Hamilton Bee from South Carolina joined a Raymond Martin (pronounced Martán) from France and both shared economic power with a Tejano, Basilio Benavides (Adams 2008, 83). But the relatively small number of such new non-Tejano elites also meant something else, best captured by the first professional historian of Laredo, Gilberto Hinojosa:

> Sharp divisions ... along ethnic lines seem to have been avoided. Interaction between Mexican Americans [Tejanos] and Anglo-Americans [former southerners] was to a great extent characterized by cooperation. ... Anglo-Americans and Europeans in Laredo, according to local tradition, learned Spanish, mixed socially with the Mexican American upper class, and intermarried with them. They often appeared more Mexicanized than Mexicanos [Tejanos] appeared Americanized. (1983, 70–71)

In 1861, Laredo's developing socioeconomic identity as an already predominantly Tejano international commercial center took a quantum jump. In what is surely one of the strangest developments in the histories of Texas, Mexican Americans and the American South history, Laredo stepped into agricultural modernity by way of southern cotton. Such an agribusiness slot had also long been occupied by a plantation slave economy in the South in which eastern Texas played its part as the economy there grew "in only one way": cotton (R. Campbell, 2003, 211). By contrast there was very little, if any, cotton cultivation around Laredo, yet, true to its social nature, the town became a trading outlet for a southern cotton economy itself already intimately tied to world capitalist markets. During the American Civil War, this predominantly Tejano town paradoxically became a Confederate stronghold in an already Confederate state (J. Thompson 2017, 80–207). As David Montejano has exhaustively shown, with the Union blockade of the Gulf Coast, Laredo's overland trade routes offered a relatively secure gateway for southern Confederate export cotton to Mexico and then to European markets (2012). However, as Jerry Thompson tells us, the landing of Union troops along the Gulf Coast threatened this vital connection and the large profits that leading Laredoans were deriving from it. Laredo's primary civic leader at this moment was the Tejano, José de los Santos Benavides. Led by newly appointed General Benavides, troops from Laredo joined the Confederacy in the fighting against the Union troops, leading to the last battle of the Civil War at Palmito Ranch near Brownsville, Texas, on May 13, 1865 (J. Thompson 2017, 203). The Union Army never got even close to Laredo.

With the defeat of the Confederacy, and not particularly interested in the racial politics of the Southern "lost cause" and reconstruction, these Laredo Mexican American, erstwhile Confederates, and their intermarried multicultural elites, simply went back to doing export-import business with the United States (Adams 2008, 80–207). Adams neatly captures a Laredo that

> in the mid-nineteenth century had prospered during wartime with the expansion of merchants, traders, and new service activities to support the commercial sector and the military. The inflow of immigrants began a second wave, following the first influx in the 1850s. The cotton business, along with the merchant exports, created the beginning of the Laredo forwarding agents and brokers, thus solidifying fast ties not just with San Antonio and Monterrey but also with shippers from New Orleans and the eastern seaboard of the United States (93).

Laredo, Texas, really never looked back from its initial insertion into an agricultural modernity by way of cotton that it itself did not grow but skillfully exploited and managed. Later, the coming of the railroad from San Antonio and Corpus Christi in 1881 and 1882 only enhanced the city's economic identity as a trading center, the very same years that serious coal mining operations began just outside the city (J. Thompson 2017, 265–68). By the 1880s, Adams suggests that Laredo might best be described as a bustling commercial center focused on trade with Mexico and already becoming a city in the modern American sense of the term (100–101). Under Mayor of the city, Refugio Benavides (José's younger brother), Laredo had a life centered on the city's plazas; it witnessed the construction of a "large and imposing" Catholic Church, but also a new post office, courthouse, and hotels. There was twice a week mail service to San Antonio, and even, in 1878, a baseball game between Laredoans and the soldiers from a nearby fort that the Laredoans won 26 to 16 (234). There was also a new elementary school called the *Escuela Amarilla* (the Yellow School) constructed with yellow brick. And the streets of Laredo were being cleaned, leveled, and planned in very orderly grid fashion (240). These gridded streets of Laredo were also now governed by city ordinances that prohibited noisy and sometimes violent dancing, and called for the arrest of vagrants and drunks. And, "anyone caught carrying a pistol or deadly weapon in the city limits would be fined from five to no more than ten dollars" or "jailed with fifty cents credit for each day of incarceration" (240). While Adams does call Laredo a "Wild West boom town," his very description in the rest of this paragraph belies this label that is more loosely metaphorical than descriptive. Since the Civil War and through the early 1880s, he tells us, Laredo's "population nearly tripled"; there was "a shortage of housing and hotels"; "over one hundred buildings, at a total valuation of $220,000, were under construction"; "city and county services were expanded to include better land use requirements"; "the first Webb County courthouse was completed in June 1882 at a cost of $41,000"; and, finally "direct capital investment in railroad facilities, land acquisition and labor . . . exceeded $1.3 million" (2008, 114). In short, postbellum Laredo, Texas, was becoming a modern site, or as Montejano puts it, in the 1880s after the railroads "reached Laredo, the town had 'blossomed' into modernity" (1987, 95). Although, perhaps paradoxically, the flower metaphor is apt, because the seeds, indeed the stem and buds of capitalist modernity, had already been implanted before the 1880s. Laredo's Civil War insertion in an agricultural modernity of export cotton had created a significantly Tejano capitalist entrepreneurial class awaiting the expanded opportunities for Laredo as a trading center afforded by the railroad.

I have detailed Laredo's entrance into modernity in part because it offers another perspective on Mexican Americans usually seen as a rural population in the nineteenth century, but also because it raises a certain conundrum about our ballad. I will have much more to say about our song in chapter 5, but, for this moment in Laredo's modernity, let us recall what is manifestly obvious in the ballad that we know: it is an anglophone narrative about two Anglo cowboys in the streets of Laredo. We are asked to imagine this modernizing commercial Laredo, heavily Tejano, as the ostensible setting for our song about anglophone cowboys who deal with death and redemption on its streets. Since they are obviously central to our song, we can reasonably imagine that such cowboys would have intersected with Laredo, Texas, at some point between their appearance in Texas circa the 1840s and toward the 1880s when the song is first detected. It is possible that its anglophone composer did walk Laredo's gridded streets, perhaps even witnessed or at least heard about such an inspiring violent incident, and then set about his artistic business. If indeed this literal intersection between anglophone cowboys and Laredo ever occurred, where did such anglophone cowboys come from?

In his commentary on the song, Jim Bob Tinsley notes that "Laredo served the Mexican ranches and haciendas on the original range of the Texas longhorn between the Nueces River and the Rio Grande" and he is correct to say "Mexican," or, what I have been calling *Tejanos* (2007, 78). Laredo was indeed serving its immediate Tejano ranching environment of present-day Webb, Zapata, and Starr counties and the owners were Tejanos (A. Alonzo 1998, 190). Indeed, the four largest ranches in Laredo's own Webb County were owned respectively by men with the names Nicolás Sánchez, Ramón Martinez, Cayetano de la Garza, and, not surprisingly, the omnipresent José de los Santos Benavides (A. Alonzo 1998, 212). I think we can also be reasonably sure that the labor force in these Tejano-owned ranches and smaller ones—the working cowboys and sheepherders (*pastores*)—would very likely themselves have been to a man—not cowboys, but *vaqueros*—Tejanos, perhaps with some indigenous workers. Why would the *Señores* Sánchez, Martinez, de la Garza and Benavides hire monolingual Anglo cowboys— if they even showed up in this area—when there was plenty of available Tejano, Spanish-speaking, familiar and familial, ranching talent who had been doing such work for generations?

If an anglophone cowboy ever did make his way into Laredo, it is far more likely that he came from the Anglo-dominated ranches to the east. This might have happened from the moment that such anglophone cowboys first began to appear in that part of South Texas since we simply do not really know exactly when the song was produced. Did, for example, a Texas Irish cowboy composer make his way some 150 miles from San Patricio to Laredo as early as the 1830s with an Anglo-Irish balladry already in his repertoire as a model? Was it some other later anonymous Anglophone, Scots-Irish cowboys from the Anglo ranches developing along the Gulf Coast after 1848 when the area finally became part of the United States? If such did so, either one would have had to come over one hundred miles on horseback or wagon—across Comanche and Apache raiding country—to a Laredo that in its incipient modernity and overwhelming ethnic Mexican identity would have seemed an unlikely destination for Anglo cowboys. If such men were looking for drink and women and/or supplies, Brownsville/Matamoros or even Corpus Christi were closer and much better known, ever since Zachary Scott's US Army left from Corpus Christi and marched into internal Mexico near Matamoros in 1846 and also established Ft. Brown on the Texas side. In short, while we cannot absolutely rule out the song's origins in Laredo, Texas, it seems highly unlikely that the song's events could have occurred in such a setting; thus, we must also correct Hand on this point as well (Limón 2022b). We are left with the question: Then why Laredo as a setting? We shall return to this point in chapter 3.

Along with others, business historian John A. Adams has been indispensable in allowing us to see Laredo in its commercial and Tejano identity, so it is a mystery and perhaps an irony of a kind, that, in an appendix to his book, he felt compelled to include the song and a bit of its "Irish" background. He seems to include it as perhaps as a bit of "local color," since he offers no evidence or analysis placing it in relation to his history of Laredo, but that is not surprising (2008, 199–200). The song's story and the Laredo he has described so well seem to have little in common. However, he does correctly note the song's probable presence among "cowboys who tended cattle on long drives through the Midwest," but clearly these were not Hispanophone Tejanos from the Laredo area; much more likely cowboys from the developing cattle kingdom east of Laredo. This Gulf Coast area is the second major instance in South Texas of what I have called agricultural modernity (199).

THE CATTLE KINGDOM: 1865-1890

Tejano, Irish, and Anglo ranchers had been taking some cattle to Louisiana, Missouri, Illinois, and even New York City in the 1840s and '50s and into the South during the Civil War (Dary 1981, 105–23). But this cattle economy greatly expanded after the Civil War in response to a greatly expanded demand for beef in a growing, industrializing, and urbanizing population base in the eastern and midwestern United States in a country now reunited. This growth included increased numbers of Anglo participants both as ranch owners and cowboys as even more Anglos were coming to Texas after the Civil War, especially from the decimated South. This expansion was led by figures like the aforementioned Richard King, whose ranch occupied a considerable part of southern Texas. At this particular historical moment, southern Texas was perhaps uniquely positioned to supply this particular commodity. As Armando C. Alonzo puts it, "It is estimated that at the end of the Civil War, there were five million cattle in Texas, most of them in the territory south of San Antonio. . . . Its ranchers soon found a new source of wealth" for such cattle "in distant national markets" and "for a period of about twenty years, the livestock industry enjoyed a renewed and unprecedented prosperity that transformed the region socially and economically" and brought "South Texas increasingly into the ambit of the expanding market economy of the United States" (1998, 196–97). South Texas witnessed the appearance and expansion of a new organization of labor as well as the conversion of nature into commodities that could be bought and sold, principally the open range and the wild Texas longhorn (R. White 1991, 270–97).

The railroad, one of the principal instrumental facilitators and symbols of such capitalist modernity, had not yet reached South Texas. Thus, the large-scale cattle

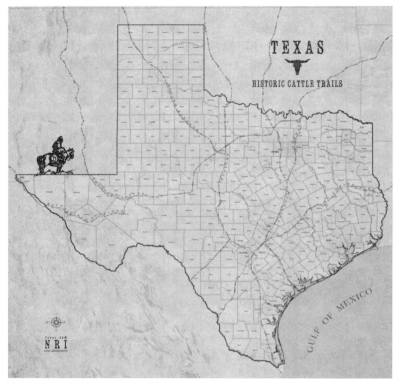

Figure 3. *Sources*: Texas Natural Resource Information System, Texas Department of Transportation, Texas Water Development Board, Texas General Land Office, Texas State Historical Association. Courtesy Natural Resources Institute, Texas A&M University.

drive was created as an organized and relatively efficient way to reach the nearest railhead distribution points in Kansas. After 1865, cattle drives took form principally along the fabled Chisholm Trail which began in this South Texas area close to Brownsville, Texas, and in close proximity to the King Ranch. There were other trails as well, but none as direct to access eastern markets. These drives then took a relatively direct line northward through Austin and Dallas-Fort Worth ending generally in Kansas where the beef would be processed and distributed by railroad (fig. 3).

Thus, we can now also recall and reject Wayland Hand's earlier mistaken observation that, as a setting for our ballad, Laredo was "an excellent choice as it lies at the beginning of the famous Chisholm trail just south of San Antonio" (1955, 4). Laredo really had very little to do with the great Texas cattle drives.[11]

THE OTHER TEXAS MODERN

In thus noting these two instances of agricultural modernity in South Texas, we must also take account of what anthropologist Richard Flores has to say on this score. In his fine book on the Alamo as master symbol, he takes up the coming of capitalist modernity to South Texas, or what he calls "the Texas Modern." However, Flores is chiefly concerned with modernity's impact in Texas in a period later than our own, but the two are not unrelated. He defines the Texas Modern as "a series of economic changes, social processes, discursive articulations, and cultural forms that result in the transformation of Texas from a largely Mexican, cattle-based society into an industrial and agricultural social complex between 1880 and 1920" (2002, xvii). For Flores, this capitalist process, centered on early twentieth-century commercial farming, offered "both promise and tragedy," the latter visited largely upon Tejanos (2).

However, when he speaks of the transformation of "a largely Mexican, cattle-based society," he seems to imply that before 1880, South Texas was fundamentally pre-modern and Mexican and that "agriculture" does not include cattle raising. Flores calls it "mercantile ranching," by which I think he means that it was an example of mercantile capitalism "engaged in long distance trade" and not defined yet as a modern capitalism "since ranch and cattle owners did not yet purchase the labor power of their cattle hands in an open market, nor did they control the labor process itself" (42). As for wages and the labor process, even on the supposedly feudalistic King ranch with its "loyal" vaqueros, Richard King complained "about the damn Mexicans always wanting higher pay," and we can certainly be sure that Anglo cowboys had even more pointed wage demands. Neither group, and certainly not the Anglo, was irrevocably bound to one ranch, and they could and did operate in an open market even if that only meant riding from one ranch to another looking for work (Moore 2010, 38–39). And, within such labor relations, ranch owners, "the Anglo cattlemen on these ranches . . . took the same measures to improve their ranches and control their men" (30).

The focus on northern markets and the organization of the economic cattle kingdom certainly intensified after the Civil War as "the business of cattle raising was beginning to take on the proportions of a full-fledged industry" and "the Texas cowmen's search for good markets would end with success" (Dary 1989, 167). In this period, external capital investment in these ranches from places like New York and London was already underway although it would not reach a high point until after 1880 (Montejano 1987, 62–63; Moore 2010, 37). Finally, there is the matter of the actual cattle drives themselves, or what Flores calls "trade." For me the cattle drive may be better reenvisioned as an organizational protocol, perhaps as a kind of conveyor belt that then brought the cattle to yet another conveyor—the railroad—which then took the animals onto a production line where more classical "industrial" workers processed them into beef commodities. At the end of the drive, there was not any sort of "trade" exchange—no opium for tea, here—but rather a cash nexus with the probability that the ranch owners may have used telegraph transfer to send the profits to their banks, most likely in San Antonio, after paying their meager cowboy wages (Standage 2007). Ironically, perhaps, after the end of the cattle drive, some of these cattlemen, but also occasionally cowboys, would sometimes take the train home, or at least as far as it would take them back to Texas (De León 2014, 15).

Moore provides us with a summation of this already fundamentally capitalist modernizing cattle kingdom between 1865 and 1880:

> The earliest cattlemen . . . often trailed their first herds themselves and knew the skills for handling cattle, but they were still businessmen with an eye to the future. Quite a few of them had attended college . . . ranching was as much an investment as a calling for them, and many had reputations for being strict with their men and ruthless with business competition. Most of the successful cattlemen experimented with breeding techniques and invested heavily in land. (2010, 37)

We thus dissent from a too strict characterization of ranching South Texas between 1865 and 1880 as somehow pre-modern, pre-capitalist, and all "Mexican." In this period of time, while not yet fully enveloped in modernity—they soon would be—Anglo-ranching South Texas and other parts of the state were certainly forging an intimate relationship with it. And we must not forget that other site of this earlier modernity: Laredo, Texas. Analyses that stress the exploitation of Tejanos or Mexican Americans in general with emphasis on farm labor do not explain postbellum Laredo and the relative socioeconomic, but also cultural, privilege or "promise" of many Laredo Tejanos that are still quite evident today. At that moment and not even today, as ethnic Mexicans, they largely did not experience the later "tragedy" that, according to Flores, almost universally befell other Tejanos downriver from Laredo under cash-crop agriculture, principally citrus, an economic colonization that historian Timothy Bowman has aptly called "blood oranges" (2016).[12]

CROSS-CULTURAL COWBOYS

In the preceding, I have addressed the impact of modernity on two locales in southern Texas, keeping in mind that "to speak of modernization with specificity is to put the accent on the material and organizational features of world capitalism in specific locales." While they may be "otherwise modern," they are still participants in it (Trouillot 2002, 223). Or, as Robert J. Foster puts it, "what we take modernity to mean will have much to do with the ethnographic particulars we hope to understand" (2002, 59). My "ethnographic particulars" have been Laredo and the cattle kingdom, but deeply implicit within the latter and modernity, we now turn to the ordinary cowboy who made the cattle drives possible and fostered our ballad to better understand his cultural role within this new economic order. Yet, the coming of modernity to Texas was part of a global process, and I also want to begin this understanding of the cowboy's society and culture relative to recent anthropological work on other parts and cultures of the world, if only because we do not often think of the cowboy in these terms, imagining him rather as out on the lonesome range. We can enlarge our sense of him by now seeing him and his experience also in a transnational dimension.

While this comparative effort might surprise some, let us recall that several such societies across the globe were first brought within modernity's ken during the very same nineteenth-century historical moment of high European imperialism when the cowboy himself came into being. Bruce M. Knauft terms these "alternative" modernities because although they were at a distance from the increasingly urbanizing centers of Euro-American modernity, the latter nonetheless exerted their influence on these peripheral sites including the American West (2002). Such societies shared a temporal moment but also shared this modernization which was not always welcome, and they reacted to this phenomenon in various ways ranging from armed conflict to acquiescence. But in between, we also find creative and sometimes critical, unconscious or semiconscious, adaptations evincing what I have been calling a discontent with modernity such as that of the cowboy, or so I will argue.

According to Foster, local sites first experience modernity's pressure as a twin process of (1) "distanciation"—the long range presence of a distant "superordinate" authority—and (2) a subsequent "disembedding"—the local articulation of that abstract market force—of localized practices or "mechanisms that disembed or lift out social relations from localized context of interaction and stretch them out or restructure them across indefinite spans of time-space" (65–66).[13] Is this not what happened to pre-Civil War small cattle ranches and therefore cowboys when in response to the demand of an abstract authority of abstract market forces after 1865, they developed the cattle drive, in this case, quite literally, to stretch out and restructure local ranching practices "across indefinite spans of time-space?"

Localized sites may then also sometimes respond to such "dis" forces by "reembedding" understood as "the constant efforts of human beings, embodied and physically located, 'to make themselves at home in the modern world'" (67).[14] Put another way, reembedding refers to practices that serve to orient and give meaning to a person or people amidst rapid social change and/or trauma. From the moment of such contact and even to the present day, such societies at times expressed their varying discontents with modernity, sometimes drawing on their native cultural resources to reembed themselves (Foster 2004, 114–15). The Native American "ghost dance" is one such example (R. White 1991, 220). However, we find other moments and places where the "natives" paradoxically found such reembedding resources within modernity itself, or, more precisely, within its contradictions, or what Foster, after Giddens, calls "bargains with modernity (Giddens 1990, 90; Foster, 67). Before turning directly to the cowboy and continuing our comparative effort, I offer an illustrating case that also has the advantage of being part of the Texas cowboy's historical background.

In his work on black slavery on sugar plantations and the early-nineteenth-century Haitian Revolution, David Scott also draws our attention to such a moment and place where the twinned processes of distanciation and disembedding together with a reembedding reaction (2004).[15] In their rebellion, the Haitian slaves drew on resources within modernity at two contradictory levels. The rebellion's elite leaders, principally Toussaint L'Overture, whose unusual literacy led him to subscribe to modern enlightenment principals of individual freedom, favored integrating a Haiti with freed slaves into the already capitalist modernity of the world sugar economy. Ironically, such an integration could happen only if the mass of slaves continued to work in the plantation economy as still coerced working-class laborers but now under an enlightened, quasi-dictatorial black leadership. Adding a large measure of salt—not sugar—to this wound, under such an elite black national leadership, such an economy would nevertheless continue be directed by a managerial class of whites, the *petit blancs*, who, of course, knew the business of modernity. In sharp dissent, the mass of slaves favored a self-subsistent small plot agriculture that they had already begun to develop, even as slaves, something in the manner of Thomas Jefferson's yeomanry, itself an inheritance from the modern West (121). That is, both the black elites and now working-class former slaves became what Scott calls "conscripts of modernity"; that is neither volunteers nor in rebellion as both drew from and struck their respective if contradictory bargains with it so as to fashion what each saw as a new and better existence within modernity at their different levels (98–131).

What Scott calls a "tragedy" resides in that their respective bargains were incompatible with each other and ultimately with an unrelenting modernity (2004, 170–208). Having freed themselves from slavery, the ordinary black population lost this second struggle. Haiti continued to be ruled as a dictatorship in favor of other new native elites sharing L'Overture's views, if not his learning and charisma, and the mass of former slaves became "free," but highly exploited, labor in a global competitive plantation economy that could underwrite Haiti's future among enlightened modern nations. This "enlightened" effort was doomed to failure as subsequent Haitian history to the present was severely marred by a continuing French imperialism that eliminated even L'Overture himself but with continuing forms of dictatorship, extreme social inequality, and foreign interference, all aggravated by recurrent natural disasters.

While obviously worlds apart in several ways, Haitian black former slaves and white nineteenth-century cowboys do share some interesting features, including the tragic. In the broadest sense, the eighteenth-century institution of slavery by the French was but another instance of an already modern agricultural project that provided sugar from the Caribbean for a developing worldwide and already emerging capitalist economy (Mintz 1985). If Caribbean slavery was so intimately tied to an emergent capitalist modernity, so was its also slave-driven cotton cousin in the US South, both members of what Immanuel Wallerstein called "the creation of a new peripheral region[,] . . . the extended Caribbean . . . stretching from northeast Brazil to Maryland" during the emergence of the modern capitalist world system (1980, 1, 166–67).

We have already seen that the nineteenth-century cowboy came predominantly from these US southern origins—this extended Caribbean—from those mostly Scots-Irish southerners, who, with slaves, then moved into Mexican Texas in the 1820s and '30s. But we must also remember, that for the most part, they came from what Randolph B. Campbell (2003) earlier called "plain folk," or, a white agricultural working class already in the thrall of modernity by way of their participation in the slave economy. Even though they themselves may not have owned slaves, they were structurally located at its lower rungs both economically and culturally, always on the verge of being "white trash," like the petit blancs (small whites) in Haiti, which is to say, in a relationship of coercion and exploitation within a developing modernity like other members of the nineteenth-century white working class and recently freed slaves although the latter had the obvious and very large additional issue of racism. But, taking their cue from vaqueros and in a first stanza of reembedding, some of these white "plain folk"—but also freed slaves—managed to move out of the cotton economy into a different kind of agricultural labor as cowboys, although as with ordinary black Haitians who remained in Haiti, modernity would eventually triumph and even that moment as cowboys would come to an end.

The parallel tragedy for cowboys which is to say the final disembedding, or elimination of the cowboy's world came with the closing of the open range and the corporatization of Texas ranching as the railroads, including the refrigerated car, finally reached southern Texas beginning in the late 1880s. Or, as Richard White clearly and emphatically noted: railroads represented "the epitome of the modern in the late nineteenth century" that brought the most material sense of an ending to the cowboy when the railroads extended into very part of Texas permitting the direct shipment of cattle thus ending the cattle drives (2011, 507). But, it was not only the railroads as other technologies played their part. Perritt had described and documented this entire process explicitly for the cowboy that, in a telling phrase, he refers to as an instance of "Creative Destruction" in a modernizing global capitalist economy (2019, 361).[16]

In perhaps the best-known Texas example, in 1866, Goodnight helped create the Goodnight-Loving Trail from western Texas to Colorado and beyond for the cattle drives he and Oliver Loving organized. (We shall revisit this partnership in chapter 4). More significantly, Goodnight then went on to establish "the first large ranch in the Panhandle in 1876 . . . in the Palo Duro Canyon" (R. Campbell 2003, 302). By the early 1890s, and financed with British capital, Goodnight's ranch called the JA had grown to "1,325,000 acres in parts of six counties and ran a herd of more than 100,000 head." As Campbell puts the matter, "Cattle raisers, as they became more business-like and sought to protect their pastures and water sources used by their herds, brought an end to open-range ranching" and thus, "made cattle raising more of a business than an adventure" (302). Such major ranches were developed by fencing off land, using windmills instead of depending on river water, depressing the wages of their cowboy labor.[17] Montejano underscores this point. "By the 1880s the work of the cowboy in Texas was increasingly irrelevant . . . as the railroad had brought the shipping points much closer, rendering trail driving an inefficient way of shipping cattle to market." Such as cowboys continued to be needed, ironically, being a cowboy seemed to revert back to Tejanos, but only as workers on local ranches and only because they could be paid "one-half to two-thirds" of the wages that had been paid Anglo cowboys (Montejano 1987, 90). The cowboy, or what was left of him, was fully enveloped by modernity; his prior existence reduced to nostalgia.[18]

But before this ending—this Texas tragedy—the cowboy did have his reembedding moment, albeit briefly, on the open range of the cattle drives from 1865 to the 1880s. Like the former slaves, cowboys also became "conscripts of modernity" (Scott, 98–131). Neither volunteers nor in open rebellion, they also participated in "the constant efforts of human beings, embodied and physically located, 'to make themselves at home in the modern world'" (Foster 2002, 67). In comparison to the Haitian slaves' failure to win small-plot agriculture for themselves, within an American democratic ethos, the cowboy had a larger measure of success in finding such respect within an otherwise degrading nineteenth-century modernity. He was handed a modernizing labor mandate to supply fresh meat to an industrializing American market. This labor process primarily took the form of the cattle drive which, in turn, required his labor but over long distances and open country and on horseback—a fortuitous and paradoxical opportunity—an unforeseen contradiction within modernity that lasted only a short time. Within this new economic order, this ordinary Texas Anglo cowboy developed a socio-culturally distinctive role—his own kind of reembedding—that put him in tension with this new modernity. Like the Haitians and their pastoralist small-plot farming, this tension—this dissent from modernity—also appealed to an inheritance from Romanticism, articulated as a cowboy emergent culture and expressed in our ballad in critical discontent as we shall see next.

Song and Signification

The foremost writer on cowboy culture tells us that

> by the early 1870s the growth of the cattle trade had firmly established the
> cowboy as a hired man on horseback[,] ... the northern markets had created
> a demand for this unique man on horseback, but those markets had been cre-
> ated by the coming of the railroad. ... It also brought civilization and all of
> the things associated with the East that most cowboys regarded with scorn.
> (Dary 1989, 196–197)

If Dary is right—and I sense he is—what is the cultural basis of this cowboy
"scorn" for "all of the things associated with the East" which, in my view, is to say
"modernity?" And was it only a negating scorn, or did the cowboys reembed against
modernity with any sort of affirmative response? In what follows, I suggest that
the cowboy did develop such an affirmative culture, or as Dary says, he was a hired
man, like millions of others across the world, but *he* was "on horseback," a "unique
man on horseback." Dary further suggests that some cowboy songs reflected
this more consciously critical attitude, but does not offer any examples (196). I
will argue that this affirmative culture of labor largely on horseback will eventually
lead us to "The Streets of Laredo."

Jack Thorp, a working cowboy and writer whom we shall meet in more detail
later, gives us a start:

> Romance has come to gather around trail driving and trail drivers. ... Viewed
> in one way, it was a life calculated to suit self-reliant free men in love with

big open country, horses, and the skills of an industry that wasn't exactly farming and certainly wasn't manufacturing, but was just as important and necessary as either. (1945, 247)

Here we began to sense at least one perception of a certain cowboy dissidence with modernity; it "certainly wasn't manufacturing," says Thorp, a dissidence he couches as "romance" even as the expression "self-reliant" also invokes Emerson's idea that the individual must stand apart from the conformity of the moment, in this instance, a gradually enveloping modernity. But between "open country" and "skills" not to be missed is the centrality of "horses."

To better understand the cowboy's special place within the nineteenth-century labor process, we can exploit and expand Thorp's use of "romance" in a way that, as a well-read poet, he might possibly have understood. In my view, nineteenth-century cowboys articulated their culture as a paradoxical and subdued expression of what we have habitually called Romanticism, which we first associate with literature, and which itself cannot be separated from the early advent of modernity in Europe. Traditional cultural criticism of Romanticism has not fully engaged this conjunction in a nuanced fashion. Or, such is the claim of two critics, Michael Löwy and Robert Sayre, who argue that Western Romanticism—most evident for anglophone readers in early-nineteenth-century English poetry and also in Emerson's American transcendentalism—has been in a continual and adversarial relationship to the materialist features of modernity and also to its rationalist inheritance from the Enlightenment (2002). For them, Romanticism always offers an alternative "in the name of pre-capitalist values" (46). While Romanticism's "values" may harken back to some pre-capitalist past such as the medieval period, it is nevertheless much a product of modernity itself, not only in the obvious sense that it is a reactive phenomenon within modernity, but that it is also "*often bound up with it in a complex way* [emphasis theirs]" (53). Romanticism may be a "value" but its very social base and discursive modes are tied to modernity: formal education; technological resources such as printing and later film; the changing organization of language itself, especially in the form of the novel; and, most fundamentally, the very idea of the Western "individual," the *cogito ergo sum* who can then experience the alienation of modernity,

for this very individual cannot but live frustrated within its constraints . . . to fulfill certain socio-economic functions; but when this individual transforms itself into a full-fledged subjectivity, and begins to explore the internal universe of its particular constellation of feeling, it enters into contradiction with a system based on quantitative calculation and standardization. (58)

From this sense of individual alienation, a protest can spring forth expressed usually in varying modes of mostly literary creativity that nevertheless, at its most florescent, posits the individual now in some harmonious connection, often with the natural order but more significantly as an "impulse to recreate the human community conceived of in various ways" (59). As classically trained literary critics, these two erudite scholars are, indeed, drawn principally to literary texts but also political philosophy for the most extensive and intensive expression of Romanticism as a worldview. Therefore, we are not surprised when they conclude "that the *producers* of the Romantic anti-capitalist world view are *certain traditional sectors of the intelligentsia*, whose culture and way of life are hostile to bourgeois civilization [emphasis theirs]" (90).

For the most part, cowboys were not such an intelligentsia, and "hostile" may be too strong a term, although there is clear evidence among cowboys, such as Thorp, of what I have been calling a "discontent" with modernity. Yet, before we divorce the cowboy from the "literary," contrary to stereotypes, while a "number of cowboys were functionally illiterate, there were others who read Shakespeare or the Bible for pleasure" (Moore 2010, 129). If, indeed, some read Shakespeare, then why not the English Romantics themselves, and/or the American transcendentalists, such as the very popular Emerson, not that far removed generationally from the cowboy? J. Frank Dobie, the foremost literary exponent of Texas cowboy culture in the twentieth century and himself a sometime cowboy in South Texas, read the English Romantics who, "although none of them had ever been anywhere near the Brush Country, they spoke directly to Dobie's soul, and he became entranced" (S. Davis 2009, 21).

Yet, such reading was probably not the principal resource to which cowboys appealed as they fashioned their own much more subdued romantic sensibility, or what Raymond Williams might have called "a structure of feeling," which refers to "a pre-emergent cultural phenomenon: a trend that is developing but is not yet clearly emergent. We may have a sense of something new developing but as yet not fully formed" (O'Connor 1989, 84). When it does emerge, we can detect a fully formed new culture clearly expressed in texts and other media. I think Williams would say, for example, that early-nineteenth-century English high Romanticism is one such salient formation resulting from a prior and nascent structure of feeling developing *contra* the Enlightenment and emergent capitalism in the English eighteenth century, or what E. P. Thompson famously called the "moral economy" of the eighteenth-century English peasantry (1971).

Thus a "structure of feeling" precedes a more public and coherent expression, but the process might also work in reverse while also moving forward into the future. That is, while an inchoate "structure of feeling" may well acquire a more fixed and observable form in a later moment such as high Romanticism, that "high" moment itself can then also disappear altogether, or perhaps attenuate into yet another "structure of feeling." In this instance, early-nineteenth-century Romanticism gradually seems to give way, in its case, to capitalist modernity but also to various corresponding literary "realisms" in the later nineteenth correlated with the harder realism of an industrializing and urbanizing modernity that we see in figures such as Dickens in England, and Howells, Crane, and Dreiser in the United States. Nevertheless, even within such hardening realism—social and literary—it is possible for the previous high moment to continue, albeit in a now attenuated form. But the word "form" may be too much, as it persists now only as, again, a structure of feeling, only as a dispersed relatively inchoate presence. Williams's "structure of feeling" also overlaps with another famous formulation of his: the "residual" in culture, where "certain experiences, meanings, and values which cannot be expressed or substantially verified in terms of the dominant culture, are nevertheless lived and practiced on the basis of the residue—cultural as well as social—of some previous social and cultural institution or formation" (Williams 1977, 122). Such a feeling is sensible, or more like "sensate," perhaps only in the social margins and/or in cultural geographies not yet fully impacted by modernity, or structurally set aside from it (Williams 1977, 122).[1]

I would argue that between 1865 and the 1880s, the cowboys indirectly drew on high Romanticism but only as a residual culture indebted to a prior "high" historical moment; a kind of Romanticism that he might have still sensed but probably did not directly know. But what more precisely was the content—the practice—of this culture, albeit residual? There are many such accounts, but since we are on the subject of Romanticism, let us take our cue from one contemporaneous observer of this culture, Walt Whitman, whose later poetry overlaps with that of the cowboy's prime era. Indeed, in his 1882 *Specimen Days*, after traveling in the American West, we see clearly Whitman's Romantic recognition of this cowboy residual Romanticism, or, what Farley has called an "objective correlative" of his poetry (Farley 2005). In *Specimen Days*, Whitman writes: "the cow-boys ('cow-punchers') to me a strangely interesting class, bright-eyed as hawks, with their swarthy complexions and their broad-brimm'd hats—apparently always on horseback, with loose arms slightly raised and swinging as they ride" (2023, 172). Their strangeness to him as a class already speaks to their cultural dissidence, but this was much less a matter of complexion or bright eyes or even their "broad-brimm'd hats" and much more that the cowboy was "apparently always on horse-back, with loose arms slightly raised and swinging as they ride."

HORSE MEN, NOT COW BOYS

While other features and practices may matter, I would submit that this residual culture of low-key Romanticism was centered on the horse, which became at once the fleshliest instrument of labor and arguably the most symbolic of nature's non-human animals in the American West. The horseman as a symbolic figure was, of course, well-known throughout world cultures although mostly as a warrior hero. In this particular instance and whatever its other antecedent sources, the cowboy's residual Romanticism might be connected to medieval Spain and the epic quest against Moors and other enemies. Such horsemen were celebrated in the medieval Spanish ballad called indeed, the *romance* (in Spanish) that, according to Américo Paredes, was then brought to Mexico and then to Tejano Texas already itself as a residual culture (1958, 129–130). The anglophone Texas cowboy probably could not really come to know the Spanish-language *romance* and its closely related form, the *corrido*, but it seems likely that anglophone cowboys inherited the sustaining Romantic tradition of the horseman as a residual culture from their Tejano teachers along with the practical skills of his artisanal culture (Leslie 1957). All of this, we need remember from chapter 1, mediated by the Texas Irish, themselves from a people associated with the "Romantic."

But it is difficult, if not impossible, to separate the cowboy on horseback from his sense of masculinity. As her subtitle indicates in *Cowboys and Cattlemen: Class and Masculinities on the Texas Frontier*, Moore views her subject through the *au courant* lens of masculinity studies. The cowboy seemed to have two kinds of masculinity. On the one hand, they "spent their leisure time in boisterous behavior designed to show masculinity through public drinking and sexual prowess" with "gambling and fighting" also as "key parts of cowboy identity" (21). However, her use of the term, "leisure," clearly suggests that such behavior was occasional—probably at the end of the cattle drive—relative to what the cowboy actually spent most of his waking time doing, which was working on the cattle drive. Here she finds another and more abundant kind of male behavior as the cowboys "saw their masculinity in terms of their skills on the job, their control over their working conditions and their ability to make independent decisions" (21). Yet this might also describe the outlook of a schoolteacher at that moment. Clearly Moore would agree that the cowboy's work setting also had a paramount character that accented his masculinity, namely the sheer physicality required and the danger it posed that would not have been the case for such a teacher. Also, unlike this teacher, the cowboy's skills—primarily riding, roping, and manhandling cattle and horses—were of a particular artisan nature learned on the job from other cowboys; indeed all of this happened in the exclusive company of men. Allmendinger has aptly called this cowboy formation a "work culture" although he largely ignores the horse (1992, 3)

Moore compares the cowboy to other nineteenth-century and truly dangerous occupations principally miners. The latter, she claims, were like cowboys in that they also defined their manliness through the risks they took and overcame while working underground (79). While such comparisons do hold, not only for miners and other occupations such as loggers, one also needs to emphasize that the cowboy's risk-taking labor was closely tied to the cattle drives in the mid-nineteenth century and made the cowboy a unique member of the working class. Moore does not take account of another more directly relevant occupational group, one with great comparative potency for emerging cowboys, especially those with a southern ancestry. As Randolph B. Campbell noted, most southerners entering Texas were "plain folk," lower middle class at best, "poor whites" at worst. For the most part, they were tied to cotton agriculture from the 1820s through 1865, some with a few slaves, most farming small plots as tenants or sharecroppers, living in simple cabins and eating simple food (2003, 214–219). They also preferred mules to horses (Dary 1989, 76). We can reasonably say that most young Anglo cowboys in the mid-nineteenth century came out of such a "plain folk" existence, either directly from eastern Texas or from the defeated Old South after the Civil War. We emphasize this population to fully appreciate what it might have meant to a young man from this kind of society to get on that horse for a long trail drive; two western folk phrases speak to mobility—to "get a leg up" into a stirrup to then "ride high in the saddle." This elevated posture was even better than "walking in tall cotton," especially if you didn't even own it. As Dary notes:

> What made the cowboy different from hired help in other vocations was the horse. The cowboy felt independent on the trail or on the open range. It has been said that he was in a position to look down on the rest of the world. Many a cowboy had contempt for any labor that could not be performed from

what Charles A. Siringo described as "the hurricane deck of a Spanish pony."
(1989, 197)

And, indeed, it was not the horse standing still but rather "on the trail or on
the open range." The long cattle drives to places far beyond Texas on the open
range and on horseback also lent a certain kind of exciting pastoral and epic quality to their productive labor not easily available to other occupations. But we must
continue to stress that this unique kind of labor was largely articulated on horseback.
Surprisingly, Moore does not foreground the horse and its esteemed place in many
world cultures. For it was the horse that presented not only the greatest physical
challenge in its initial domestication but also afforded the cowboy the utmost display of his artisan skills, a freedom of movement across time and space, but also a
literal elevation, all of which put him above and beyond other working men in
industrializing America and made the horse the cowboy's most prized possession
even as he could also be emotionally possessed by his horse (McGuane 1999). Yet,
we must never forget that, while, in our contemporary moment, the residual may
be now relegated to areas of "leisure," for the cowboys, it was wholly imbedded as
part of a challenging labor process. As noted earlier, like their not-that-far-removed
English peasant ancestors, they too developed a moral economy closely intertwined
with their practical one (Thompson 1971).

One does not have to idealize the cowboy or worse yet, indulge in the
stereotypes and caricatures that would come later, to note that in an industrializing
nineteenth-century America, the real living cowboy was a distinctive working class,
sociocultural figure, and that he was aware of himself as such. We are not surprised
that for young Texas boys in the nineteenth century, "cowboys were irresistible, and
tangible, heroes [emphasis mine]" (Moore 2010, 50). As the distinguished historian
of Texas, Randolph B. Campbell, also noted, "The life of a cowboy, regardless of the
reality, had mythic appeal *even then* [emphasis mine]" (2003, 299). As such, and
only for a brief historical moment, the cowboy was set apart from an industrializing
capitalist modernity that was taking off in Euro-America at the same nineteenth-
century historical moment of his emergence and his most salient presence on the
long cattle drives. And in thus being set apart, he also stood as a critical commentary on that modernity offering not only a different but a humanly better, less alien-
ated, mode of labor in comparison to other sectors of the working class.

One might be tempted to think of the world of cowboys as a liminal category. It is hardly a coincidence that interest in liminal spaces took off as modernity intensified in the twentieth century. Even with its focus on non-Western

principally African tribal societies, such an interest in spaces away from time, labor and regimentations could not help but have relevance to unfulfilled needs within modernity, and soon enough we saw such an interest turn in that direction (Turner 1982). Yet liminality does not adequately account for what we sense in the cowboy between the short span of years roughly 1865 to the late 1880s, and a large part of the reason is that at his utmost, the cowboy was not ever in any version of "time out" but rather centrally involved in labor. Yet this was a form of labor literally practiced in elevation but that also elevated the cowboy above the ordinary, which is to say, the modern form of most labor. I know of no fully adequate term to name this particular state of being, but during the mid-twentieth-century period of intensifying modernity, a famous American sociologist offered the idea of the *craftsman*, the worker who

> becomes engaged in the work in and for itself; the satisfactions of working are their own reward; the details of daily labor are connected in the worker's mind to the end product; the worker can control his or her own actions at work; skills develop within the work process; work is connected to the freedom to experiment; finally, family, community and politics are measured by the standards of inner satisfaction, coherence, and experiment in craft labor. (Mills 1951, 220–222)

I would like to believe that this most famous sociologist, C. Wright Mills, would think so of cowboys. Mills was a native Texan from Waco, sitting astride the Chisholm Trial, and he spent a good portion of his adult life in Texas, most notably as a graduate student in philosophy at UT–Austin in the 1930s.[2]

ROMANCE AND CONTRADICTION

I can already hear certain kinds of critics over to my left objecting to even this restrained affirmative understanding of the Texas cowboy. We can readily acknowledge that his inherently critical posture toward modernity did not make the cowboy a paragon of progressivism in other respects any more than many other members of the white working class at that moment and even into our time. For the most part, we can be sure that at least some cowboys often had less than salutary or expansive views on matters of race and gender, and these must be addressed. We can critically note four distinct and perhaps predictable instances, but I also wish to put these in relation to his discontent with modernity.

Gender relations were perhaps the most fundamental of these. Here Moore is also of the greatest assistance in noting the cowboy's obvious participation in a prevalent patriarchy even as she notes its distinctive role in the cowboy's cultural stance toward modernity. According to Moore, cowboys might sentimentalize their mothers, but they were anxious about "respectable" and marriageable females, keeping them at a distance as if a threat to the cowboy way of being. While they might "settle down" in later life, to be a cowboy was essentially to be free from the civilizing effects of women, which is to say from the project of modernity as carried by women (141–167). Indeed, "marriage often meant the end of a cowboy's career" (162). Prostitutes were obviously in a different category. "Cowboys were aware that their relationships with prostitutes were mainly financial ones," and of course sexual, but without any expectation of long-term affection and love although on occasion such could happen (156–162). Thus, while subordinated within a prevalent patriarchy, women played a role as agents of a suspect modernity from the cowboy's point of view.

There was also the question of race, especially in the central iconography so intimately associated with the cowboy, at least in my generation, which is the child's play of "cowboys and Indians" and casts the cowboy as an unremitting agent of the internal colonialism and genocide directed against indigenous peoples in the American West (Yellow Bird 2004). Clearly cowboys did occasionally fight Native Americans on the cattle drives and may possibly have even engaged in atrocities although, as in the Sand Creek massacre, the US Army and paid mercenaries of the *Blood Meridian* variety were probably far more culpable than working cowboys (Hoig 2005). Indeed, from 1865 through the 1870s, the US Army and buffalo hunters did far more to exterminate or drive Native Americans out of Texas (Campbell 2003, 293–294). While such actions did make the cattle drives possible, the working cowboy does not appear to have been central to this process. He had other things on his mind. Then there is also the often-overlooked story of Native Americans themselves becoming cowboys (Iverson 1994).

For the white cowboy, ethnic Mexicans, or Tejanos, and African Americans had more racial salience, if only because of their greater everyday presence and proximity. We have already noted Anglo violence in the areas north of the Nueces, especially after the wars for Texas independence and annexation. This sometimes carried over into the 1870s, and cowboys may have been involved in this particularly racist contact zone closer to the Nueces River as J. Frank Dobie himself documented by way of the cowboy, John Young (1929, 69–85).[3] However, as the New West historian, Richard White demonstrates in detail, a great deal of social violence in the ranching American West was instigated by cattle men who hired professional gunmen and not cowboys (1991, 344–345).

Nevertheless, in more face-to-face interactional zones such as eating and drinking, a clear social distance was maintained, certainly with African Americans, but also with Tejanos (Montejano 1987, 83; Moore 2010, 134–138). As Frank Maynard, a working cowboy poet whom we will soon meet more fully, candidly noted, in the Texas of the 1870s, "the [Mexican] 'greasers' did not stand in much favor with the white population in general" (Maynard 2010, 85). Yet, for the ordinary cowboy, Moore notes the variability in these particular relations, which ranged from outright racial hostility and violence to begrudging respect for Tejano and African American ranching skills, especially with the Tejano legacy of ranching (2010, 134–140). She makes this specific point that illustrates the complications of class, race, ethnicity, and also gender in the world of the Texas cowboy: "white cowboys were themselves social outcasts . . . which could work to blur racial barriers[;] . . . they were willing to acknowledge talented cowboys when they saw them, regardless of ethnicity" and, then makes a critical point that reminds us of Marty Robbins and "El Paso": "certainly, many white cowboys had no difficulty in courting Mexican or Indian women" (134).

African-Americans and ethnic Mexicans might also lend a further dimension to the cowboy's critical encounter with modernity. Given their distinctive cultures at that moment, did these subaltern cowboys share the white cowboy's stance toward modernity? That is, did they also think of cowboying as a distinctive and indeed prized occupation relative to a sensed alienation from modernity? There is precious little primary data on these two groups to really know. Moore says little on this question about African Americans except to note that "black cowboys were attracted to the work for much the same reasons as Anglo cowboys" (40). Here modernity may also play a paradoxical role as it did with women. One may also surmise that African Americans still recalled their relatively recent experience with slavery, and their very proximate awareness that many "freed" blacks were still bound to the East Texas plantation cotton economy might have led to a greater appreciation of their higher cowboy status much like the white cowboy.

For their part, Tejano vaqueros may have had a very different relationship to modernity given their longer history in the region. What evidence is available of their attitudes toward their own work clearly suggests they were highly valued for their skills and undoubtedly had a sense of pride in them. Américo Paredes also tells us of a nineteenth-century corrido, or Mexican folk ballad, about a cattle drive from Texas to Kansas in which thirty Anglo cowboys are not able to manage a hundred steers together, a task then easily accomplished by just *five* Tejano vaqueros (1976, 25–26, 53–55). More fundamentally, did vaqueros share the white cowboy's residual romanticism and his discontent with modernity? We also have other evidentiary sources on this matter that Moore does not use. The early-twentieth-century folklorist and historian, Jovita González reports that "an old vaquero told me once of what to him was paradise: the open prairies with no fences to hinder the roaming of cattle and the wanderings of cowboys" (1927, 11). However, while they may have shared at least some of the white cowboy's discontent, they may have differed in another important respect. One also has the impression that Anglo cowboys tended to be on the nomadic side, perhaps even in flight from the "plain folks" existence of toughened families eking out a living in cotton, a distancing accentuated by the cattle drives.[4] By contrast, vaqueros were much more closely affiliated with the ranches where they worked. Their ranches tended to be wholly congruent with an extended and patriarchal family that sometimes could include nonfamiliars who were nevertheless close, or what even into my day we would call "*arrimados*," those, not exactly kin, but close by. Tejanos, says Armando C. Alonzo, "cherished traditional values, such as love, honor, and respect for every family member. They were also united in purpose, egalitarian in their treatment of family members in matters of property rights and fair in their dealing with each other and with outsiders" (1998, 113). Within this kind of kinship, vaqueros also "were often married, and the presence of their wives and children created a strong sense of community and family responsibility." Thus, the vaqueros on the large ranches of South Texas gained "their sense of manhood from their roles as husbands and fathers" in contrast to most white cowboys. Vaqueros "also saw their work as a defining part of their masculinity," and "spent a good portion on their work week away from their families in all-male cow camps," but "they also did not spend the same time in town carousing that the other cowboys did," (Moore 2010, 30). Alonzo's and Moore's descriptions clearly suggest that the vaqueros had domestic cultural resources that may have shielded them from the growing adversarial alienation of modernity on the cattle drives. Even those Tejanos who did go on the cattle drives had something to come home to that was not as evident with Anglo cowboys.[5]

RECOGNIZING THE COWBOY

Over time, it has become almost obligatory to assess all modern cultural phenomena in terms of race and gender, and this is what I have tried to do in the immediately preceding section, especially when these categories had clear implications for the cowboy. Inevitably there will be those who might believe I am teasing things out too much in creating a distinct and more affirmative space for the white cowboy. Indeed, I am, but in doing so, I would like to think that I am responding to Rita Felski's call for "recognizing class" (2021). From her reading of the social theorist Didier Eribon's autobiographical sociology, *Returning to Rheims*, she distills the idea of recognition as a currently absent relationship between a broadly conceived academic "left," especially among literary critics and a white Euro-American working class. In its continuing enthrallment with an early, usually not cited, Frankfurt School perspective, the former is very inclined to dismiss the latter as hopelessly entrapped in a false consciousness, usually of race and gender. This largely humanities world has turned "its gaze away from the empirical complexity and messiness of the social world" of this white working class in a way that has also recently been critically noted of the national Democratic Party (100). Felski would have us turn to a *second* generation of the Frankfurt School represented by Axel Honneth who does fully acknowledge such white complexity and messiness. This messy complexity should also not be taken in purely socioeconomic terms—lost jobs, reduced health benefits, childcare, etc., for, among other injuries of class, it also includes the often inchoate "relevance of moral feelings—anger, disappointment, the desire for dignity, resentment at unfairness" (104). As we have learned the hard way in our presidential politics, we have ignored this world at our common peril. It is in this spirit that I have called attention to the American cowboy who undoubtedly experienced this range of feelings, but I have lent more emphasis to his claim on dignity if only by way of his horse, a not small matter. He emerged out of his sociocultural complication with modernity with all manner of contradictions yet with a strong, if muted, sense of his critical difference, always within the labor process, or as Felski, after Honneth, puts it, "critical consciousness is *ordinary*, part of daily life rather than estranged from it [emphasis hers]" (101).

Such a critical consciousness can, however, become less "ordinary," which is to say more artistic, in the working-class aesthetic, creativity that we have habitually called folklore, especially folksong. At some point during his time in the saddle on the Chisholm Trail or a similar site, and from his still active residual romanticism, the Texas cowboy generated a number of folksongs, including some version of "The Streets of Laredo." More recent scholarship has neglected cowboy song, a neglect much remedied by Joanna Ray Zattiero's recent and very useful overview of the subject in which she argues that "nineteenth and early twentieth century cowboy songs are part of a vibrant and active musical tradition that developed alongside the cattle industry boom of the 1870s–1880s" (2020, xi). Moore notes the importance of singing for cowboys, and perhaps only slightly overstates when she says, "it was not possible for a cowboy to get a job in some outfits unless he could sing," also noting that tunes were not as important as lyrics (2010, 129). "Such songs," says Dary, "were a good gauge of the mood and thoughts of the nineteenth century Texas cowboys who made the long trail drives to Abilene and other railheads in Kansas and elsewhere" (1989, 196–197). Yet, we cannot entirely discount the charge that the always hardworking cowboys had neither the time nor the requisite education to compose such songs, and admittedly most did not, nor that these songs accurately reflect the cowboy's daily reality (Barsness 1967). However, as in every culture, and as Moore already noted for the cowboy, there undoubtedly were those with some educated literacy and, frankly, with an artistic temperament and inclination for poetics and music. As for "reality," the whole point of a Romantic sensibility is to create an imaginary world, not escapist, rather one that critically questions the origins and moral status of "reality" even while acknowledging it with realistic descriptors such as gambling, drink, and death as in "The Streets of Laredo." For even in questioning the realism of most cowboy songs, John Barsness acknowledges that some such songs demonstrated the "strained retention of older folk traditions," specifically he notes, "The Streets of Laredo" (1967, 56–57). Tinsley tells us that our ballad quickly "spread . . . after its re-creation and was sung everywhere on the trail and the range, becoming one of the favorite songs of the cowboys" (2007, 78). More specifically, Lomax and Lomax refer to "The Streets of Laredo" as "the most popular Western ballad . . . after the Chisholm Trail" (1947, 248). Later, I propose to raise some serious questions about the specific textual accuracy of these assessments, even as they all speak of its fame, but for the moment, let us take them at face value for the purpose of an immediate understanding of our song, an understanding later requiring a more detailed and nuanced inquiry into its evidentiary base.

THE SIGNIFICATION OF "THE STREETS OF LAREDO"

Over half a century ago, the distinguished folklorist, Alan Dundes of Berkeley, scolded folklorists for paying insufficient attention to the literary merits and meanings of folklore, calling on them to interpret such folklore as literature (1965). In fact, cowboy songs in general have been much noticed but not specifically discussed in critical literary terms. The usual summations are to the effect that such songs were used for entertainment, camaraderie, and calming cattle, but not much on what a close reading might tell us about the cowboy and his world (Moore 2010, 129).

I propose to interpret "The Streets of Laredo" within the cowboy's residual Romanticism and his encounter with modernity using as my text the 1947 Lomax and Lomax version with which we began. I do so at this juncture to take advantage of our immediately preceding discussions of agricultural modernity and residual Romanticism while they are fresh in the reader's mind. Yet, my interpretive exercise might be seen as a kind of presentism because one must fully acknowledge that this particular text was never directly field collected amongst nineteenth-century cowboys, at least as far as we know. Nevertheless, I beg the reader's indulgence, for in a more textually and biographically detailed account that follows in the next chapter, I hope to demonstrate a series of collecting and editorial linkages that connect this 1947 text to its nineteenth-century origins to provide what I hope is a sufficient basis for my interpretation in that historical context.

With this interpretive warrant, I suggest that the song's thematic outlook and its elegiac tonality correlates well with the cowboy's sense of himself in the world, that which I have designated as a residual Romanticism. "The Streets of Laredo" expresses a contradiction between the cowboy's culture and a modernity represented most immediately by the drinking and gambling that led to his death in the town. This critical encounter with modernity is at the heart of our song as it is in no other example of the cowboy's song repertoire, an antithetical relationship played out in the song's narrative but also in its musical tonality.

In an opening and framing stanza, we meet two cowboys in dialogue. One of them is also our narrator who speaks the stanza. The other the "young cowboy," at first appears to be dying, although "wrapped up in white linen as cold as the clay" he would seem already dead. We can possibly imagine that the principal narrator is himself really voicing what the young cowboy would have said if he could still talk, so in some sense, he might be the only true speaker in dialogue with reported speech. Nevertheless, after the framing of the first stanza, the young cowboy is given voice in the second, especially in its first two lines where we see him dashing and gay in the saddle, only to learn that he has been shot in the breast. His misfortune is probably the result of some altercation resulting from drinking and gambling, but more specifically in the "dram house" and the "card house" which is also to say in the town and not on the open range.

We then enter the fourth and fifth stanzas which greatly amplify the song's emotional appeal in the evocative funeral rites that follow. He does not wish to be buried in the town. Rather, he asks to be taken to the "green valley" in a pastoral moment accentuated by his pall bearers—his fellow cowboys and six pretty maidens—who will place red roses on his coffin. We also witness this funeral procession to the mournful sound of drums and fifes but that are also tonally replicated in the solemn lento tempo in which "The Streets of Laredo" is usually sung. The fifth and sixth stanzas then offer a final articulation of a collective cowboy identity in his invitation to the other cowboys to "swing your rope slowly and rattle your spurs lowly" and reminds us again that he has "done wrong." In one final part, he continues this cowboy identity by asking for "cool water," much as he might have on the range. The first cowboy speaker then returns to close the song in a final framing stanza, more reportorial than imagistic, as "we" and the others "bear him along" to his final resting place. Even as they testify to their love of their cowboy representative "comrade, so brave, young, and handsome," they also remind us one final time that "he'd done wrong." Given the Texas religious culture of that time, one might see this song in moralistic terms. From a more Protestant (Baptist) point of view, the cowboy has been sinful in drinking, gambling, and perhaps even fornication and thus merits his punishment, but then the story should end there, perhaps adding only a consignment to hell. Instead, this section invites, not our castigation or even forgiveness, and much more our understanding that something more tragic has happened here.

As we saw earlier, as part of the cattle drives, the cowboy was already configured by modernity at a macro level with the organization of the cattle drives, but here he directly encounters it at a local level—a micro-modernity—and really the only such encounter he would experience on the cattle drive. It is the town itself, but really the gambling and drinking specifically designed to take the cowboys' meager wages for profit, especially given their youthfulness (Dary 1989, 209). In the guise of entertainment, saloons "were arguably the most prevalent kind of retailing outfit in the West." Richard White continues: saloons were "always a business enterprise and a retail establishment[,] . . . an example of how retailers tied together local consumers and regional or national suppliers. Saloon keepers were businesspeople in search of profits" (White 1991, 275). In all of this, the aforementioned profitable prostitution was also not a small matter for the furtherance of modernity "as a source of additional revenue not only for the saloon owners who managed the women but also "for the towns and cities that fined and taxed them" (307).

Clothing also became a commodity. At the beginning of the cattle drives, "Texas cowboys wore whatever kinds of nondescript clothing they could obtain or make from available materials," although, continues Lawrence Clayton, "distinct patterns of clothing made for the task began to appear, and the outfit of the Texas cowboy soon began to emerge because it fitted the work." Indeed, Clayton turns to our ballad to make the point that one cowboy to another "could see by your outfit that you are a cowboy" (2001, 103). However, given the wear and tear of the cattle drive, when in town, and preferably after a bath, cowboys also wanted to look good, or at least better. New clothes and boots were *de rigueur*, such that "clothing was the second largest consumer industry in the cattle towns as a result of its cowboy customers, and boot making made up a sizable portion of the market as well" (Moore 2010, 169).

The town thus stands in a metonymic relationship with a modernity that by transporting cattle had already brought the cowboys into a larger and anxious conscription, one in which, as I have argued, they developed a countervailing culture as part of a labor process that nevertheless ultimately furthered the modern project by literally feeding it. To say all this is not to deny or diminish the pleasure cowboys may have taken in town, but in our song, it is also evident that the young cowboy thinks he "has done wrong" in thus partaking of the town's site of modernity, a refrain that will be repeated for emphasis. The emotional core—the funeral, the drums and fifes, but perhaps even more so, the imagery of a young handsome cowboy, gay and dashing in the saddle, offer an alternative and better way of life from which this young cowboy momentarily and fatally lapsed, but that, nevertheless, is still offered in a vibrant contrapuntal imagery to modernity. As with the Mexican corrido, even the lento tempo of "Streets" suggests a contrapuntal relationship to the intensifying faster, at times chaotic, rhythms of modernity as do its traditional ballad rhyme scheme (a-b-c-b) and iambic meter (Limón 1992, 34–35). It is against this town-sanctioned modernity that cowboy kinship and occupational values create comradeship and perhaps a utopian sphere but one that is concretized through the most compelling image in the ballad recalling the centrality of the horse:

"It was once in the saddle I used to go dashing,
It was once in the saddle I used to be gay

I suggest that the cowboys who sang this ballad sensed the tenuous, precarious but still vibrant, state of their horseman's culture against the growing presence of modernity and its towns, and that is why they loved this song that spoke to that encounter in such a vivid manner.

However, I am not the first to venture an interpretation of this famous ballad. As we have already seen, there is a plentiful literature on our ballad's genealogy and diffusion, but I have come across only one extended critical analysis of this ballad in relation to its most central subject—the American cowboy and his social context (Tatum, 1994). We acknowledge Tatum's precedent and persuasive interpretive work even while taking hopefully productive issue with its conclusion (1994). He first suggests that the ballad's "narrative of sin, death and remorse indicts popular pleasures—in this case drinking and gambling—in a manner that reminds us of how an underlying sense of Christian righteousness persistently locates the cowboy's life in service to an official bourgeois morality." But there needs to be more, or as Tatum himself tells us that "what needs further to be said has two aspects:"

> (1) how the song identifies . . . the merger of kinship and occupational values in the face of death, this desired merger accomplished through an oral performance; and
> (2) how the utopian impulse through comradeship coursing through the song takes substantial shape precisely because of and in opposition to the absent but felt presence of an official morality (97).

Again, I can readily agree that the dying cowboy's kinship with his fellow cowboys but also the maidens as well as the evocation of his occupational value of the horse are at the core of the ballad's affirmation of the cowboys' culture but, for Tatum, these are seen as critically substituting for and thereby opposing an "official bourgeois morality" that, however, remains unspecified. In my view—as I have argued above—and to now paraphrase Tatum's words, "what needs to be further said" even more so is that we also have the very evident presence of a capitalist modernity underwriting drinking and gambling and deriving a profit that is also socially sinful and deadly. As we have seen throughout American history and even in the present moment, Christian morality and capitalist modernity are quite capable of coming into collusion as they so evidently did in the settlement of the American West. This ballad gives evidence of both, but it is the modern capitalist dimension that is quite specified and against which cowboy kinship and horse culture are offered as a critical alternative.

¿LAS CALLES DE LAREDO?

The song fails only in one respect and that is in its use of the town of Laredo, and even here there may be some measure of redemption for the cowboy. Let us recall my earlier extended provocation about Laredo concerning its modern and ethnic unsuitability for cowboys. The cowboys encountered one kind of emerging modernity in the saloon, gambling, and prostitutes in real cattle towns such as Abilene, Dodge City, or Wichita. These railhead towns also had yet another "alternative" modernity inimical to cowboys: the often-Anglo Protestant farmers, merchants, and lawyers who wanted to "settle" these towns into sites of bourgeois civilization that did not include cowboys. As I noted in chapter 1, Laredo was not such a railhead town and was already well enmeshed in modernity, which, together with its overwhelming Tejano identity, put the town at too much of a remove from the world of the cowboy. I suggest—and only suggest—that the song's cowboy composer was probably never in Laredo. So why is Laredo in the ballad?

I suggest two possible reasons not mutually exclusive. Perhaps the song is asking its Anglo listeners, then and now, to imagine Laredo as a pulp fiction Mexican border town where all sorts of bad things happen, mostly because of bad *hombres* and *señoritas* sex starved for white men, an irony given what we know about Laredo and its entrepreneurial, multi-cultural population at that moment. Nothing says that even cowboy ballad composers were not susceptible to stereotyping. In this kind of sensational, literate but historically unknowing imagination, Laredo might be said to occupy Michel-Rolph Trouillot's "savage slot" (1991). Even with most scholarly commentators on the song today, it is quite amazing how often the word "dusty" is used in describing nineteenth-century Laredo.

Poetically, there is an additional ironical possibility for the choice of Laredo that has to do with cultural phonetics in the American West applied specifically to the name, "Laredo." The composer was probably never in Laredo, but very likely had heard of it and simply liked the phonetics of the name when uttered in English. As an English utterance, it has three major and aspirated gliding syllables ending in soft vowels. My Webster dictionary defines "aspirated" as the creation of "a sonorous speech sound" generated by pronouncing a consonant followed by a vowel sound creating "a puff of suddenly released breath": /ləˈreɪdoʊ/ lə-RAY-doh, a sonorous effect enhanced when joined to the also aspirated English-language "Streets" and "of." Pronounced in formal Spanish, Laredo simply sounds a bit stiffer since Spanish vowels are not typically aspirated: [laˈreðo]. It is one of those ironical but not at all infrequent instances where a formal Spanish gives poetic/phonetic way to an anglicized Spanish. I would further suggest that such a poetic phonetics prevailed in the American West and may explain why the dominant Anglos kept so many Spanish place names but pronounced in English. It is as if the phonetic anglicization of the native formal Spanish made this racist imperial dominance subconsciously more pleasurably acceptable to all.[6] By this measure, the anglicized pronunciation, ironically perhaps, adds to the romantic ethos of the song and serves well in the cowboy's funereal redemption, much as Marty Robbins's famous protagonist met his heroic and romantic death "out in the West Texas town of El Paso" (/ɛl ˈpæsoʊ/; El pAAAHsooo).

Thus, the phonetic "Laredo" in "The Streets of Laredo," has a paradoxical function that nevertheless does not detract and may even phonetically advance its imagistic expression of the cowboy's residual Romanticism and its morally political calculus of right and wrong. While the young cowboy knows he has "done wrong," the overall effect of the song is to isolate and distance his confessed transgression within modernity and bring redemption from his residual culture. The song's vivid images make this argument, but we cannot overlook the lento tempo and aspirating vowels of the tune and the cowboy singer himself, for politics also reside in "a character, personality, or mood [rather] than a scene or a story[,] . . . its vehicle primarily the sound of the singer's voice" (Peart 2015, 697). And never to be overlooked: to the degree that the guitar was the primary instrument for this singing, it was a Mexican instrument brought to the New World from its origin point in Spain. Quoting Carl Sandburg, Andrew Peart notes that its "low Mexican thrumming" produced the "sound/potential of profound contemplation" (708). All of these, including the phonetic Laredo, served to enlist the singer's fellow cowboys— and now us—in that redemption for "we all loved our comrade so brave, young, and handsome . . . although he'd done wrong," even as it might leave us all with the question: If the cowboy has "done wrong," what does it now mean to do right?

I have argued that this "right" is the projection of a different kind of human existence beyond modernity expressed in the song's residual Romanticism and the cowboy's own real daily life on the open range and on horseback. This kind of moral economy may also have been part of the song's Anglo-Irish ancestry. D. K. Wilgus closely examined the *aisling* tradition of seventeenth- and eighteenth-century Irish visionary folk poetry where a mystical female figure appears in a vision to the poem's speaker/narrator. More often than not, she is an allegorical figure for Ireland itself, *ériu*, and she speaks of England's subjugation of a defiant Ireland that nevertheless must deal with her fate (1985). Wilgus concludes with a surprising linkage to "The Cowboy's Lament," suggesting that the dying cowboy comes to occupy the role of this female figure, further implying that he also is a contradiction of subjugation and defiance even as the gender identity has been reversed. The distance between the Irish earth goddess" he says, and "the cowboy shot down in the back street of a dusty western town, is great, but it is spanned by the tenacity of the folk tradition[,] . . . in this case the Irish tradition of vision" (300). Wilgus does not spell out the nature of the cowboy's subjugation and defiance inherited from this high romantic Irish tradition, but I would argue that it lies in his residual Romantic adversarial sense toward modernity.

I have offered the 1947 ballad as my primary text in a tentative fashion while adducing Tatum. Although it is not clear what text Tatum is using, it appears to be 1947 or close to it. Nevertheless, we must stress again that, as far as we know, this 1947 ballad was not directly collected from cowboys in the nineteenth century. Put another way, in our overlapping interpretations, both Tatum and I are relying on an unreliable text. We can lend this 1947 version greater reliability by reconstructing an evidentiary base composed of various parts of texts with their highly probable origins in the later nineteenth century, but then reconstructed in the twentieth leading directly to Lomax and Lomax in 1947 and from there to Wayland Hand where we began but also to other folklorists.

Modernity's Song

In Part I of this chapter, I take up this process of establishing our ballad in the nineteenth century, followed by a Part II tracing the ballad's twentieth- and twenty-first-century transformation in various other expressive genres, all in relationship to an intensifying urbanized modernity.

PART I

Paradoxically enough, the argument for the ballad's nineteenth-century status is premised on modernity's enabling role in the printed retrieval of the song, a retrieval process made possible by the gradual emergence of amateur and professional folklore scholarship; the latter as part of modernity's intensification of higher education in the twentieth century especially after World War II. Folklorists often distinguish between *folklore*, the vernacular expressive activity among various groups such as cowboys, and *folkloristics* as the self-conscious disciplinary action of collecting and reflectively working with such collecting either artistically, academically or as public cultural advocacy. In large part, this Part I is also intended as a contribution to the history of folkloristics centered on this one instance of folklore: "The Streets of Laredo."

There are now several histories of folkloristics which understandably lend emphasis to its major academic conceptual developments and institutions (Bronner 1986; Bendix 1997; Zumwalt 1988; Ben-Amos 2020; Sawin and Zumwalt 2020). However, Dan Ben-Amos also advocates for a simultaneous enlargement of the social scope and a sharpening of the focus of such potential histories. But he also cautions against "listing facts that relate to each other only in calendric succession. The resulting narrative would be a chronicle but not a history of folklore" (2020, 100). Rather, he calls for a critical accounting of "the complex social relationships between the students of folklore and their subjects, the intersection of different disciplines, and popular social movements in our field" (103). In this Part I of what follows, I examine the emergence of this ballad, not as a list of calendric occurrences, but as an historical instance of "complex social relationships" within folkloristics centered on this ballad principally during the first half of the twentieth century, to account for the emergence of "The Streets of Laredo" into a famous ballad. Part II then tracks the influence of the ballad on other non-folkloric forms of discourse, principally the American novel.

Where it concerns "The Streets of Laredo," the "complex social relationships" noted by Ben-Amos also included prevarication, error, and creativity, all in relation to the growing pressure of modernity. Thus, I am also mindful of Ben-Amos's admonition: "why should we expose past debates, forgotten failures, and wished-to-be-forgotten errors, and air them again in print . . . ?" (2020, 99). In the case of "The Streets of Laredo," these problems have not been fully exposed, or better yet, not critically and comprehensively examined as a chapter in the history of folkloristics. These practices evolved from a nineteenth-century vernacular phase of folkloristics to mid-twentieth century when such studies attained what Regina Bendix called "disciplinary coherence" and became far more professionalized as part of modernity's reshaping of higher education (1997, 5). Led by the University of Indiana, this formation of disciplinary coherence was then institutionalized in colleges and universities with full-fledged programs in folklore including the PhD (Zumwalt 2020, 63–64). Not surprisingly, Wayland Hand, whom we have already met, was one of these disciplinary mid-twentieth-century folklorists, he at UCLA (Bendix 1997, 188–194).[1] We can now see this grouping as a constellation, which is but a metaphor for a set of "stars," or what has been called "the great team of American folklorists," which emerged "within the development of specific graduate folklore programs in the United States in the 1960s at a time of organizational efflorescence in academia" (Zumwalt 2020, 63). Several of them will appear in these remarks, but it was Hand who first provided an analytical entry into these vexing questions for this ballad. Bendix also associates this mid-century moment with a continuing folkloristic insistence on the "authenticity" of collected folklore texts, particularly focusing on Richard M. Dorson, the ostensible *pater familias* of this gathering (Bendix 1997, 188–194).[2] But let us first look at the earlier vernacular phase that overlaps with poetry and will lead us to our ballad.

ON FOLKLORE AND POETRY

Among others, the Grimm brothers in Germany are often credited with the beginnings of the discipline of folklore in early-nineteenth-century Germany as it even then began to encounter modernity (Bendix 1997, 49–67). But it was an Englishman, William Thoms who, writing in the literary journal *Athenæum* in 1846, coined the term "folk-lore" on the eve of capitalist modernity saying that such "folk-lore" was "by no means extinct in England, and that in districts, if there be any such, where steam-engines, cotton mills, mail coaches, and similar exorcists have not yet penetrated, numerous legends might be collected" (Winick 2014).[3] This early consciousness of folklore in tension with modernity also characterizes the advent of an American modernity around the Civil War, as noted in chapter 1, even more so in the already industrializing, urbanizing, northeastern United States. At this stage of a still nascent "discipline," folklore was closely intertwined with literary practice as it had been in England with figures like the English Romantics. Lecturing on balladry at mid-nineteenth century at Harvard, the well-known American poet, James Russell Lowell, showed "his infatuation with the authentic natural voice he felt in the ballads," but also "coupled with statements betraying disappointment and alienation with his own time," replicating "the enthusiasm and simultaneous fear of loss that had stirred scholars such as the Grimms," and where the impulse toward retrieving, better yet, salvaging is evident, if only by writing and printing the otherwise oral (Bendix 1997, 78). Lowell may also be taken as an example of the early blurring between the professional and amateur folklorist, but in his case, this distinction is also overcome by his better-known identity as an elite poet attracted to balladry as a poetic form.

Lowell's later-nineteenth-century life overlapped with the emergence and high point of a cowboy culture where, unlike Lowell with respect to his sources, we find cowboy poets native to their own culture. They attempted to collect cowboy balladry even as they created their own and saw little distinction between the two. Both collection and creativity were also undertaken in support of the cowboy, especially on the eve of his passing as the great cattle drives were coming to an end with the advent of the same alienating modernity that motivated Lowell, especially with the expansion of the railroad in the American West (R. White 2011, 502). Thus, I see these practitioners as poets but also folklorists—native folklorists—to the degree that they engaged in the conscious collecting of ballads among their own even as they themselves also authored such items, the latter sometimes entering oral tradition. Lowell hesitated to print the results of his folkloristic poetics, seeing print as a kind of corruption (Bendix 1997, 78–79). These cowboys had no such ideological hesitation in printing the results of their work; indeed, they avidly sought it out and may now be seen as the beginning point of a minor industry of such poetry well into our own time (Stanley and Thatcher 2000).

DUELING COWBOYS I

Frank Maynard (1853–1926) and N. Howard "Jack" Thorp (1867–1940) were two such cowboy poets/folklorists who played key roles in the eventual appearance of "The Streets of Laredo." Yet two other writers also figure in this discussion: the well-known Owen Wister, novelist not poet, and the lesser-known memoirist, John Callison. At the center of these literary efforts, however, we find John Avery Lomax, the very well-known Texas folklorist, who first collected and printed a lengthy version of the ballad, doing so through a kind of editorial poetics even as he also laid some claim to a cowboy identity (1910, 74–76). Maynard and Thorp participated in cattle drives as cowboys, and respectively and publicly claimed to be the primary sources of two very different versions of what later turned out to be "The Streets of Laredo." Originally from Kansas, Maynard claimed that he heard the "Bad Girl's Lament" in Kansas from Texas cowboys while working in a trail drive in 1876 (2010, 135). As Maynard said, "One of the favorite songs of the cowboys in those days was called 'The Dying Girl's Lament,' the story of a girl who had been betrayed by her lover and who lay dying in a hospital" (2010, 136). In his account of the cattle drives on the Chisholm Trail, Wayne Gard includes a chapter called "Songs of the Punchers" and suggests that "Bad Girl" was known to the "punchers" (1954, 247).[4] Maynard also furnishes a telling clue when he tells us that this particular trail drive was coming from "Matagorda Bay," Texas, which, as it happens, is in the midst of the historical Texas Irish settlement along the Gulf Coast, approximately mid-way between present-day Corpus Christi and Houston that we discussed in chapter 1 (2010, 135). It would not at all surprise if these cowboys were working for the O'Connor family that we also met in chapter 1, who were still active Irish ranchers in 1876. We cannot be sure as to what exactly Maynard heard, but here is one version as collected by Goldstein (1960, 1).[5]

"The Bad Girl's Lament"

As I walked down to St. James Hospital,
St. James Hospital early one day,

l spied my only fairest daughter
Wrapped up in white linen as cold as the clay.
CHORUS:
So beat your drums and play the fife lowly,
And play the dead march as you carry me along;
Take me to the churchyard and lay the sod over me,
I am a young maid, and I know I've done wrong.
Once in the street I used to look handsome;
Once in the street I used to dress gay;
First to the ale house, then to the dance hall
Then to the poor house and now to my grave.
(CHORUS)
Send for the preacher to pray o'er my body,
Send for the doctor to heal up my wounds,
Send for the young man I first fell in love with,
That I might see him before I pass on.
(CHORUS)
Let six pretty maidens with a bunch of red roses,
Six pretty maidens to sing me a song,
Six pretty maidens with a bunch of red roses
To lay on my coffin as they carry me along.

Maynard said he kept the "Bad Girl" tune but changed the words to make it a song about a dying cowboy, and, indeed, called it just that, "The Dying Cowboy," but also referred to it later as "The Cowboy's Lament." However, he does not say when exactly he composed his version, but it first appeared in 1911 in his self-published collection *Rhymes of the Range and Trail*, for which there is no publication data. His version below is now available in a more recent and accessible edition of his work (Maynard 2010).

"The Dying Cowboy"

As I rode down by Tom Sherman's bar-room,
Tom Sherman's bar-room so early one day,
There I espied a handsome young ranger
All wrapped in white linen as cold as the clay.
"I see by your outfit that you're a ranger,"

The words that he said as I went riding by,
"Come sit down beside me, and hear my sad story,
I'm shot through the breast and know I must die."

Chorus:
The muffle the drums and play the death marches;
Play the dead march as I'm carried along;
Take me to the church-yard and lay the sod o'er me,
I'm a young ranger and I know I've done wrong.

"Go bear a message to my grey-haired mother
Go break the news gently to my sister so dear,
But never a word of this place do you mention,
As they gather around you my story to hear.
There is another as dear as a sister,
Who will bitterly weep when she knows I am gone,
But another more worthy may win her affection,
For I'm a young ranger—I know I've done wrong."

Chorus:
"Once in the saddle, I used to be dashing;
Once in the saddle, I used to be brave;
But I first took to gambling, from that to drinking,
And now in my prime, I must go to my grave.
Gather around you a crowd of gay rangers,
Go tell them the tale of their comrade's sad fate.
Tell each and all to take timely warning.
And leave their wild ways before it's too late."

Chorus:
"Go, now, and bring me a cup of cold water,
To bathe my flushed temples," the poor fellow said.
But ere I returned, the spirit had left him,
Had gone to its Giver—the ranger was dead.
So we muffled the drums and played the dead marches,
We bitterly wept as we bore him along,

For we all loved the ranger, so brave and so handsome,
We all loved our comrade, although he'd done wrong.
(2010, 155–156)

We cannot be sure as to what exactly Maynard heard from those Texas cowboys, but his version does loosely correspond to "Bad Girl." Yet, one immediately
notices that Maynard's version does not include the now iconic opening lines about
Laredo. Rather, as he said, he placed the events in a place called Tom Sherman's
"dance hall and saloon" in Dodge City, Kansas (2010, 136). Nevertheless, Maynard's
editor believes Maynard's adaptation led to "The Streets of Laredo."

> Maynard's most notable contribution to the heritage of the American West
> is without question his adaptation of what he called "The Dying Cowboy,"
> and which most of the rest of the world knows as "The Cowboy's Lament,"
> or better still, "The Streets of Laredo." (Hoy 2010, 135)

However, as if sensing he has overreached, Hoy then notes that "Maynard's ranger
(that is a cowboy who ranged the prairies, not a lawman) was dying at the doorway
of Tom Sherman's barroom in Dodge City, not on the dusty streets of a Texas border
town." But, "how the dying youth got to both places is described, if tangentially, in
Maynard's own words," to wit: "after I had finished . . . the song, I sang it to the boys
in the outfit[;] . . . it became popular with the boys in other outfits . . . and from that
time on I heard it sung everywhere on the range and trail" (2010, 135–136). This
indeed is tangential and does not explain how, why, and where a specific Laredo version appeared; for example, did a later cowboy say something like: "I heard the Tom
Sherman song and decided to reset it in Laredo"? There is simply no warrant for
crediting Maynard with "Streets," other than the most circumstantial of evidence, if
that. Without any such evidence, later scholars like Tinsley support Maynard's very
questionable claim (1981, 78). An even later scholar says, "there is no evidence to
either support or refute Maynard's claim to authorship," but then repeats Maynard's
claim "that the cowboys to whom he sang his new version apparently liked it well
enough to carry it back to Texas, where with the passing of time the locale was
changed to the streets of Laredo" (Logsdon 1989, 290). Yet another more recent
scholar goes even further asserting that "Streets of Laredo" itself "was written by
Frances Henry Maynard in 1876" which, of course, is wholly incorrect (N. Cohen
2005, 188). There is no evidence that directly and conclusively links Maynard's

version to "Streets." The latter did, of course, become the famous song, and one senses a belated effort to credit Maynard with it (including by Maynard himself) even though it is set in Tom Sherman's saloon in Kansas. Hand offers a circumspect assessment of Maynard's composition.

> Given the many directions the ballad took, we must weigh carefully the opinion of F. H. Maynard of Colorado Springs, Colorado, who claims he rewrote "The Cowboy's Lament" to fit with the older song, 'The Dying Girl's Lament." No further information is given, but as Mr. Maynard was at least 79 or 80 years old when he made this comment, in about 1928, his opinion can be accepted. (1955, 156)

Maynard's 1876 creation probably did not lead to "The Streets of Laredo." Indeed, it appears to have largely disappeared until its recent posthumous publication, but it—or at least its setting—may have possibly and momentarily entered oral tradition as he claimed, "I heard it sung everywhere on the range and trail" (2010, 136). As it happens, in 1914, one John J. Callison published a dime-novel book about the adventures of a cowboy, Bill Jones, who witnessed a shooting in a saloon on Dodge City resembling Tom Sherman's.[6] The only date offered is "in the summer of 188–." The marshal of Dodge City, one "mysterious Dave," killed another man in a gambling dispute. In this instance, however, and most unfortunately, the bullet went right through him and killed the saloon owner's very popular dog sitting on top of the bar (1914, 155). According to Callison, the Dodge City folk held a proper funeral for the dog where some cowboys sang "The Cowboy's Lament" with these verses:

> Once in the saddle I used to go dashing,
> Once in the saddle I used to go gay.
> First took to drinking and then to card playing,
> Got shot in the neck and now here I lay.

> Beat the drum slowly, play the fife lowly,
> Play the Dead March as you bear me along.
> Take me to the Boothill and throw the dirt over me
> I'm but a poor Cowboy, I know I done wrong.
> (1914, 158)

Callison offered no source for his verses. Notwithstanding the somewhat humorous use of the ballad, that the alleged incident happened in a Dodge City saloon about ten years after Maynard supposedly wrote his ballad might suggest his influence, but we must also note that Callison's verses differ enough from Maynard's version to suggest yet another alternative source.

In his 1897 novel *Lin McLean*, Owen Wister, the famous novelist of the American West, tells of the death of a woman held in high esteem by the local cowboys whom they knew as a "biscuit-shooter," cowboy slang for a cook or waitress (Lambert 1970, 229; Whipp 1990). At her funeral they sing the following which they simply call "the Lament."

> Once in the saddle I used to go dashing,
> Once in the saddle I used to go gay:
> First took to drinking, and then to card-playing;
> Got shot in the body, and now here I lay.
>
> Beat the drum slowly,
> Play the fife lowly,
> Sound the dead march as you bear me along.
> Take me to boot-hill and throw the sod over me—
> I'm but a poor cowboy, I know I done wrong.
> (Wister 1897, 274).

Unlike Callison's humorous use, here the ballad is sung "as a genuine human response to the problem of death" (Lambert 1970, 230). Yet Wister's verses are an almost exact match with Callison's, and both are at some textual distance from Maynard's, so it is entirely possible that both Wister and Callison's Bill Jones heard the song elsewhere, all of which might then suggest that some version was available in oral tradition in that later-nineteenth-century moment, a point to which I will return with some force later.[7] If all of this is so, it would then also be the case that, in 1897, Wister appeared "to be the first to put these famous lines between the covers of a book" although we must note that these famous lines are only eight in number and do not include the words, "the streets of Laredo" (J. White 1989, 37).

In his commentary on Wister, John I. White then conveniently affords us a transition to our penultimate writer/folklorist/cowboy when he tells us that "ten years later, N. Howard Thorp included six stanzas and a chorus [of the ballad] in his pioneer anthology, *Songs of the Cowboys*" published in 1908 (1989, 37). Like Wister,

Thorp was an upper-class easterner who came west, but, unlike Wister, he did so explicitly to take up the cowboy life as a job and became "a veteran cowhand" (Slowik 2012, 207–208). Or as Guy Logsdon also puts it, Thorp learned "the ways of the West and the techniques of cowboying" (1989, 296). He then conducted what amounted to rudimentary fieldwork among working cowboys, as he said, "on horseback trips that lasted months and took me hundreds of miles through half a dozen cow country states, most of the time being spent in cow camps, at chuck wagons and line camps" (Thorp 1945, 22). Thorp then "rode toward Texas, carrying a notebook into which he jotted the words to any cowboy song" (Logsdon 1989, 296). He conducted this mobile, participatory fieldwork in 1889 "as the trail-driving years were coming to a close," but he was still active (quoted in Logsdon 1989, 296).

In 1908, Thorp published his findings but also songs of his own in a collection, *Songs of the Cowboys*, with some hand-written annotations. Thorp's original book is now a rare edition, and although I have examined it at the University of Texas at Austin's Humanities Research Center, I draw on the more accessible, comprehensive, and annotated 1966 edition of his 1908 book produced by Austin and Alta Fife.[8] It includes a facsimile reprinting of the original 1908 booklet including this version of the ballad.[9]

"Cow Boys Lament"

'Twas once in my saddle I used to be happy
'Twas once in my saddle I used to be gay
But I first took to drinking, then to gambling
A shot from a six-shooter took my life away.

My curse let it rest, let it rest on the fair one
Who drove me from friends that I loved and from home
Who told me she loved me, just to deceive me
My curse rest upon her, wherever she roam.

Oh she was fair, Oh she was lovely
The belle of the Village the fairest of all
But her heart was as cold as the snow on the mountains
She gave me up for the glitter of gold.

I arrived in Galveston in old Texas
Drinking and gambling I went to give o'er

But, I met with a Greaser and my life he has finished,
Home and relations I ne'er shall see more.

Send for my father, Oh send for my mother
Send for the surgeon to look at my wounds
But I fear it is useless I feel I am dying
I'm a young cowboy cut down in my bloom.

Farewell my friends, farewell my relations
My earthly career has cost me sore
The cow-boy ceased talking, they knew he was dying
His trials on earth, forever were o'er.

Chor. Beat your drums lightly, play you pipes merrily
Sing your death march as you bear me along
Take me to the graveyard, lay the sod o'er me
I'm a young cowboy and know I've done wrong.
(Fife and Fife 1966a, 29–30)

As noted, Thorp wrote some of the songs in his 1908 collection, but he clearly noted these in his table of contents by marking them with a "+" and an accompanying statement "songs marked + are by the Author" (1966a, title page and "Contents"). His "Cow Boy's Lament" is not so marked and thus appears to have been collected in the field at some time in the later nineteenth century although no source is credited. Again, as with our other nineteenth-century sources, we see variation but also some consistency in the verses, most notably in the funeral march with pipes and drums of an unfortunate cowboy who had ridden his horse happy and gay. Thorp's version is quite singular in its introduction of a "belle of the village" and certainly in its racist deployment of a Mexican "greaser." All this said, Thorp's version, like Maynard's, also does not use the key phrase "the streets of Laredo," as that key title and first line had yet to emerge.

DUELING COWBOYS II

Thorp's and Maynard's efforts intersected with those of the Texan, John Avery Lomax, as he was launching his famous career as the primary collector and popularizer of American folksong (Porterfield 1996). While much more is typically made of his work with African Americans, "it was Texas and its cowboy lore that first set him on the path to fame and fulfillment" (Porterfield 1996, 1). His first major publication, *Cowboy Songs and Other Frontier Ballads*, appeared in 1910, shortly after Thorp's booklet and included a version of our ballad where the key phrase "streets of Laredo" first appears—and as the first line—even though its title is still "The Cowboy's Lament" (1910, 74–76).

"The Cowboy's Lament"

As I walked out in the streets of Laredo,
As I walked out in Laredo one day,
I spied a poor cowboy wrapped up in white linen,
Wrapped up in white linen as cold as the clay.

Oh, beat the drum slowly and play the fife lowly,
Play the Dead March as you bear me along;
Take me to the graveyard, and lay the sod over me,
For I'm a young cowboy, and I know I've done wrong.

"I see by your outfit that you are a cowboy,"—
These words he did say as I boldly stepped by—
"Come, sit beside me and hear my sad story;
I was shot in the breast and I know I must die.

"Let sixteen gamblers come handle my coffin,
Let sixteen cowboys come sing me a song,
Take me to the graveyard and lay the sod over me,
For I'm a poor cowboy, and I know I've done wrong.

"My friends and relations they live in the Nation,
They know not where their boy has gone.
He first came to Texas and hired to a ranchman,
Oh, I'm a young cowboy, and I know I've done wrong.

"Go write a letter to my gray-haired mother,
And carry the same to my sister so dear;
But not a word shall you mention
When a crowd gathers round you my story to hear.

"There is another more dear than a sister,
She'll bitterly weep when she hears I am gone.
There is another who will win her affections,
For I'm a young cowboy, and they say I've done wrong.

"Go gather around you a crowd of young cowboys,
And tell them the story of this my sad fate;
Tell one and the other before they go further
To stop their wild roving before 'tis too late.

"Oh, muffle your drums, then play your fifes merrily;
Play the Dead March as you bear me along.
And fire your guns right over my coffin;
There goes an unfortunate boy to his home.

"It was once in the saddle I used to go dashing,
It was once in the saddle I used to be gay;
First to the dram-house, then to the card-house:
Got shot in the breast, I am dying to-day.

"Get six jolly cowboys to carry my coffin;
Get six pretty maidens to bear up my pall;
Put bunches of roses all over my coffin,
Put roses to deaden the clods as they fall.

"Then swing your rope slowly and rattle your spurs lowly,
And give a wild whoop as you bear me along;
And in the grave throw me, and roll the sod over me,
For I'm a young cowboy, and I know I've done wrong.

"Go bring me a cup, a cup of cold water,
To cool my parched lips," the cowboy said;
Before I turned, the spirit had left him
And gone to its Giver—the cowboy was dead.

We beat the drum slowly and played the fife lowly,
And bitterly wept as we bore him along;

For we all loved our comrade, so brave, young, and handsome;
We all loved our comrade, although he'd done wrong.

Lomax provides very little contextual information for this ballad, so we are left to wonder how Lomax came by this very long version that eventually became the ballad with which we began in our introduction. To answer this question, we now need to intersect Lomax with the with the aforementioned cowboy poets, or at least one of them. His work also had to deal with the newly emergent and developing profession of folkloristics both during and after his death in 1947. Indeed, in 1955, from Westwood, California, Wayland Hand first attempted to ride analytical herd on all these Texas-based folkloristic mavericks with mixed results as we shall see.

SCHOOL OF "DISCIPLINARY COHERENCE"

Lomax's works have not been without controversy for his free-wheeling methods for gathering his materials, including appropriating the work of others, and also for his editorial shaping of his folkloric texts. This criticism took full force in the mid-twentieth century, arguably beginning with Hand's 1955 essay and the emergence of what Bendix has called the school of "disciplinary coherence" (1997, 5). However, as we shall see, this folkloristic formation did have its moments of incoherence and "The Streets of Laredo" might be taken as a prime example. While critical of Lomax's practices in general, this criticism also focused on his relationship to Thorp. One of these mid-twentieth-century folklorists, John O. West, noted that Lomax reprinted *nineteen* of the songs in Thorp's 1908 collection with only minor changes and without crediting Thorp (1967, 114). As Logsdon notes, "One of Lomax's weaknesses was in not crediting his sources," in this instance evoking "Thorp's anger" (1989, 300). That anger is expressed sarcastically in Thorp's autobiography where he says that after his own 1908 book, "a very learned professor brought out a big book of cowboy songs which he claimed to have collected with great labor" (1945, 42). Although Lomax denied Thorp's claims, another distinguished mid-century folklorist, D. K. Wilgus, said, "the weight of the evidence is with Thorp" (1959, 165).[10] Most of these folklorists, however, spoke of this misappropriation in general terms and none specified "The Cowboy's Lament" as one of these uncredited appropriations and with good reason. If we compare Thorp's 1908 "Greaser" version to Lomax's, it is abundantly clear that whatever else Lomax may have used from Thorp without credit, the six verses of Thorp's "The Cow Boy's Lament" simply do not match Lomax's lengthy version, and, therefore, it was not among the nineteen that Lomax may have appropriated. Lomax simply did not use Thorp's 1908 version.

In 1955, however, that very evident discrepancy did not seem to stop Wayland Hand from making exactly this very specific criticism of Lomax, charging him with the misappropriation of Thorp's "The Cow Boy's Lament," saying "although Lomax gives no source for 'The Cowboy's Lament,' he seems to have taken Thorp's version almost word for word" (1955, 144). "In any case," he continues, "John A. Lomax made the song more widely known in his 'Cowboy Songs'" (1955, 1).[11] But, how could any of this be the case, when it is absolutely clear that Thorp's 1908 version does not at all match Lomax's? The mystery deepens when Hand then says that Thorp claimed that his version "was *supposed* to have come into the hands of a certain Troy Hale, of Battle Creek, Nebraska" and that this happened "around 1885"; that is, one Troy Hale was Thorp's primary informant for this ballad, but then Hand further adds, "Whether the version of the song that Thorp published in his "Songs of the Cowboy" in 1908 in Estancia, New Mexico, corresponds exactly with the Nebraska version or whether the text is precisely that of the supposed author is not known" (1955, 1). At first it is not at all clear what Hand is talking about because neither "Troy Hale" nor "Nebraska" appear with the 1908 version noted above, nor do two of the subsequent and posthumous editions of this exact 1908 book add such information (1966a; 2005). That exact version is in fact attributed to no one and no place.

However, we soon discover that in his own lifetime, Thorp produced a second edition of his 1908 volume, and we first learn this from Hand's very first footnote to Thorp's book, quoted here in full: "I do not have access to the first edition of this rare work; the citation is therefore from the 1921 edition published in Boston and New York" (1955, 144). It now becomes crystal clear that Hand is working with a *1921* edition of Thorp's work and not with the original 1908 booklet. In 1921, Thorp did indeed include a song called "The Cowboy's Lament," but not the one that appeared in 1908. This later version is a much longer and altogether different, indeed one that actually begins with

> As I walked out in the streets of Laredo,
> As I walked out in Laredo one day,
> I spied a poor cowboy wrapped up in white linen,
> Wrapped up in white linen as cold as the clay.

Oh, beat the drum slowly and play the fife lowly,
Play the Dead March as you bear me along;
Take me to the graveyard, and lay the sod over me,
For I'm a young cowboy, and I know I've done wrong.

"I see by your outfit that you are a cowboy,"—
These words he did say as I boldly stepped by—
"Come, sit beside me and hear my sad story;
I was shot in the breast and I know I must die.

"Let sixteen gamblers come handle my coffin,
Let sixteen cowboys come sing me a song,
Take me to the graveyard and lay the sod over me,
For I'm a poor cowboy, and I know I've done wrong.

"My friends and relations they live in the Nation,
They know not where their boy has gone.
He first came to Texas and hired to a ranchman,
Oh, I'm a young cowboy, and I know I've done wrong.

"Go write a letter to my gray-haired mother,
And carry the same to my sister so dear;
But not a word shall you mention
When a crowd gathers round you my story to hear.

"There is another more dear than a sister,
She'll bitterly weep when she hears I am gone.
There is another who will win her affections,
For I'm a young cowboy, and they say I've done wrong.

"Go gather around you a crowd of young cowboys,
And tell them the story of this my sad fate;
Tell one and the other before they go further
To stop their wild roving before 'tis too late.

"Oh, muffle your drums, then play your fifes merrily;
Play the Dead March as you bear me along.

And fire your guns right over my coffin;
There goes an unfortunate boy to his home.

"It was once in the saddle I used to go dashing,
It was once in the saddle I used to be gay;
First to the dram-house, then to the card-house:
Got shot in the breast, I am dying to-day.

"Get six jolly cowboys to carry my coffin;
Get six pretty maidens to bear up my pall;
Put bunches of roses all over my coffin,
Put roses to deaden the clods as they fall.

"Then swing your rope slowly and rattle your spurs lowly,
And give a wild whoop as you bear me along;
And in the grave throw me, and roll the sod over me,
For I'm a young cowboy, and I know I've done wrong.

"Go bring me a cup, a cup of cold water,
To cool my parched lips," the cowboy said;
Before I turned, the spirit had left him
And gone to its Giver—the cowboy was dead.

We beat the drum slowly and played the fife lowly,
And bitterly wept as we bore him along;
For we all loved our comrade, so brave, young, and handsome;
We all loved our comrade, although he'd done wrong.
(1921, 41–44)

Thorp says very little about this 1921 version of the song, really only, as Hand noted, that he collected it "about 1886" in a barroom in Wisner, Nebraska, from one Troy Hale from Battle Creek, Nebraska, who claimed authorship of the song (1921, 41).[12] Hand then wonders "whether the version of the song that Thorp published in his 'Songs of the Cowboy' in 1908 . . . corresponds exactly with the Nebraska version" and tells us that this correspondence "is not known" and offers footnote 1 as an explanation (1955, 1). Yet, the most perfunctory of comparisons between Thorp's 1908 and 1921 clearly indicates that these are two very different

ballads in length and complexity. Because he did not examine Thorp's 1908 collection, Hand—not too unreasonably—assumed that the 1921 publication had
simply reproduced 1908, perhaps with minor changes, which is why he asks
whether 1908 "corresponds exactly with the Nebraska version" of 1921.[13] Of course,
it did not, because 1921 is an almost entirely new ballad as we can now plainly
see, but Hand could not, because, as he says, he did not have access to 1908.[14]

However, another kind of comparison is revealing and indicting. Hand saw
this one immediately—and we can as well—and that is between Thorp's 1921 and
Lomax's 1910 versions. Hand's central error, as we have seen, is that he wrongly
believed that Thorp's 1921 version was probably the same as his 1908 *without
having seen the latter*. But he then compounded this initial and forgivable error
when he further concluded that Lomax therefore must have misappropriated his
lengthy 1910 version from 1908 Thorp. That is, Hand simply assumed that
Lomax knew Thorp's 1908 work (which he did), and, thinking that Thorp's 1908
was basically the same as Thorp's 1921, he wrongly surmised that Lomax had
pilfered this particular song two years later in his own big 1910 book, possibly
along with others, as West and Wilgus noted. Thus, in 1955, in effect, Hand
thereby also credited Thorp with the first version of this ballad that uses the
phrase "the streets of Laredo" although not yet as a title.

There is one further large piece missing in this pilfering, prevaricating puzzle.
If Thorp's 1908 version differs substantially from his supposed 1921, then how did
he come by the latter which, as it happens, is almost exactly Lomax's 1910? One
can already suspect what happened. Since we already know that Lomax did not
take his particular version from Thorp's 1908, we can only assume that his 1910 is
his alone, although it remains to be seen how *he* came by it. Yet Lomax 1910 is
reproduced almost in its entirety in Thorp 1921 with only three words changed in
the second stanza: "carry me along" to "*bear* me along"; "green valley" to "*graveyard*"; "*there* lay the sod" to "and lay the sod" (1910, 74–76). Thorp also abandons his
1908 title, "Cow Boy's Lament" and now uses Lomax's "The Cowboy's Lament."
So how did this close correspondence occur? The Fifes adjudicated and answered
this question. They included Thorp's autobiography, "Banjo in the Cowcamps" in
their edition of his work in which Thorp makes a sarcastic reference to Lomax as "a
learned professor." In a footnote to that reference, they first chide Lomax saying
that he "did make liberal use of Thorp's booklet in his 1910 collection . . . without
giving credit," but then they say that in his 1921 book, "Thorp returned the compliment even to the point of abandoning some of his genuine 1908 texts in favor
of 'the learned professor's' synthetic specimens" but also, they might have added,

without crediting Lomax (Thorp 1966b, 24–25). A bit later in their own commentary on the ballad, they explicitly offer "Cow Boy's Lament" as a case in point (Fife and Fife 1966b, 151). Writing much later, Mark L. Gardner also concludes that "Thorp made free use of John Lomax's book without citing the noted scholar" (2005, 16). That is, for his 1921 edition, Thorp abandoned his own 1908 text, "Cow Boy's Lament," instead reprinting Lomax's long version *as his own*. Hand then came along to give Thorp full credit for collecting the first extended version of the ballad which turned out to have the iconic first line "As I walked out in the streets of Laredo." And what about Troy Hale, the supposed field source for 1921? We can only assume that Thorp knowingly used him—a real person—to authenticate this very long version, that he unabashedly had taken from Lomax.[15] Thus, it would seem that Thorp prevaricated on three counts: taking Lomax's version as his own, making up an informant for it, and then dating it circa 1886.

Wayland Hand's error was a rare lapse, but perhaps understandable in the disciplinary coherence of the moment that was predisposed against Lomax as we shall see. Oddly enough, in the development of their Thorp edition, the Fifes thank Wayland Hand for "his encouragement and wisdom all along the way" suggesting he surely must have read their book (1966b, 2).[16] One would think that at some point, he would have acknowledged his oversight in overlooking Thorp's first edition now made available to him in 1966, that is, if we assume he read the Fife volume and was still interested in the fortunes of "The Streets of Laredo." One wishes he had done so and in a more accessible manner, which is to say in English, not German, perhaps in a *mea culpa* note in *Western Folklore*, the journal where much of the work on this ballad appeared, including his own. Had he done so, Lomax would have emerged as the undisputed collector of "The Cowboy's Lament" where the classic first line, "As I was walking the streets of Laredo," appears in print for the first time.[17] To summarize this textual and institutional history, which can be confusing, I offer the following simplified chronology of these events:

1876—Frank Maynard hears "The Bad Girl's Lament" from Texas cowboys on the trail and is inspired to write his own "The Dying Cowboy" set in Tom Sherman's saloon in Dodge City, KS. It is first published in 1911.

1880s—John Callison writes a dime novel, *Bill Jones of Paradise Valley, Oklahoma*, in which one verse of the ballad appears. It is published in 1914.

1890s—Owen Wister writes his "western" novel, *Lin Mclean*, in which one verse of the ballad appears.

1886—N. Howard "Jack" Thorp collects the ballad "Cow Boy's Lament." It is published in seven verses in his collection, *Songs of the Cowboys*, in 1908 with no contextual information.

1910—John Avery Lomax collects and publishes his *Cowboy Songs and Other Frontier Ballads*, including one called "The Cowboy's Lament" where the words "the streets of Laredo" appear for the first time. Lomax's material came from various sources. According to most folklorists, Lomax does appear to have "collected" several of these songs from Thorp's 1908 collection without attribution. However, in comparison to Thorp's 1908 seven-verse version, Lomax's very lengthy and complex "The Cowboy's Lament" cannot be one of them.

1921—N. Howard "Jack" Thorp publishes a second edition of his 1908 *Songs of the Cowboys*, in which he discards his original "Cow Boy's Lament" and substitutes one called "The Cowboy's Lament." A close examination shows that it is an almost exact match for Lomax's 1910 version, an observation supported by folklorists. Adding insult to injury, Thorp claims to have collected this 1921 version in 1886 from one Troy Hale.

1955—Folklorist Wayland Hand publishes his study "The Streets of Laredo" in German. He fails to examine Thorp's 1908 publication. Working only with the 1921 edition, he mistakenly thinks that Thorp's 1908 "Cow Boy's Lament" had simply been reprinted in 1921 and thus concludes that this lengthy version was Thorp's all along and, ironically, that Lomax took it from Thorp in 1910, whereas the reverse is true.

THE FOLKLORIC EDITORIAL POET

If more evidence was needed of Thorp's prevarication, one could also say that the long 1921 (Lomax) version that he falsely claimed as his could not have been reasonably collected in the field from Hale nor anyone else. Thorp's songs were probably never collected as complete songs, "since no cowboys could ever remember a complete song[,] . . . the complete cowboy song exists only as an archive of separate cowboy verses in Thorp's book." And thus, "the object that Thorp defines as a cowboy song (a complete version) is not that which is sung by cowboys" (Slowik 2012, 209). Largely a working cowboy, Thorp often collected his material piecemeal, in Thorp's own words, "a verse or two here, and another verse or two there" (1966b, 13). Thorp's true 1908 "Cow Boy's Lament" indeed reads as a song that he might have written down as he heard it sung in the field. In their own comparison of Thorp's 1908 and Lomax's 1910 versions, the Fifes actually favor Thorp's "seven stanzas of 1908" because they "have a stamp of authenticity," dismissing Lomax's "longer and smoother synthetic text" (Fife and Fife 1966b, 151).

Lomax's version of "The Cowboy's Lament" does have an extended and flowing narrative movement that even Thorp found more attractive than his own, enough so, as we have seen, to claim it for himself! But these very qualities also tell us that Lomax's 1910 version was also not very likely collected directly in the field in a sung performance. Lomax quite simply took stanzas mostly received in the mail and edited them into a much longer ballad than could have been heard in any given performance. So how, but also why, did he come to produce such a text? Lomax was quite candid in addressing this question.

> As for the songs in this collection, I have violated the ethics of ballad gatherers, in a few instances, by selecting and putting together what seemed to be the best lines from different versions, all telling the same story. Frankly, the volume is meant to be popular. (1957, xxix—xxx)
>
> The songs have been arranged in some haphazard way as they were collected—jotted down at a table in the rear of a saloon, scrawled on an envelope while squatting around a campfire, caught behind the scenes of a bronco-busting outfit. (1910, xxix-xxx)

But how did he come by these "best lines from different versions" and once in hand, what did he do with them? Lomax did not mean that the songs were collected directly from the singing lips of cowboys on the cattle drives, for these had long since passed by early twentieth century. What he seemed to mean is that he believed that his material had come from such lips at some point but now came to him mediated through others who recalled these songs in various forms and which he then collected courtesy of the US Postal Service. According to his foremost biographer, "the bulk" of his cowboy songs and ballads "had come to him through the mail, from friends, former students, businessmen, teachers, and local officials, mostly in Texas, to whom he had written[;] . . . other songs were gleaned from scrapbooks and newspapers." However, a "few had come from the lips of ex-cowboys" (Porterfield 1996, 153). Lomax's bit of dramatics about saloons and campfires seems to refer not so much to his own field activities but rather to the imagined sources of those individuals in Texas who had sent him material in various forms and amounts. He largely did not gather these songs firsthand; the people who sent him verses did in various ways, including from memory, and this sourcing may have varied enormously from song to song.

Lomax's way of gathering folklore also came under predictable criticism from the school of disciplinary coherence that expected a more direct and preferably verbatim recording of such material from its performers, preferably electronic or written down *in situ*, but also far more contextual information on his sources than Lomax provides. There are other problems as well. As Wilgus noted, "Lomax was extremely careless and inefficient in preserving his field material," a situation not helped by the management of his collection in the 1950s.[18] His collection "was once well organized and indexed" but, "whether its present state is due to the work of writing *Adventures [of a Ballad Hunter]* or to the rifling of a careless researcher is not clear" (1959, 160–161). More importantly,

> the papers do *not* contain complete documentation of the texts of *Cowboy Songs*. There are many texts without dates or sources, or both. The changes in an overwritten base text cannot always be accounted for by other texts available; nor does the revised text always agree with the text in *Cowboys Songs*. . . . Lomax was then, as later, the recipient of material from other collectors, which he then did not properly document, even in manuscript. His editing ranges from exact transcription to extensive collation with personal "improvement." A few examples will indicate the range of editing. (160–161)

Unfortunately, Wilgus did not select "The Cowboy's Lament" as one of his examples, but he well could have.

There is one file in the collection containing some ten contributions to Lomax's request from disparate geographical sources and consisting of one or two verses, each as if that was all his informants could recall (Lomax 1948, Box #D 177, File # 5). All of them are undated, and, for the most part, Lomax and/or his literary executors did not think to keep the postmarked envelopes in which these arrived. For indeed and fortunately, this same file offers one text that does not appear to be a submission, but rather a version in progress of what will eventually appear in 1910. Like the published version, it carries the title "The Cowboy's Lament." Unlike his other materials, it is enclosed in a clear plastic folder, almost as if Lomax wanted posterity to especially value this prepublication version. I offer it here, as figure 4, comprised of two pages.

Based on other examples in the papers, this is clearly in Lomax's handwriting and shows him editing and amending it for publication. For example, what will appear in print as the second stanza beginning with "Oh beat the drum slowly" is labeled a "chor" in the handwritten version, which is to say a "chorus," although it is not marked as such in the final print version. The third printed stanza is written

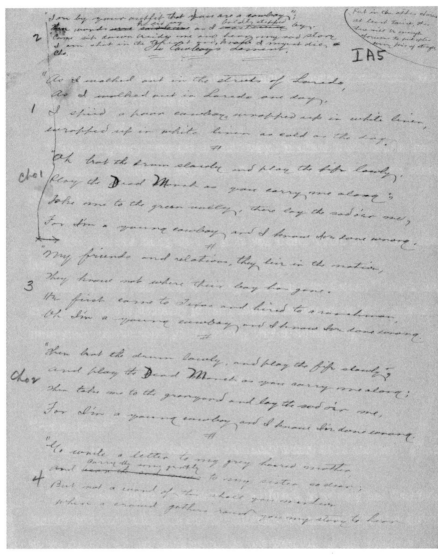

Figure 4. Prepublication version of "The Cowboy's Lament" that will appear in *Cowboy Songs and Other Frontier Ballads* in 1910. *Source*: camh-dob—01672–0001_ pub and camh-dob-01672-0002_pub (Lomax 1948).

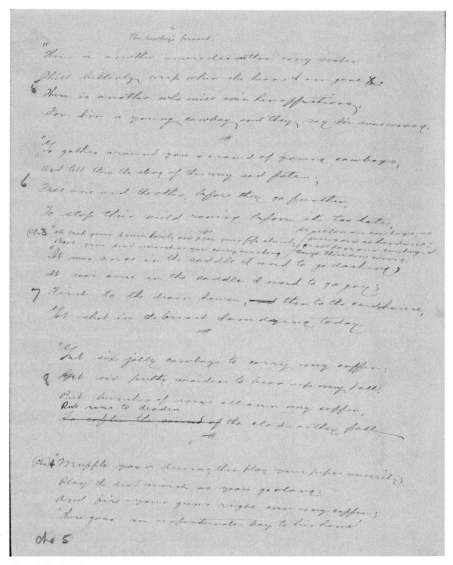

Figure 4. *(Continued)*

out at the very top of the working draft and inserted after the chorus with a verti-
cal arrow in the left margin pointing downward. In the published version, stanza
number 4 which begins with "let sixteen gamblers come handle my coffin" does
not appear in the handwritten text, and while most of the rest do, they were
not published in the same exact order as they were written. Finally, we also note

that this editorial work in progress carries the same title as the published version, but it also has the iconic first lines: "As I walked out in the streets of Laredo / As I walked out in Laredo one day." We still cannot be certain about the authorship of these two famous lines, which will later furnish a title, but among the various contributions in this same file, we find the following (fig. 5):

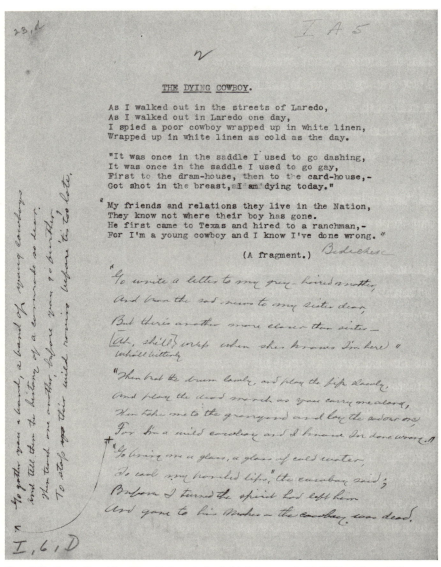

Figure 5. "The Streets of Laredo" version sent to Lomax by Roy Bedichek. *Source*: camh-dob-016173-pub (Lomax 1948).

I could find no page 1 corresponding to what seems to be a number 2 at the very top of this document. The entire thing appears to carry the title "The Dying Cowboy," but these verses are not those of the song traditionally associated with this title, more often than not also known as "Bury Me Not on the Lone Prairie." Such a song with this title does appear in Lomax's collection (1910, 3). Rather, these are clearly verses to "The Cowboy's Lament," but it reads like an editorial work in progress toward what will eventually appear as such in Lomax 1910, including the iconic lines: "As I walked out in the streets of Laredo / As I walked out in Laredo one day." The first three verses are obviously typed and labeled "a fragment," also typed, as Lomax then continues to add his own handwritten verses, an odd, disconcerting practice seen elsewhere in his editing as "Lomax chose the not altogether wise course of amending freely" (Wilgus 1959, 163). But, in this instance, Lomax also writes in the name "Bedichek" right under the typed verses, suggesting that this person is the source of that typescript portion. Who is "Bedichek"? The use of only a last name is instructive, because it suggests a familiarity, especially among men of that period, although perhaps not in personal address to each other.[19] As usual, the contribution was undated, but in this instance, the envelope was saved. The very faded postmark seems to read 1907, and it has a return address in San Angelo. Undoubtedly, this contributor is Roy Bedichek who attended the University of Texas at Austin from 1898 to 1903 as Lomax's fellow student and fraternity brother and remained a life-long close friend (Porterfield 1996, 41). After graduation in 1903, Bedichek taught high school in San Angelo even as Lomax was working on his book. He later returned to Austin and the university for more than less the rest of his life (Hudson 1976).[20] But, again, why did Lomax identify "Bedichek" at the end of the typed stanzas? If Bedichek did indeed submit these verses to his friend in Austin, had he heard them somewhere as he was growing up in the 1880s in Falls County, Texas, just north of Austin, close to the Chisholm Trail? Or, even more of a speculation, as a creative writer, was he possibly the author of these verses? Lacking other evidence, we must at least entertain the possibility that Bedichek was the source for the iconic lines that will appear in Lomax 1910 and thereafter.

Finally, as if to reinforce the appearance of these lines, this same file also contains the following, again without any contextual information (fig. 6).

This is clearly a musical score, and the name "Lomax" at the top would seem to suggest that he produced it, but there is no evidence that he has such musical abilities. Rather, I suspect that we are looking at another work in progress—in this case,

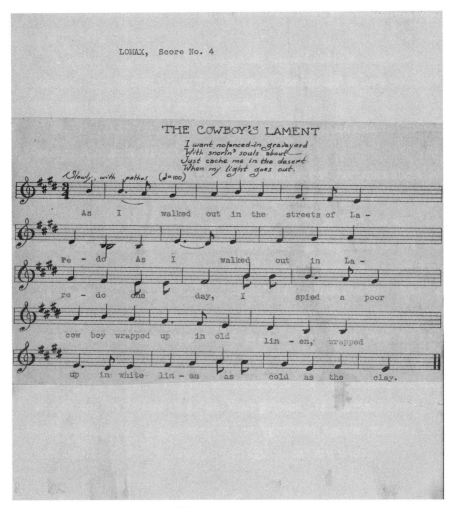

Figure 6. *Source*: camh-dob-016174-pub (Lomax 1948).

"Score No. 4"—but this one probably led to the final musical score that accompanies the Lomax and Lomax 1947 version first noted in my introduction, and which we will discuss more fully below. That version, it will be recalled, was also musically produced by Charles and Ruth Seeger, accomplished musicians. Finally, and frankly, I have no idea why the hand-printed verse right under the title was put there, nor what it refers to. It begins with the line "I want no fenced-in graveyard," and reads almost like a parodic response to the verses in "The Streets of Laredo" where the dead young cowboy is buried in a graveyard.

THE FOLKLORIST AS "COWBOY"

While Lomax's unorthodox methods drew the fire of mid-twentieth-century folklorists, a later critic—not a folklorist—Michael Slowik also looked askance at his methods so as to question Lomax's representation of the cowboy in a kind of internal postcolonial criticism. For him, Lomax

> selected the best lines[;] . . . his role as a collector of songs causes him to manipulate the components of a song to the extent that he becomes a creative force in their production. Not just a man retrieving untainted songs in the shadows, Lomax implicitly posits himself as *producing* songs for a mass audience . . . in stark opposition to Lomax's ostensible goal: to retrieve unmediated songs representing the life of a group of people who have been rhetorically marked by their Otherness vis-à-vis mainstream society. By manipulating the text for widespread circulation, Lomax erases the civilization/Other dichotomy that served as his original justification for documenting the lifestyle of the Other. (2012, 211)

Slowik thus chastises "the contradictory actions of the song collector" such that Lomax's work "detaches itself from any form of truth" (211). For Slowik, Lomax claimed that his songs offer a "genuine" picture of the cowboy life, "an unmediated trace" in contrast to "mediated representations of the cowboy as the press and theatre" (211).

In Lomax's defense, we must first note that the word "genuine" is Slowik's, not Lomax's, and that what the latter actually claims is that his songs "coming direct from the cowboy's experience . . . will afford future generations a truer conception of what he really was than is now possessed by those who know him only through highly colored romances" (1910, xxviii). Much hinges here on how we are to interpret what is "coming direct from the cowboy's experience." And, while the dichotomy between civilization/Other certainly obtained in the case of poor African Americans that Lomax also worked with, it does not hold up for the collection of these cowboy songs mostly from Texas. In that instance, Lomax was not erasing "the civilization/Other dichotomy" because, in this cowboy instance, it never fully existed in the first place, or at least not as the sharp binary Slowik suggests.

The people who sent him contributions were mostly rural or had such recent experience much like himself, notwithstanding his university education at UT-Austin and Harvard (Porterfield 1996, 1–32). Even his education at a turn-of-the-century University of Texas at Austin and then teaching at Texas A&M would not have taken him that far away from his ancestral culture. Of Austin and the university, founded in 1883, Porterfield notes that "dust from the cattle trails was still settling, figuratively at least, and everywhere there was lingering evidence of frontier days" such that,

> When a writer for the student newspaper stopped coming to work, the editor posted a notice, only half-humorously, in language cowboys understood: "A reward is offered for the discovery and return to this staff office of one Robert E. Goree, lost, strayed, or stolen. Description: Twenty-three years old, 16 hands high, dun and muckled roan, branded BTP on left vest." (38)

Lomax did not really leave Texas until he went to Harvard in 1907 at age forty where he arrived carrying his collection of cowboy songs, and it remained his native home until his death (Lomax 1947). Abrahams avers that Lomax "could righteously claim" the appellation, "cowboy" based on "his interest in cowboy songs as well as his having grown up near the Chisholm Trail" (2000, 108). It is as if Abrahams had read the following from Lomax's correspondence with one of his mail-in informants:

> I grew up in West Texas on a cattle ranch and one of the old trails from Texas to Kansas ran close to my father's door. The experience of those days has kept me interested in the cowboy and everything that concerns him. Soon the cowboy will be a thing of the past and his songs, unless they are written down and preserved, will perish utterly. I am no longer a cowboy, although I feel I should be. I love my kind and wish to contribute something to the perpetuation of his name and fame (Lomax 1948, Box #3D 176).

This claim to cowboy identity is a bit exaggerated as is perhaps Abrahams' assessment of him. Lomax's father was a homestead farmer, but the farm did sit astride the Chisholm Trail, and, as his biographer puts it, in his early years "there was a steady procession of covered wagons, trail herds and riders on horseback. Cowboys ... often spent the night in the Lomax home" (Porterfield 1996, 17). At best, we have a child's close identification with cowboys carried into adulthood, although Lomax was, of course, never a working cowboy. Nevertheless, among his papers, we also find a book-length manuscript entitled *The Cattle Trail*, a narrative of cowboy life on the nineteenth-century cattle drives.[21] The narrative has several verses of songs inserted, illustrating various aspects of this life. These songs also appear in full in a kind of appendix.

Beyond the debatable question of Lomax's Texas cowboy identity, the quality and character of his cowboy material may be a better test of his work. His various commentators almost necessarily generalize about his entire collection as to its cowboy "authenticity," and for them, it generally falls short. A further question that needs to be asked is what were the sources for each song in Lomax's collection, in this case "The Cowboy's Lament"? A generalization across all of Lomax's material will not do, especially when we are dealing with the most famous of American cowboy ballads. But does "The Streets of Laredo" itself testify to an origin among cowboys even with what the Fifes called its "longer and smoother synthetic text" (1966b, 151)? While we cannot speak for all of Lomax's collection, given our recent review, there is more than enough reason to believe that some forms of this particular ballad were circulating in oral tradition in the later nineteenth century as the evidence offered by Owen Wister and John Callison indicates.[22] I suggest that Lomax may have received mail-in contributions based on this oral tradition from cowboys only one generation removed from his Texas correspondents. While we do not have a full "authentic" textual version collected directly in the field, there was probably some "there" out there.

Wayland Hand certainly seemed to think the ballad was "authentic," in this nineteenth-century sense, although as we have seen, he mistakenly thought that Thorp had collected it from Troy Hale, a presumably working cowboy. We have an even better-informed assessment from another and perhaps surprising quarter. Abrahams' close colleague and my mentor, Américo Paredes, was another great University of Texas at Austin folklorist, yet another member of the mid-twentieth-century school of "disciplinary coherence," but he was native to southern Texas, the ancestral home of the cowboy in his Mexican and Anglo versions that Paredes knew well (Paredes 1958; Limón 2012, 72–99; Stoeltje 2012.). Indeed, in an article with the germane title, "The North American Cowboy in Folklore and

Literature," Paredes commented on Lomax's 1910 collection. For Paredes, for the most part, Lomax's songs were not "acts of cooperative composition"; many of them have "no merit, neither artistic nor folkloric and came from disparate sources not at all folkloric. They were largely culled from written sources by ordinary individuals inspired by the idea and image of the cowboy but not by his real everyday life" (1963, 236). Yet even as he largely rejects Lomax's work, he notes an exception—"The Streets of Laredo"—as though he does not wish us to assume that it is simply another bad song in the Lomax collection. The collection does have some traditional songs, he tells us,

> that have suffered significant changes and can be considered typical cowboy variants. One of these is the famous "The Streets of Laredo,"... one of a series of variants made in the United States of the Irish song, "The Unfortunate Rake"[;] ... songs like these were sung as part of the cowboy's repertoire ... even though, there are not very many that could be considered part of the cowboy's song book." (236)[23]

Based on the foregoing evidence and argument, it seems not unreasonable to conclude that "The Cowboys Lament," later "The Streets of Laredo," did emerge among working Texas cowboys at some point during the cattle drives, sung undoubtedly with varying numbers of stanzas and changes in diction and tempo among varying numbers of cowboys and for different occasions. While one would have preferred several versions collected at different moments over the course of the cattle drives, this was not to be given the nonexistence of systematic, modern, professional folklore studies in the later nineteenth century. Yet as we saw, Wister and Thorp had some considerable awareness of the ballad. In the nineteenth century, and in all probability so did Lomax's correspondents, especially Roy Bedichek. In editorially composing his 1910 ballad, Lomax was not working in a folkloric vacuum nor an ideological one.

I close this section with another, perhaps even conclusive affirmation of the ballad's probable nineteenth-century presence among cowboys. As we shall soon see, the ballad inspired written modern literature in the twentieth century, but in the nineteenth century, our ballad may have inspired a written poem which in turn offered its own critique of modernity. From 1879 to 1886, a small newspaper—*The Cheyenne Transporter*—appeared in the town of Darlington in then Indian Territory, later Oklahoma. According to the Library of Congress, this small four-page newspaper was started by the Darlington Indian Agency following the removal of those two tribes to the Territory. It was primarily dedicated to "Indian Civilization and Progress"; that is, fostering respect for the Indian while assisting in the Indian's inevitable encounter with modernity (Oklahoma Historical Society 2023, 1). But the small four-page newspaper actually had a double mission: it "opposed opening the territory for white settlement and called on the government to protect the interests of Indians and the cattle industry" (1). Several articles in the newspaper attest to these interests, but also clarify that by "cattle industry," the newspaper was referring primarily to the livelihood of working cowboys.

As further and compelling testimony to this cowboy advocacy, in its very last issue in 1886, the newspaper printed the following poem. Since it has no authorial identification, I will reference the two editors of the newspaper, George West Maffet and Lafe Merritt. I have numbered the stanzas for clarity.

"The Cowboy's Lament"

1.

Through progress of railroads,
Our occupation's gone,
We put our ideas into words,
Our words into a song.
First comes the cowboy,
He's pointed for the west;
Of all the pioneers I claim,
The cowboy is the best.
We miss him on the round-up,
Gone is his merry shout.
The cowboy's left the country,
And the campfire's going out.

2.

No railroad nor graders,
Nor anything to mar
Our happiness in camping out,
Or trav'ling with the star—
When I think of the good old days,
My eyes do sometimes fill,
When I think of the tin by the campfire,
And the cayuse on the hill.

Imagination takes me back,
I hear the merry shout;
But the cowboy's left the country,
And the campfire's going out.
    3.
You freighters are companions,
You'll have to leave the land,
Can't haul your loads for nothing,
Through seven feet of sand.
Railroad's bound to beat you,
Do your level best;
So, give it to the granger,
Shake hands before you leave us,
And give a merry shout.
Freighter's left the country,
And the campfire's going out.
    4.
In times when freight was higher,
Old-timers had a show,
Their pockets full of money,
No sorrow did they know;
But, O! how times have changed since then;
You're poorly clothed and fed;
Your wagons are all broken,
And your mules are almost dead.
The cowboy and the freighter
Soon will hear the angels shout:
"Here they come to heaven,
And their campfire's all gone out."
(Maffett and Merritt 1886, 1)

I always taught my students to begin their understanding of a poem with close consideration of its title, if only to ask how the poem is related to it. In this instance, I trust it is perfectly clear that this poem shares its title with our ballad. That this could be mere coincidence seems impossible. My supposition is that the ballad inspired this poem, and the poet more than hints at this inspiration with the lines "we put our ideas into words / our words into a song." But it is precisely

these "ideas" which is to say, the poem's argument, that firmly establishes this relationship. Running throughout the poem is the imagery of the cowboy as a hero
pitted against the forces of modernity represented, again, by the railroad, but also
by the key word "graders" in the first line of the second stanza. In this context, it
meant then in the nineteenth century what it means today which is a tractor-like
machine for flattening the ground, usually for construction projects such as the
building of towns. At that time before the combustion engine, they would
have been pulled by horses, a sad ironic commentary on the horse in cowboy culture. Against such modernity, for this poet, "the cowboy is the best," but by 1886,
one can now only imaginatively hear his "merry shout," for with modernity's inevitable triumph and the end of the cattle drives, "the cowboy has left the country"
and his "campfire's going out." The poem could have easily ended with the second
stanza, but the speaker also wanted to create alliance in the face of modernity by
turning to the freighters also known as teamsters. Like the cowboy who drove
cattle to capitalist markets, the freighter was perhaps also a conscript of modernity. While not on horseback on long cattle drives, the freighter hauled a variety
of goods from place to place using oxen or mule-drawn carts and wagons, usually over trails on the open range. Fundamentally, the freighter/teamster was a
small business owner or entrepreneur but working out in the open. To some
significant degree, like the cowboy, the poem envisions the teamster as a semi-
pastoral figure whose livelihood was also imperiled by the railroad. In Texas at
this time, "the railroad freight rates were about half of those charged by teamsters" (Texas State Library 2023, 2). The poem's ending has both figures greeted
by heaven's angels after their discontent with modernity. If I am correct in posit-
ing our ballad, "The Streets of Laredo"—in this instance as "The Cowboy's
Lament"—as the inspirational source for this poem, then it is further evidence
that in some discernible textual fashion, our ballad circulated in the later nineteenth century.[24]

THE EMOTIONAL CORE OF 1947

But our history does not end with 1910 and 1921. In 1947, Lomax and his son,
Alan, then produced a more accessible version of the ballad included in *Folksong U.S.A.*[25] For the first time, as far as I know, the ballad appears with the title
"The Streets of Laredo," which will then effectively take over. This version is a
distillation of the previous quite long 1910 text into what amounts to its "emo-

tional core." The concept of a ballad's "emotional core" was first developed by Tristam Coffin, yet another member of the school of "disciplinary coherence" and then amplified by the aforementioned Américo Paredes (Coffin 1957; Paredes 1972). More recently, Elliot Oring has referred to this idea as one of the possible "four laws of folklore," to wit: over time, "in a chain of oral transmission, a ballad will contract into a lyric centered on its emotional core . . . as interest is focused on those aspects of a song that arouse emotion" (2022, 56).[26] Paredes offered greater specificity in his study of a Mexican ballad which "contains an emotional core, essentially lyrical, which is more important to its evolution than are its narrative parts. With the passing of time, the narrative parts are forgotten and nothing remains but the emotional core, which finally becomes a lyric rather than a narrative song" (1993, 146).[27] By "lyric," Paredes clearly means verses that are of "lyric beauty," richly metaphorical and evocative in comparison to more "pedestrian" stanzas (145). However, while the lyrical is foremost, some narrativity remains, and "the emotional core functions as a focal point or constitutive principle that structures the total composition during the act of re-creation each time a song is performed in a folkloric context" (159). Referring back to Coffin, Paredes then makes a crucial comparative point, noting the presence of "the emotional core in the British ballad, which shares significant characteristics with the *corrido* in spite of differences in culture and language" (162).

I believe that in 1947, Lomax and Lomax arrived at their own more economical and far more aesthetically competent version stressing the song's emotional core. The first two stanzas constitute an opening frame while the last one and possibly the last two are the leave-taking frame. Everything else in between may be taken as the emotional core, although the number and order of these stanzas in actual performances can vary from singer to singer. That this distillation may have also responded to publication requirements only suggests that the Lomaxes addressed both issues in one editorial practice.

Given what evidence we do have, including the later endorsement of distinguished ballad scholars such as Abrahams and Paredes, I am comfortable in speaking of this 1947 ballad, as I did at the beginning of this chapter, as an articulation of the nineteenth-century cowboys' cultural consciousness of their situation within modernity. While he may not have been fully conversant with this folkloristic history, as we have seen, the distinguished critic of Western Americana, Stephen Tatum, also articulated this cowboy critical consciousness as well. This linkage was made possible by John Avery Lomax who, with his perhaps unorthodox editorial poetics, recovered various verses and fragments of a ballad that surely existed but could also be reimagined later as he did. Roger D. Abrahams, the great folklorist, and my also esteemed teacher, who spent most of his distinguished career at the University of Texas-Austin, acknowledges that Lomax's "publishing practices . . . sometimes appeared unprofessional and didn't seem to cleave to the standards of authenticity . . . of folksong scholars . . . whose mixed reception of Lomax's work . . . also rested in large measure on what was perceived as his unseemly self-promotion and his slippery way of reporting texts," perceived, that is, by what Abrahams identifies as "the purists of the first half of the twentieth century" who "feared that the Lomaxes constructed composite texts from those they collected from a number of performers." Abrahams then asks a rhetorical question: "Should songs be printed as found, or changed to make them more consistent, readable, appropriately representative of the best of the tradition from which they grew?" (102).[28] In asking this question, Abrahams allows us to continue our interrogation of folkloristics.

ON PERFORMANCE AND POLITICS

I have charted the manner in which folklorists of different persuasions and degrees of professionalization, including cowboy poets, participated in the identification and the textual emergence of "The Streets of Laredo" from its Anglo-Irish ancestry to its articulation within a twentieth century modernity. John A. Lomax was at the center of this enterprise, but the work of Wayland Hand first led us into this history fraught with controversy, prevarication, ambivalence but also creativity. This review has also furnished an occasion for me to recall that particular period of mid-twentieth-century "disciplinary coherence" which included several other "star" folklorists. Yet, as Bendix reminded us, this mid-twentieth-century moment was still largely invested in idioms of authenticity centered on the folkloric text. From that mid-century moment, we then progressed through a 1970s performance-centered folkloristics toward our own fin de siècle, a time of "representation," intertextuality, and a reflexive politics of culture in the humanities that I myself lived through professionally. However, I would argue that this progressive flexibility was always present, at least within what Richard Bauman has called "the Texas School" of folkloristics at whose center was Roger D. Abrahams which is why he was so open to Lomax's work (2020).[29]

Ironically enough, in his seeming disregard for canons of textual authenticity and disciplinary coherence, Lomax himself may have anticipated these later developments including "performance" folkloristics such that he may now be seen as an oddly early member of the "Texas School."[30] Frank De Caro and Rosan Augusta Jordan noted that, writing in the 1930s, both Zora Neale Hurston and J. Frank Dobie "actually anticipated some of the trends in current folklore research" and the same may be said for Dobie's colleague, John Lomax (2004, 260). For example, he offered this observation of how a ballad might have been sung even as his last line suggests that he had "The Streets of Laredo" in mind:

> Whatever the most gifted man could produce must bear the criticism of the entire camp, and agree with the ideas of a group of men. In this sense, therefore, any song that came from such a group would be the joint product of a number of them, telling perhaps the story of . . . some comrade's tragic death. (1910, xix)

Which, for me, resonates with this perspective offered by the leading theorist of performance:

> performance as a mode of verbal communication consists in the assumption of responsibility to an audience for a display of communicative competence[;] . . . from the point of view of the audience, the act of expression on the part of the performer is thus marked as subject to evaluation . . . for the relative skill and effectiveness of the performer's display of competence. (Bauman 1975, 293)

For Lomax, however, the group's evaluation also contributes to the performer's display of competence and thus, "in this sense," the ballad is the "joint product of a number of them," a certain kind of collective production and not to be confused with a Gummerian "singing, dancing, throng" (Gummere, 1901, 139).

In an even wider sense, the composition of a ballad in a shared performance "seemed to offer . . . a mechanism for practicing communitarian alternatives to a modern society predicated on bourgeois individuality" (Peart 2015, 696). Thus, in Lomax, we also sense a more democratic principle at work than is evident in performance theory, which also tended to neglect the social forces that produce folklore in the first place (Limón and Young 1986). The school of disciplinary coherence predictably charged Lomax with "usurping the function of the folk artist" (Wilgus 1959, 218). In this later and more fluid instance, however, it may be that the rural Texan Lomax envisioned himself as yet another audience participant *cum* performer. With this charter of "authenticity," he then rendered his own performance in a very popular print version that he fully expected would be sung, especially with the music notation provided for the 1947 "emotional core" version, a version of folklore in literature (Abrahams 1972). As a third stage in the development of contemporary folkloristics, Bendix proposes such an elaboration of performance theory into what she calls a "politics of culture" saying, "what performance scholars have isolated as a key element in aesthetic performances also holds true for folkloristic practitioners—responsibility in the face of an audience" (1997, 217). At least as it concerns "The Streets of Laredo," Lomax was such a practitioner who faced a national and international audience with responsibility but also responsibly acknowledged his methods in the conviction that he was also being responsible to the Texas cowboy, his "folk."

Bendix has also well-charted the recurrent malady in folkloristics of searching for the "authentic" (1997). The search for the authentic reminds us of Slowik earlier when he also charged Lomax with manipulating "the components of a song . . . for widespread circulation" thus "*producing* songs for a mass audience" (2012, 211). Slowik's criticism seems misplaced. Clearly Lomax knew that he was indeed producing his own text; there was nothing hidden about his method as he himself tells us rather explicitly. His 1910 text as a narrative whole is obviously not fully "authentic" although, as I have suggested, it was likely based on oral tradition at least indirectly, but Lomax freely conceded and eschewed this point even as he fashioned his own claim for a certain authenticity. While most of Lomax's stanzas likely did come originally from cowboys, now once removed, its overall narrative structure is a product of his own aesthetic judgement. Whatever his other motives, this "Streets of Laredo" that Lomax candidly composed from a probable oral tradition—and later distilled to its "emotional core"—affords us at least a persuasive sense of the cowboy's measured outlook on a time of great change. Moreover, while he does not intend the characterization as a compliment, Lomax was indeed, in Slowik's words, "a creative force," who had every intention of "producing songs for a mass audience" (211). We turn now to the ballad's even more intimate dance with modernity in the later twentieth and twenty-first centuries, still by way of Lomax, but also several others well into recent time. While some of these will take us away from Texas, we will return in a decisive manner by way of Larry McMurtry.

PART II

Abrahams has offered an affirmative recognition of Lomax's work and influence which was based "on the values of those who worked on the land away from the contagions of bureaucracy and industrialization," which is to say modernity (2000, 103). "It is time," he continues, "to put behind us the misgivings and mis-readings of John Lomax's enterprise." For "in good part," he continues, "this reputation arose because of Lomax's decision to write as a public intellectual and not in the approved academic presentation style" (107).[31] As such a public intellectual and publishing between 1910 and 1947, Lomax creatively manipulated our ballad and several others to reflect on the cowboy past but also to insert himself and later his son into a continuing twentieth-century discontent with modernity. The more important question may not be one of textual authenticity, but rather to what end did he produce this book and our song in this fashion? What, if any, was the point of his editorial poetics as public performance? Lomax had more lucrative ways of making a living, principally as a university administrator and an investment banker, such that his considerable time spent in folkloristics now seems almost extravagant (Porterfield 1996, 217–230). Whatever personal financial reward or ego gratification he surely received from the latter must now also be measured relative to the book's importance in the general American culture of that moment. Wilgus was the most pungent of Lomax's critics professional limitations, but conscious of his controversial practices, he nevertheless averred that "we could multiply the examples of obfuscation in *Cowboy Songs* without destroying the importance of the book" (1959, 165). Lomax's book, Logsdon tells us, "became the most widely circulated collection of cowboy songs ever published and exerted much influence on later generations of cowboy singers" (1989, 300). I would argue that this influence went far beyond "later generations of cowboy singers," depending on what Logsdon meant by that, if this influence is to be measured solely by its reputation within folklore's later disciplinary coherence. Even though this reputation would come under question by mid-century, it is more than worth remembering Lomax's popularity as a lecturer at major universities including his alma mater Harvard and also Yale as well as scholarly forums such as the American Folklore Society and the MLA (Fenster 1989, 268–270).

But what made Lomax's book, and even Lomax himself, so popular? Jerrold Hirsch takes Lomax's biographer to task for not exploring "the intellectual and cultural discourse in which Lomax participated" (1998, 531). Indeed, Benjamin Filene and Hirsch himself had already done so almost simultaneously although both place far more emphasis on Lomax's work on African Americans in the US South (1991; 1992). Lomax took note of African America's "creative contributions . . . to American folksong," which were in tension with a New South modernity that might destroy such folklore that paradoxically also depended on their continuing social segregation (Hirsch 1992, 187). Adducing neither Filene nor Hirsch, Peart also focuses on African Americans and Lead Belly, but he does draw a more stringent relationship between Lomax's work and modernity saying that in the salon "all understood black folksong in particular as a kind of antinomian outside to the forces of industrial capitalism that seemed to threaten the national project of becoming a more perfect union" (2015, 708). One might even say that Lomax's work is the folkloristic equivalent of the work of the Southern Agrarians such as Allen Tate and John Crowe Ransom who, at that same moment between the world wars also opposed modernity offering high literature—both classical and modern—as the humanistic counterweight to such modernity with the Old South as the "natural" home of such literature (Gray 2000). Of course, Lomax added African Americans to this southern struggle with modernity, an irony perhaps, for even as he worked directly with African Americans, he also shared the Agrarian's deep ambivalence on race (Porterfield 1998, 169). As it happens, Lomax's fellow Texan and UT alum, the well-published writer Laura Krey, was also an Agrarian in these same terms, although it would seem the two never crossed paths (Limón 2022a).

Lomax scholars have focused on Lomax's work on African Americans and say relatively little about his cowboy songs. What commentary there is has a marked tendency to associate this work, principally *Cowboy Songs and Other Frontier Ballads*, with a turn-of-the-century populist American nationalism best exemplified by Theodore Roosevelt, and the latter's admiration and endorsement of Lomax's book certainly support this linkage (Bronner 2002, 3–8). This connection is most evident in Lomax's dedication of the book to Roosevelt and Roosevelt's handwritten endorsement that also appears in the book (1910, 11, 13–14). Yet he would have nothing but contempt for that other Roosevelt's New Deal and its own version of modernity by way of a vast federal bureaucracy (Porterfield 1998, 424–426). Congruent with his paradoxical though muted racism toward black people, Lomax also certainly had nationalistic and at times jingoistic tendencies, part of what Porterfield aptly calls his "mass of contradictions" (1).

Yet clearly, for the white-cowboy-identified Lomax, cowboys and their songs were different and cannot be separated from the general and well-rehearsed role of the cowboy within American modernity in the first half of the twentieth century. Cowboys represented an "an imaginary escape to a simpler era, the removal from the buzz and hum of urban life in a real or imagined countryside close to nature and the earth," and especially "when the crushing weight of the Depression began . . . the issue and image of freedom and independence of the cowboys began to mean so very much in music and film" (Green 2002, 22). I suggest Lomax's work on cowboys was one such reading for an American public perhaps ill at ease with an increasingly enveloping modernity bereft of a full human fulfillment. Melanie Dawson and Meredith L. Goldsmith have also recently invited us to reconsider the way in which we have habitually thought of what counts as American literature from the turn of that century in response "toward the changes of modernity" (2018, 3). They note the very many different kinds of noncanonical texts that were available to a reading public marked by "the sheer diversity of the era's print culture, which underwent considerable expansion in terms of the voices it newly included" as "debating modernity's boundaries was a large part of this culture of expanded representation" (2018, 10). Lomax's work became part of this debate.

We must also note the special role of Texas in this larger confrontation with modernity. Probably no other place in the United States so abruptly experienced the transition from an already modernizing agricultural society to one increasingly urbanized, involved in mass communications and petrochemical industrialization, the latter obviously keyed on the newly discovered abundance of oil all over the state, but oil fueled the entire process. But "as the country's traditional agrarian society crumbled before the onslaught of industrialization . . . there was a counter-movement afoot," and "the leaders in this movement were folklorists . . . at the University of Texas, John A. Lomax . . . chief among them" (S. Davis 2009, 53).[32] He was soon joined by an acolyte in this dissent, J. Frank Dobie, also in the English department at UT, who, in Lomax's own words, eventually "supplanted me in everything pertaining to the Southwest," and, he might have added, as it concerns modernity (64). Eventually the two would quarrel over Dobie's support of FDR and the New Deal (157–158). The far more agrarian-style-conservative Lomax tended to conflate a capitalist industrial modernity with a state-sanctioned bureaucracy as did the Southern Agrarians, and I have already noted his fellow Texan, Laura Krey, in this same stance (Limón 2022a).[33]

THE STREETS OF LAREDO REDUX

Within this ideologically effective popularity of Lomax and his work, there may have been a particular place for our primary concern, "The Streets of Laredo." Let us recall that, even though he thought (wrongly) that Lomax had misappropriated the ballad from Thorp, Hand did give Lomax begrudging credit for making "the song more widely known" through his 1910 collection (1955, 144). And in negative but revealing fashion, the conservative Fifes also noted that Lomax gave the ballad "much more influence upon the twentieth century than it deserves" (1996b: 151). Throughout the first half of the twentieth century, it seemed to have become something of a cowboy Kalevala, that is, authorially fashioned in controversy and from an indirect oral tradition, but, as with the Kalevala, such a ballad paradoxically acquired a growing social significance although perhaps not of the nation-building kind (Anttonen 2005, 153–154, 165–166).[34] Yet, the Fifes also acknowledged that "'The Cow Boy's Lament' comes about as near to supplying the elements of an epic of the American West as any other single song" (1996b, 150). Or, as Lomax's contemporary, Wallace Stevens, might have said, "a larger poem for a larger audience" (1954, 465). In the context of modernity, however, less may be more, lyric more effective than epic. As noted in the previous chapter, in 1947 the ballad's singularity was undoubtedly enhanced when Lomax and his son, Alan, produced a compendium—"a sampling of America's folk songs"—that included our ballad in its cowboy section, the ballad now condensed into its emotional core (1947, viii). While its inclusion does not surprise, what is notable is that the title "The Streets of Laredo" appears for the first time, replacing "The Cowboy's Lament." However, it must also be noted that John Lomax did not particularly refer to the ballad in any of his other writings with one exception. While collecting ballads from African American convicts in Texas, he reports a prisoner with the nickname, Clear Rock, who sang the "famous cowboy song entitled 'The Streets of Laredo'"(1947, 153). Lomax's retrieval and production of the ballad then placed it within the more evident modernity of mass media— radio, electronic recording, film, and eventually television and social media. The song was recorded for the first time for mass popular consumption in the 1920s and would be many times again. It must also be noted that the 1947 Lomax book, reprinted in paperback in 1966, also came on the eve of the American folksong revival (Cantwell 1996; R. Cohen 2002).[35] With the very popular imprimatur of 1947, this much more manageable version then seems to have become a kind of urtext for even more subsequent recordings and transformations of the song (Goldstein 1960). These versions, however, were largely contained within the orbit of leftist circles and the coffeehouse "folk" world, and I say this as one of its participants as a student at the University of Texas at then truly weird Austin in the mid-1960s.

The ballad then became fully enmeshed in an advanced modernity through its central inventions—sound recording, radio, and later television—even as it continued to question that very modernity (Ives 1941; Livingston and Evans 1949). In 1960, the song had a far more significant "break out" moment when melded as "folk," "country-western," and "pop," it reached a much larger audience by way of

Marty Robbins's extremely popular album *Gunfighter Ballads and Trail Songs*, an album that also included "El Paso." Subsequently the song was also recorded by Johnny Cash, and both men sang it as a duet in 1969 on Cash's television program (Cash and Robbins 1969).[36] Cash and Robbins are closely identified with the proletarian "cowboy" West but also the Scots-Irish South and thus they "returned" the song to something resembling its cowboy roots (Danker 1975; Diekman 2012). Writing on "country musicians and their markets," Neil V. Rosenberg says,

> the very nature of a professionalized music which draws its workers from an identifiable group will inevitably affect and reflect the music traditions of the group. In other words, the music continues to function as folk music[;] . . . it speaks for the group, articulating the concerns, beliefs, attitudes and world view of the group. (1986, 152)

In this case, what are these "concerns, beliefs, attitudes and world view" that might account for the song's popularity in this new popular culture ambience that we know as "country-western" and even beyond through the Robbins/Cash "crossover" careers? We can only suggest the continuing recognition of a better way of life—then and now—that the Texas cowboy momentarily expressed in his labor on horseback as his song with its emotional core was now shared with a wider audience. Twentieth-century musicians recorded the song and thus made it very accessible to the general public with possible ideological consequences akin to that of the nineteenth-century cowboy in his discontent with modernity.

In my view, the most interesting of these is that offered by Anna Domino, a very accomplished American singer and a feminist who has also written on women and balladry (2005, 69–80). In a duo called Snakefarm with her husband, Michel Delory, she recorded a wonderful version of "Streets of Laredo" for their 1999 album *Songs from My Funeral* (Domino, 1999). She faithfully follows the now traditional lyrics in a lower key, while he flows in and out of the sung narrative with beautifully impulsive electric guitar sequences. In a manner quite germane to the album's title, the effect is a haunting quite contemporaneous rendition in a style variously called "Blues Rock, Lounge, Down tempo or Pop Rock" according to the album notes. As the famous music critic, Greil Marcus, puts it, "The Streets of Laredo" and the other songs on this album, "were remade—felt through—with modern sound effects, shifting them into a dimension where they could be heard as if they had never been played before." Domino's "cool, regretful, unhurried" narration allows her to inhabit the story much as the traditional narrator does such that "she and the rest bear his coffin through the streets, covered with roses ... even though he done wrong" (2005, 353). We take great comfort in imagining that, at the turn of the century and with a feminist female narrator, our song as musical performance may have still been doing its critical work in a manner more accessible to younger audiences.

Yet for all the ideological resonance that musical performances can offer, often with great variation in tempo, rhythm, and versification, they do not really transform the song's story—its narrative structure and theme—for that is not their primary or even secondary purpose. Nevertheless, we are obliged to note that at least two of many later musical performances do transform the ballad by way of parody, itself a recognition of and compliment to the ballad. As reported by Wayland Hand, one replaces the cowboy with an electrical power lineman who falls off a pole and must die, while the other features a college professor who dies on the campus of UCLA, saying "It was once on the campus / I used to go dashing / It was once on the campus I used to go gay," but now that he is dead,

> Get six happy colleagues to carry my coffin,
> Get six pretty coeds, short medium and tall;
> Put acres of bluebooks all over my coffin,
> Put bluebooks to deaden the sods as they fall.[37]
> (1958, 204–205)

But the ballad did have a far more transformative appeal to other kinds of artists. Film would seem to offer the possibility of drawing on the song's metaphorical structure and thematics in a creative transformation. Such an accounting would almost necessarily take us to the popular commercial cowboy movies and television shows of the first two thirds of the twentieth century. While there is a voluminous literature on this subject, I am afraid I cannot add to it with our song. There is one very minor exception. The 1949 *Streets of Laredo*, directed by Leslie Fenton and starring William Holden, obviously needs to be mentioned here, as its very title would seem to suggest a recreative engagement with the ballad. The song appears chiefly in its title. This forgettable film has little to do with Laredo, and while *a* song is performed on the film that repeats the line, "the streets of Laredo," it is assuredly not our ballad, but rather a saccharine love song about a Texas Ranger and a *señorita* in Laredo that also has nothing to do with the film's plot, which winds up as lawmen confront bad guys in the streets of Laredo. But these popular films from the 1930s and '40s also brought forth the "singing cowboy" such as Roy Rogers and Gene Autry and a host of other faux cowboy singers individually and in ensembles for which Mark Fenster gives Lomax much credit (1989). Although both Rogers and Autry recorded the song, neither integrated it into any of their films. Douglas B. Green reports one such popular singer in the 1940s and '50s, Rex Allen, whose "greatest recording success during his singing-cowboy years was his commanding version of the old warhorse 'The Streets of Laredo'..." (2002, 302). That Green refers to the ballad as "the old warhorse" clearly suggests its legacy and continuing wide popularity, but again, these were strictly musical performances without any transformative creative intent. For the most part, these films and musical groups paid little attention to the working cowboy and the cattle drives, instead focusing on the lawman and/or the heroic pistol-in-hand lone "cowboy" as the central character (Green 2002, 12).[38] Perhaps this is why the song is never heard in any of these films, for the hero of our ballad is not "heroic" in this manner. In a manner paralleling the cowboy film, the twentieth century also saw the popular development of another articulation of the "cowboy": the rodeo. The rodeo was in some ways a celebration of the working nineteenth-century cowboys in its physically demanding mimicry of the older artisanal crafts minus branding and just plain herding. Beverly Stoeltje has shown how this festive form was also the site of a continuing cowboy discontent with modernity expressed in their performative replication of the cowboy's artisanal culture and also in labor disputes (2012). Yet, as far as I know, the song was not, and probably could not be, addressed in any reasonably creative manner within the rodeo where such a lament would not be a good fit with the festive competition.

THREE AMERICAN FICTIONS IN SEARCH OF A BALLAD

American fiction may offer us another and better way of tracking and exploring a continuing twentieth-century discontent that explicitly draws on and creatively transforms the song. By its very nature, narrative allows us to witness a creative use of key symbols or metaphors such as that famous white whale—or, in this instance, our ballad—as part of an extended thematic argument for an audience engaged in a presumably more deliberate reading and reflecting process. For such a use of our ballad, we find three major examples of American fiction in the respective novels of Mark Harris, Larry McMurtry, and John Irving in chronological order (1956; 1993; 2015). All three of these writers straddle that tenuous ground between "serious" and "popular" fiction that focuses on well-known instances of public culture—in this case, baseball, cowboys, and, for Irving, the writer him/herself as a celebrity public figure.[39] Two of them, Harris and McMurtry do so through a realism that adheres closely to a kind of ethnographic observation (Harris) or historical research (McMurtry). That it is fiction, and not disciplinary history or sociology, is, of course, not a small matter, but it may matter less when the writer is obviously aware of these distinctions *and* is empirically and/or historically informed. As Louis Gerard Mendoza notes, "imaginative reconstructions of daily life examine the particulars of identity formation as they are shaped by ritual, emotional relations, spiritual beliefs, and relations of power outside the traditional domain of political and economic relations" but also the received literary canon (2001, 16). As compared to various "modernisms," popular literary practice is simply more accessible to a general public and therefore potentially more ideologically efficacious.

All three writers offer us a nexus within folklore, mass media, and now fiction which then leads to the question: How did these writers come by this song? Since none of the three had anything to say on this point, we could be content to simply say that they "heard it somewhere," but it may be possible to home in on a more specific moment when the song came to their notice. It cannot be proven conclusively, but for Harris and McMurtry, at least, it may be of some interest to consider the not entirely forgotten figure of Burl Ives. He was the best-known mass media singer of anglophone folk songs from the 1940s through the early '60s until Joan Baez came along, although it must be said that in comparison to most "folk" singers such as Baez, Ives did spring from a clearly rural, working class, midwestern upbringing in which traditional music was valued and which he learned at a very early age (Ives 1948; Cantwell 1996, 175–177). Mark Harris was in the US Army during part of World War II, and, as it happens, in his own richly complicated life, Burl Ives had a radio show, *G.I. Jive*, that he hosted during World War II in which he played such songs. It was transmitted to all American military at home and abroad. We do not know if his radio play included our ballad, but Ives had also just recorded his first album in 1941, *The Wayfaring Stranger*, on the small OKeh Records label which contained the ballad as "The Cowboy's Lament." It would probably be the largest mass audience for our song before the Marty Robbins version of 1959. For his part, McMurtry was five years old in 1941, but *The Wayfaring Stranger* was reissued for a much greater national market by Columbia Records in 1944 and again in 1950 (Daniels 1985, 37).[40]

It is also possible that Harris and/or McMurtry came across the Lomax and Lomax 1947 collection, or saw the 1949 film *Streets of Laredo*, although, as noted earlier, the latter uses nothing from the song except for its title. By 1959, Harris had already published his principal novels, but McMurtry could have also heard the song from Marty Robbins in 1959, although I suspect he already had some sort of acquaintance with it, possibly even firsthand from the cowboys on his father's small ranch in North Texas. Or perhaps he read Lomax. As for Irving's knowledge of the ballad, we can only assume that by the twenty-first century, any number of sources would have been possible for him, including, by the way, McMurtry's own novel *Streets of Laredo*, possibly facilitated by both writers having Simon & Schuster as their primary publisher.[41] Scholars have long been interested in the respective relationships of folklore to written literature and of folklore to mass media culture (Dundes 1965; Abrahams 1972; Narváez and Laba 1986; De Caro and Jordan 2004). In this instance there may have been a continuum from folklore through mass media to written literature: that is, from our cowboy song *in situ* in Texas, from there to folklore collection and editing such as Lomax's, followed by commercial musical media including Burl Ives, and then on to our novelists.

In their use of the ballad, Harris and Irving take us to other places and other arguments that, while intriguing, nevertheless would prove only ancillary at best to my general argument concerning the ballad, cowboys, and Texas. Here I will offer only a few summarizing words about those other arguments and places which I discuss in much more detail elsewhere.[42] Harris is best known for a series of four baseball novels from 1953 to 1970, the most famous of which takes a line from the ballad as its title, *Bang the Drum Slowly* (1956). In that novel, "The Streets of Laredo," becomes part of a critical commentary on the modern professionalization of baseball, but it is also marshaled toward a rejection of racism and anti-Semitism (Limón 2021). For his part, John Irving, arguably the best-known of the three, explicitly draws on the ballad in his novel, *Avenue of the Mysteries*, in such a way as to render it as an instance of mordant humor in what seems to be his penchant for recording the general vacuity of postmodern global culture (2015).

For our purpose, McMurtry is by far the more central writer, principally by virtue of his *Lonesome Dove* tetralogy of novels, of which the second is, indeed, called *Streets of Laredo* (1993). McMurtry will offer much more than Harris or Irving, much closer to what the distinguished literary critic, Frank Kermode, once called "the sense of an ending," experienced by a legion of writers in Western culture at the passing of what they saw as momentous epochal shifts in culture, as such writers and intellectuals consciously identified with the passing of some large moment in human history and thought (1967). For Kermode, the transition from the nineteenth to the twentieth century was one such key global moment, the often-noted fin de siècle in the global West (1967, 97–99). McMurtry's particular segment of this larger moment was no less than the history of the American West, especially Texas, and his entire writing project was dedicated to its delineation in fiction and essays. However, as a twenty-something, not yet well-read young writer, and as such writers often do, he began this long project with what he experientially knew firsthand, and/or could sense, which is the *mid-twentieth-century* consequences of this Texas fin de siècle. From here, he then programmatically circled back to its actual nineteenth-century genesis with this best-known and most admired work, the *Lonesome Dove* tetralogy, including its remarkable use and transformation of "The Streets of Laredo." His far more substantial relationship to our ballad, but also his well-established identity as a Texan and an advocate for the cowboy, merit its own chapter, which follows and will then also allow us to provide a kind of closure to the history of Texas, modernity, and "The Streets of Laredo," where we began.

Siren Song

The late Larry McMurtry's reputation as the leading writer of the American West, especially Texas, is now based principally on his tetralogy of novels centered on *Lonesome Dove* with prequels and sequels (1985, 1993, 1995, 1997). Two of these four, *Lonesome Dove* (1985) itself, but especially and obviously its sequel, *Streets of Laredo* (1993), will be my principal texts in this chapter as will two unpublished 1972 film treatments for *Lonesome Dove*.[1] Fictive though it is, this work is clearly informed by McMurtry's own extensive research on cowboys and ranching in that critical period, the subject of our first chapter. As Esther Allen has recently noted, "successful works of fiction tend to handle history with great care" (2020, 22). I believe that McMurtry's work is one such example although we will also note those moments when he takes historical poetic license.[2] His novels put some large measure of narrative flesh and blood on this history, such that we can imaginatively better understand the cowboy's ambivalent conscription into modernity in the later nineteenth century, an ambivalence that McMurtry shares (Busby 1995). In what follows, I want to lend emphasis to that ambivalence within gender relations but still focus on our ballad. As his major critic and biographer, Mark Busby notes, McMurtry "kept his eyes focused on male-female relationships" (1995, 50). These relationships also have much to do with modernity and with our song, which will emerge in his *Streets of Laredo*, but paradoxically enough in a revisioning of such gender relations.

McMurtry's strong and continuing interest in the ballad "The Streets of Laredo," has not received much attention, if at all, although it has been present throughout his career in a way that makes me think of our ballad as his siren song.

Indeed, with an allusive Homeric title for his essay, one critic has called McMurtry's Western novels an "odyssey of plain and prairie" (Dyer 2020, 4). In this odyssey, McMurtry has lived largely in a fictional world of men, and it was, of course, men who principally sang our ballad. My comparative classical conceit would seem initially thwarted because, of course, the sirens were famously women, but women have also sung to McMurtry, and we come to my central argument.

Beyond ordinary "male-female relationships," our author has also been especially and acutely conscious of women, not in fearful desire like Odysseus to the sirens, but rather in artistic attraction and supportive affirmation. His novel *Streets of Laredo* creatively completes his affirmative vision of women in a remarkable manner that draws on our ballad. With its self-evident title, in this novel our author takes this song from its traditional male habitat into in an appropriating and haunting transformation in which the singing of Texas women marks the passing of the cowboy life and the public emergence of women within modernity in late-nineteenth-century Texas. We can best enter into these issues in McMurtry's later fiction of the nineteenth century with a brief review of his twentieth-century work where both of these concerns—women and the song—already begin to appear. For any reader wholly unfamiliar with McMurtry, such a review might also be very helpful.

THE THALIA NOVELS

He launched his prolific career with three novels in fairly rapid succession—*Horseman, Pass By* (1961), *Leaving Cheyenne* (1963), and *The Last Picture Show* (1966)—amplified by film versions of two of these, all set in a fictive Texas town called "Thalia," in the 1940s and '50s, one closely resembling McMurtry's hometown of Archer City, Texas.[3] What John M. Reilly has called the "Thalia novels" record the almost total disappearance of a nineteenth-century world of working cowboys, the world of chapter 1. McMurtry's twentieth-century Thalia is largely in a fallen state from this prior world. Whereas cowboys in the nineteenth and early twentieth century may have been conscripts of modernity, as I have argued, their youthful descendants in the late 1940s and early '50s appear to be more-than-willing volunteers to a now twentieth-century capitalist modernity, "an intrusive new culture" represented "by such signs as the oil industry[,] ... the attraction of urban excitement in Fort Worth, and the increasing friction between those who live on accrued wealth and the wage earners who serve them" (Reilly 2000, 40).

There is a well-developed gendered dimension to Thalia. Expressing the view of his leading, mostly male characters, women are circumscribed largely to sexualized or maternal figures, and most of these offered in the most unflattering portraits (Busby 1995, 81; Reilly 2000, 34–35). But Reilly also sees a "paradox to be glimpsed in these female characterizations" where women "follow conventional scripts, but the amassing of singular details in their portraits gives the characters an unexpected individuality." There is, he continues, "a suggestion of McMurtry's sympathy in their portrayal, sympathy which encourages readers to discover that the motivation of their scripts actually is an urge to struggle against the conventions of constructed views of women as men's appendages" (35). I believe that Reilly is thinking of women such as Halmea, the housemaid in *Horseman, Pass By*; the young woman, Molly, who narrates her own story in *Leaving Cheyenne*; and, Genevieve, the waitress in *The Last Picture Show*.

We also get the first glimpse of our ballad in McMurtry's consciousness in the first of these novels, *Horseman, Pass By* (1961). His central character is a teenager named Lonnie Bannon. In one scene, Lonnie and some friends go to the one movie house in Thalia (which of course, will also be featured in *The Last Picture Show*), and they watch *Streets of Laredo* (1961, 48). Given the time frame, undoubtedly, this is the 1949 "Western" directed by Leslie Fenton and starring William Holden noted in the previous chapter. However, Lonnie could not have heard our ballad in this film, because it is not at all sung. Nevertheless, I think we can be quite certain that McMurtry knew of our song at least by his early twenties, if not sooner. Although it is not clear where and when he first came to know "The Streets of Laredo," he was also obviously aware of country-western music as amply demonstrated in *Horseman, Pass By* (1961, 195–208). Perhaps, like so many other young Americans, including myself, he heard Marty Robbins's version in 1959 although it is entirely possible he knew it from other sources, perhaps even the work of John Lomax.

Old Cowboys and Narrow Graves

After the "Thalia" novels, McMurtry's next major writing was not fiction but rather his 1968 collection of essays, *In A Narrow Grave*, where his interest in women and gender relations continues, but where his second public interest in the song also emerges. In serious writing, epigraphs and their placement matter. McMurtry opens his collection with two epigraphs, the first taken from the cowboy song, "The Dying Cowboy," which also gives his collection its title.

By my father's grave there let mine be,
And bury me not on the lone prairie.
"Oh, bury me not–" And his voice failed there.
But we took no heed of his dying prayer;
In a narrow grave, just six by three
We buried him there on the lone prairie

As with the Thalia novels, there can be no sharper articulation of the stark burial of the cowboy past, and McMurtry continues to develop this theme in these essays. But then there is a second epigraph where he turns to our principal subject, "The Streets of Laredo," albeit by its earlier name, "The Cowboy's Lament."

We beat the drums slowly
And shook the spurs lowly,
And bitterly wept
As we bore him along;
For we all loved our comrade,
So brave, young, and handsome,
We all loved the cowboy
Although he'd done wrong[4]

Here, of course, the young cowboy also dies, but there is a difference, for unlike the disavowal in the first epigraph where "we took no heed of his dying prayer," in this second song—our song—we see McMurtry's admiring recognition of the ritual honor bestowed upon one "brave, young, and handsome" even with the acknowledgement that "he'd done wrong."

In the best one of these essays, McMurtry says that "the cowboy is a tragic figure," and I think we agree that the cowboy's conscription to modernity was the stuff of tragedy, the fall from a vernacular heroism, "oriented toward the past" and facing "the present only under duress." But, McMurtry adds "one element of the tragedy is that this same cowboy was committed to an orientation that includes but does not recognize the female" (1968, 148–149). Elsewhere, McMurtry also notes that cowboys had "a commitment to a heroic concept of life that that simply takes little account of women," as if to say that women's equality is paradoxically tied to the cowboy's full, if reluctant, conscription into modernity; one will not come without the other (1977).

In the final essay, he nevertheless pays loving homage to his ancestral cowboy family, making it clear that "he still has a strong, sentimental attachment to what cowboys represented" (Busby 1995, 116). He offers a "gesture of recognition" to this older culture, but does so in a telling metaphor, offering "a wave such as riders sometime give one another as they start down opposite sides of a hill" (McMurtry 1968, 142–43). Thus, this self-described "bookish" young man wishes to imagine himself somehow still a "rider," still in some relationship, if now distanced, to a cowboy culture represented by his own family, even as he is now writing/riding elsewhere to the opposite side of this hill. As Busby summarizes the matter: "With *In A Narrow Grave* . . . McMurtry tipped his hat toward Old Texas, bade it a symbolic farewell, and signaled a major change for both himself and Texas literature[;] . . . he was ready to turn away completely from rural Texas, and his next group of novels moves to McMurtry's favorite city, Houston" (1995, 117).

The Ride to Perdition

There followed a series of "Houston" novels that chart the trials and tribulations of an urban Texas little affiliated with its cowboy past (1970, 1972, 1975). This is a Houston world wholly immersed in late modern vapidity; of mostly human wreckage, "atomistic, alienating, materialistic, violent, decadent, corrupt, and driven by a consumer economy that fosters classism and mass production of objects and entertainment" (Busby 1995, 54–55). Indeed, in the popular culture of the time, the only "cowboys" in sight were *Midnight Cowboy* which appeared in 1969, as McMurtry was entering this phase of his career, and John Travolta's 1980 *Urban Cowboy*, as it was coming to a close.[5] However, within such a vapid urban culture, women do not fare much better than in Thalia, although two female characters do emerge with some strength, resolve, and attractiveness: Aurora Greenway and her daughter Emma Horton in *Terms of Endearment* (1975). Although they have their faults and are represented as women living *in* the American West but not *of* that West, nevertheless they serve to signal McMurtry's willingness to articulate such a female presence in more affirmative terms.

His break with the past is even more evident in the next series of novels that he wrote which are only loosely set in Texas, the last one, *The Desert Rose*, mostly in Las Vegas (1978, 1982, 1983). The one "cowboy" in this grouping, Jack McGriff in *Cadillac Jack*, is a drug addict and spends most of his time . . . well, in his Cadillac . . . driving all over the country, a seeming parody of the cattle drive. But McMurtry's seeming and progressive development of women also seems to give out. In this flattened postmodern moment, his women characters "are not given a capacity for reflection that would make it possible to see them as commentators on the culture they inhabit[;] . . . they seem to be entirely the products of a showbiz culture that establishes women as commodities for the entertainment trade" (Reilly 2000, 75). It does not surprise that these three novels were critical failures, "more generally abused by critics than the others" (Busby 1995, 151). For Clay Reynolds, for example, this last body of work "exhibits a certain flatness, a loss of the inspiration, that gave his early books their freshness and appeal" (1989, 281). However, in *Cadillac Jack*, loosely based in Texas, Reynolds also notes that "McMurtry may be signaling, perhaps unconsciously, his awareness of this authorial identity crisis, and the careful reader can perceive a recognition on McMurtry's part of the need to return to his roots and make peace with his homeland" (281). McMurtry did indeed make what Busby also calls a "return," not just to Texas, but, for the first time, to the nineteenth-century moment of the great cattle drives (1995, 178). But this return was not abruptly taken. It occurred in three phases, the first of which has gone largely unexamined in McMurtry criticism, probably because it remains unpublished. McMurtry's concerns with modernity, women, and the song first become salient in this early work.

Lonesome Dove: First Take

While the first and central novel, *Lonesome Dove,* appeared in 1985, its major critics agree that it had its "inception" circa 1972 by way of a McMurtry screenplay called "The Streets of Laredo" (Lich 1987, 51–52). Yet, notwithstanding its title, they seem to assume first, that it was *one* screenplay, and, that it is simply *Lonesome Dove* writ small, in large part influenced by McMurtry's own summary in a 1980 interview they all cite (Graham 1989, 312–313; Busby 1995, 179–180; Reilly 2000, 88). "I did a script," says McMurtry, ". . . called *Streets of Laredo* for John Wayne, James Stewart, and Henry Fonda. It was an end-of-West Western. Three old men stumble into a last adventure, and they're old, and the West is over" (Bennett 1980, 34). While the existence of this work has been thus briefly noted, it has not been examined closely as far as I know.

In fact, McMurtry developed two such treatments for a possible film to be directed by Peter Bogdanovich, who had also directed the film version of *The Last Picture Show*. Both were called *Streets of Laredo*. McMurtry calls one of these a "scenario," a preliminary outline or first draft, which presumably was then rendered as a separate and later "original screenplay" according to their respective title pages. In both cases, Bogdanovich is credited as a coauthor, but given the content, in all probability, McMurtry was the lead author, and he does get first credit in reverse alphabetical order on both title pages (McMurtry and Bogdanovich 1972a, 1972b). Indeed, we find this McMurtry cursive note on the scenario's title page: "This is the first draft, done with Peter Bogdanovich, for John Wayne, James Stewart, and Henry Fonda, in 1972—it became the novel *Lonesome Dove*—L. McMurtry" (1972a, title page). But the most cursory of readings of these two treatments soon reveals that while they indeed led to "the novel, *Lonesome Dove*," as published in 1985, they are rather two early and very different anticipatory *versions* of that novel and obviously with a very different title, not yet *Lonesome Dove*, but instead, *The Streets of Laredo*.

At the time of their writings, it would appear that McMurtry scholars did not have access to either and therefore could not really be aware of major and interesting differences between these treatments and the later novel although the former's very title already suggests such differences. Both are now available in university archives, and they are both very relevant to my present argument.[6] The first of these early anticipatory filmic treatments—the scenario—allow us to see McMurtry's first sustained textualized interest in the song and his continuing interest in women. The second treatment—the actual screenplay—introduces us to a key female character, Lorena, who will later become the central figure in my overall argument.

For both versions, *The Streets of Laredo* is actually a more accurate title because the narrative action in both treatments begins and ends in Laredo, Texas. Indeed, the first line in the scenario is: "The streets of Laredo, in the late spring of 1874." It is also very hot: "The high, noon sun seems to hold absolute power over the town—the streets are white with heat" (1972a, 1). If we recall the history of Laredo, the "heat" will be about the only thing that McMurtry gets right about Laredo, especially in regard to its citizenry. We are then introduced to three men in their sixties (as we will learn later), who run a livery stable, selling and outfitting horses: Augustus Evans, James Lee Driskill, and their leader, John McCray.[7] They are all former Texas Rangers—McCray was a Captain—now trying to make a go of it in post-Civil War Texas along with a group of more ordinary working cowboys including Hoot Crane, Christian Pete, and Speedy Blue.[8] We also meet the Clancy brothers (Paddy, Liam, and Tom), who recently arrived from Ireland and who also provide musical entertainment for the group. When we first meet them, they are singing a popular song called "Lorena," no doubt reflecting their recent fighting for the Confederacy in the Civil War (8).[9]

However, the name "Lorena" will soon return. They also serve to remind us of the Irish in Texas and the origins of our song, although McMurtry does not make this explicit linkage here. Amidst all these men, we also find two females. Evangeline Brown is a young, blond "whore" who provides her services to all comers in Laredo, but clearly has a first attachment to the McCray outfit, especially to Driskill. However, she longs to move to Denver. And then, there is Marcia, Evans's pet pig, who likes to eat rattlesnakes.

We need a plot line to get things going, so one Thornton Wilberforce rides into town, a middle-aged range foreman, "a person of some authority," who wants to buy some sixty ponies for an upcoming cattle drive north to Montana (1972a, 31). McCray has only six on hand, so he promises the remainder in a month. Wilberforce is decidedly unhappy. He reluctantly agrees, but not before Augustus, who does not like Wilberforce, sardonically offers sixty pigs instead as his very distinctive character begins to develop. The group decides to cross the Rio Grande into Mexico to steal the horses from a wealthy *hacienda* although Evans is also thinking sex: "Whores on this side of the river is all too tough. What I want is a *señorita*" (1972a, 27). The prospect of violence with the Mexicans also serves to remind Driskill that he once killed a dentist in Arkansas, and he is a wanted man (34). Indeed, there is some considerable shooting as "the Mexicans scream, shout and beat their dogs. From the hacienda, the women yell the names of saints" (55). Driskill surprises a Mexican man in bed with a woman and says, "I ain't going to steal a man's horse while he's fucking. Not even a Mexican's—any human's got some rights" (60). With vaqueros in hot pursuit, the group retreats to Texas with only seven horses.[10]

Still mindful of their deal with Wilberforce, Hoot Crane says that he knows there are many wild horses in the Palo Duro Canyon in the Texas Panhandle. They get ready to leave for the Palo Duro, but not before Speedy Blue makes another foray into Mexico by himself, not for horses, but for sex with a special *señorita* he spotted the last time. He soon runs into trouble, and stereotyping in the other direction, McMurtry has some "resplendent Mexican cowboys" dressed in "silver ornamented" outfits chasing Speedy. He barely makes it into the Rio Grande and emerges soaking wet and bedraggled on the Texas side of the river to be greeted by McCray (1972a, 107). And, at that moment, the song briefly appears, as McCray, in ironic humor, takes a line from it and says to Speedy: "Well, I see by your outfit that you are a cowboy" (108).

The group soon starts toward the Palo Duro, aiming first for San Antonio. Evangeline comes along with Driskill's promise that he will take her to Denver after they capture the horses. Along the way the group will identify themselves to strangers saying "we hail from Laredo. The streets of Laredo," almost as if they are facetiously demonstrating their awareness of the song (218). They will ride past the Alamo, not taking much notice because, according to the narrator, it is "not yet, for Texans, a holy place" (136).[11] Once north of San Antonio, things begin to fall apart. It is 1874 and much of northwest Texas is experiencing white settlement, much to Augustus Evans's consternation as his contrarian personality further emerges. He cannot stand the sound of church bells from nearby towns, and he also asks, "What's wrong with the Indians?" because they cannot keep white settlers out of Texas, as if he was a reporter for the *Cheyenne Transporter* newspaper noted in the previous chapters (138). From his point of view, things get better when they finally reach the Palo Duro and the fort at Adobe Walls, the scene of a recent battle between white soldiers and buffalo hunters against the remnants of the Comanche.[12] There they also find an old female friend, Kate, whose husband, named Martin Dean, is dying from a horse kick in the head.[13] They have a little girl named Cecilia, and after her husband dies, she and Cecilia will join McCray's company.

The cowboys and company finally find and capture the promised horses although not before Augustus has also managed to rope and capture both a buffalo and an antelope simply because he likes them. But belatedly, he also reveals his surprising hostility toward their entire enterprise. Like some latter-day abolitionist and animal rights activist, he angrily compares having captured horses to having slaves that you can buy, sell, and trade (1972a, 202). They begin to make their way back to Laredo, following the Pecos River to the Rio Grande, but one night while everyone is asleep, Augustus sets the horses loose into nearby Mexico. Awakened, the company thinks they are facing rustlers, and in the process, Hoot accidently shoots and kills Christian Pete (1972a, 212). They manage to recover only a few of the horses.

With his pet antelope and buffalo in tow, Augustus is pleased with the outcome, but McCray is livid:

> Don't talk to me about your wild-life! That's all I've heard out of you this trip. Some trip. Lost a man. Never even seen an Indian. Lost our horses thanks to you. Settlers everywhere. . . . All we got to show is a goddamn antelope an' a buffalo an' handful of horses. Goddamn waste of time, if you ask me! (1972a, 233)

To which the sardonic Augustus replies: "On the other hand, a journey's a journey" (233).

McMurtry offers one final episode as he comes to a full acknowledgement of the song/title for this scenario, *The Streets of Laredo*. Earlier, while still on their way back to Laredo, Marcia the pig was attacked by a wolf, and Speedy rode to defend her by attempting to lasso the wolf, as "he sees his chance for glory: to rope a lobo wolf, and at night, too[,] . . . a feat almost beyond mortal ambition." It is reckless as well, for his horse stumbles and falls on top of him causing him grave injuries (1972a, 228). The company continues back to Laredo with Speedy on a makeshift stretcher. Back in Laredo, they learn that not much has happened since they left. One old man tells them, "Oh, politics, mostly. Had a shoot-out day before yesterday. Sixty-two Mexicans killed one another off" (237).[14] The rest of the story centers on Speedy who is cared for by some of the women, although this cowboy is dying. One of them asks him, "How you feel, hon?" Speedy "scarcely focuses, rolls his head" and answers with a partial line from the song, "It was once in the saddle . . . *señorita* . . ." but cannot complete the rest of the line, "I used to go dashing" (239). He knows he will have a funeral soon, and he asks Captain McCray if he could "fancy it up a little bit, like party," perhaps getting together "some reckless cowboys an' a bunch of pretty whores an' some roses," in another allusion to the song (251). As he is finally about to die, Speedy asks for water with yet another line paraphrased from the song: "Could you bring me a cup . . . a cup of cold water? Boys, I'm kind of parched" (252). As if to underscore the death of this cowboy, lawmen from Arkansas show up to arrest Driskill for the killing of the dentist for which he will surely hang, and Augustus, ironically, is killed by one of the wild horses they are trying to tame as if in ironic retribution for his self-indulgence in freeing the group's horses earlier (280). In the words of the song, it would seem that all of these cowboys have "done wrong."

In this film scenario, McMurtry is a long way off from the novel *Lonesome Dove*, as we shall soon see, but nevertheless, it serves us well in its delineation of the key issues in this chapter. First and foremost, we have the obvious presence of the song although perhaps too obviously so. That is, its placement as Speedy's commentary on his plight and as a statement of the group's failure seems forced and too literal, undercut by his turn to the comedic and parodic such as trying to lasso a wolf. The ultimate effect of this episode will be also to diminish the full thematic and poetic weight of the song that accompanies Speedy's pointless death. It is as if, in 1972, the song is too much with this then still very young writer. He cannot fully come to terms with it in more disciplined creative fashion. Then there is the question of women who are given relatively short shrift in this masculine world, although in doing so, McMurtry perhaps does capture their exact situation in nineteenth-century Texas. Toward the end, however, he does give a more affirmative, if still tentative, voice to his two principal female characters. Evangeline says, "I got to build somethin' up high. I can't stand to live without nothing high" (201). Later, Kate avers with some irony: "Three things a woman can do in this country. Have kids, another is teach school, and the third, I'm too old for[,] . . . at least as a profession. I guess that leaves teaching school" (281).

We may also note the scenario's early development of the question of modernity and its conscripts. Clearly, the principal characters, particularly John McCray and Augustus Evans, are aware of the changes that are coming to Texas and the American West. The land is being settled by farmers; the Indians are being defeated; and the natural environment is already under stress, most evidently in the emerging disappearance of wildlife. Yet it is also clear that Evans is the more knowing and critical conscript demonstrating clear signs of rebellion at his conscription even as he also clearly recognizes the inevitability of modernity. But his impulsive rebellions—wild animals as pets and horses as slaves—are ultimately overdone and unpersuasive relative to cowboy culture.

That same year of 1972, McMurtry followed up this scenario with a formal screenplay also called *The Streets of Laredo*. The screenplay opens again with "Laredo, Texas, the late spring of 1874," a "town consisting "of a few wide-spaced, one-story adobe buildings" (1). Here and throughout, McMurtry seems determined not to grant—or he simply does not know of—Laredo, Texas, or its modernity in 1874 as I described it in chapter 1. With more clearly defined speaking roles, the cast of characters remains largely the same as does the plot line to capture wild horses for Wilberforce in the Palo Duro Canyon, although it is now the latter's idea and not Hoot's. But there are significant changes. Mexico still figures in the drama as the cowboys' first option for horses, but, as in the scenario, they fail. Oddly enough, it is now in Mexico that the group discovers the three Irishmen, formerly the Clancy brothers, now renamed the O'Donovan brothers: Frances, Aloysius, and Sean. We learn that they came from Ireland hoping to disembark in Galveston on the Texas Gulf Coast but wound up in Mexico because they landed in the wrong place on the Mexican Gulf Coast instead of Galveston, Texas. He does not say so, but I wonder if McMurtry had these Irishmen bound for the Texas Irish colony I discussed in chapter 1? Drunken and singing, they are made part of the group and brought back to Texas when all return "in a sorry state," with only three horses, a mule, and a donkey (1972b, 16–22).

McCray decides they are going to the Palo Duro after all, and Augustus agrees only because, again, he hopes to see buffalo and antelope although this time we also learn that he is concerned about the buffalo's extinction. He even hopes to get an armadillo for a pet (42). James Lee Driskill will still bring his girlfriend, but Evangeline has been replaced by a "blond and pretty" young woman named Lorena Tyler who is still the local "whore" (12). As in the scenario, the group departs for the Palo Duro; they find Kate at Adobe Walls, but in this screenplay, the two women now get an extended and much more affirmative presence. McCray's cowboys capture their horses only to have Augustus free them as before. The group finally makes its way to Laredo where Augustus still dies in the horse accident and Driskill, still a wanted criminal, is also taken away to Arkansas by the marshals.

The most significant change has to do with Speedy Blue. As in the scenario, he makes a foray into Mexico to see a *señorita*, but the episode does not end with McCray greeting him at the river's edge with the line from the song. "The Streets of Laredo" has wholly disappeared in this screenplay. The scenario's closing death scene with Speedy has been completely changed, indeed eliminated. Instead, Speedy Blue rides out of their camp one night into Comanche country and recovers all the lost horses. In the screenplay's closing scene, he rides triumphantly into Laredo with his large herd of horses, much to McCray's delight. While a decided improvement over the scenario, the screenplay, nevertheless still insists on the comedic in its overall tone, accentuated by its gratuitous, continuing engagement with what has been called "the stage Irishman" (Welch and Stewart 1996). Yet for my purposes, it is extremely interesting that McMurtry has obviously suspended the previous engagement with the song as if recognizing his failure to incorporate it in a more creatively interesting manner. That remained to be done.

LONESOME DOVE, THE NOVEL

As noted earlier, the screenplay was submitted for the approval of three potential leading men—John Wayne, James Stewart, and Henry Fonda—who turned it down according to McMurtry in a 1980 interview with Bennett. He also told Bennett "I've sometimes thought I'd might see what would happen if I did it as a novel" (34).[15] Five years after this remark, such a novel appeared. The novel, *Lonesome Dove,* and its sequel, *Streets of Laredo* are generally regarded as McMurtry's "singular achievement," in Steven Frye's words (2017, 73). But, before we even enter the work itself, there is this on the dedication page with two lines from the song in memory of his ranching family as death again is an occasion for the song.

> For Maureen Orth,
> and
> In memory of
> the nine McMurtry boys
> (1878–1983)
> "Once in the saddle they
> Used to go dashing . . ."[16]

In comparison to the 1972 film treatments, we see definite changes in the 1985 Pulitzer Prize winning novel most immediately its title. There are now two major cowboy characters. The former Texas Rangers, John McCray and Augustus Evans, are now renamed Woodrow Call and Augustus "Gus" McCrae, respectively. James Lee Driskill has been replaced by a very similar, though now secondary character, named Jake Spoon. Speedy now appears to have become "the slow but steady Pea-Eye (Parker)," particularly loyal to Woodrow, or "Captain Call" (Busby 1995, 182). These central figures are joined by a host of other secondary cowboy figures and collectively call themselves the Hat Creek Cattle Company, operating a not-too-successful livery stable near the village of Lonesome Dove in South Texas. And, again, we have a central female figure, no longer Evangeline or Lorena Tyler but Lorena Wood. She is still a "whore" and has her room above the Dry Bean saloon in Lonesome Dove, an establishment owned by a Frenchman, Xavier Wanz. Nevertheless, she is unhappy in South Texas and like her predecessors in the screen treatments, she also longs to move, not to Denver, but to San Francisco.

The plot has also been decisively changed. The Wilberforce character has been replaced by a local rancher named "Wilbarger," who, again, shows up wanting to buy horses for a cattle drive to Kansas.[17] The Hat Creek outfit will supply them, but not from the Palo Duro. This time they do manage to steal them from the Flores hacienda in nearby Mexico, but they will also steal many for themselves, because they are planning their own cattle drive to Montana, also with stolen Mexican cattle. The relatively simple screenplay horse hunt in the Palo Duro now is transformed into the far more arduous cattle drive to Montana, and it will no longer be from the streets of Laredo, but rather from Lonesome Dove. It is still close to the Mexican border but now decidedly to the east of Laredo in the Gulf Coast area where the famous Texas cattle drives actually originated as we noted in chapter 1, as if McMurtry is now taking more care with the historical facts.

The journey, of course, provides the principal plot, including fearsome river crossings, a wild bull, bears, bad white men and Indians in general, but especially two pathological, renegade half-Indian villains, named Blue Duck and Mox Mox. But in this journey, "the nearly continuous presence of Gus and Call thus establishes them as the normative characters[,] . . . that is, they work as the reader's reference point" (Reilly 2000, 100). As in the screen treatment prototypes, they have their differences although here they are far more developed. Reilly describes these as "the voluble and self-confident Gus . . . balanced by the taciturn, generous, and realistic Call, and thus, the two cowboys offer a balanced view of the history they will experience" (101). More may be said about these men and this history in terms of modernity, for there is more to their difference than personality traits.

The year is circa 1877.[18] While there is no recall whatsoever of Laredo and the horses from the screenplay, Call and McCrae have "prospered in a small way" in cattle ranching in South Texas in response to the demand for beef in a post-Civil War modernizing, industrializing United States. We learn that "there was enough money in their account in San Antonio that they could have considered themselves rich, had that notion interested them. But it didn't," as the narrator continues to signal their conscription rather than their open acceptance of modernity even as there is also a difference between these two conscripts: Augustus continues in his more aware conscription, for he "knew that nothing about the life they were living interested Call, particularly" (1985, 81).

> It was that they had roved too long, Augustus concluded when his mind turned to such matters. They were people of the horse, not of the town; in that, they were more like the Comanches than Call would ever have admitted. . . . They were not of the settled fraternity, he and Call. (81)

It is this unsettledness that will then impel the long cattle drive to Montana, to a new frontier, but it is the very cattle drive itself rather than its economic outcomes that also constitutes what Lich calls "their region beyond the Jordan, their Promised Land" (1982, 54). It is primarily Call in which the idea "to strike out for Montana . . . had taken hold of the man," but again, it is not Call alone (McMurtry 1985, 82). For McCrae it is a more conscious knowledge that also drives him toward the paradisiacal Montana and the cattle drive itself before the encroaching forces of modernity change everything. I agree with Busby that "Gus is existentially aware of the central paradox of their lives," but it is an existential awareness perhaps more Marxian than Sartean (1995, 192). Early on we learn that "Augustus had spent a year in a college back in Virginia somewhere, and claimed to have learned his Greek letters, plus a certain amount of Latin" (McMurtry 1985, 35). He simply does more reflective thinking and shows more awareness of the political economy they are living through, of their situation as "conscripts of modernity." Speaking of "women, and children and settlers" as "cannon fodder for lawyers and bankers," he says,

> They're part of the scheme. After the Indians wipe out enough of them you get your public outcry, and we go chouse the Indians out of the way. . . . Finally the Army will manage to whip 'em down to where they can be squeezed onto some reservation, so the lawyers and bankers can come in and get civilization started. Every bank in Texas ought to pay us a commission for the work we done. (83)

I agree with Busby that Call and McCrae tend toward the mythic cowboy by being "physically strong, loyal, creative, diligent, self-reliant, resourceful and courageous," but they also share a skepticism toward modernity with Call as the less critical conscript. I leave as an open question the degree to which McMurtry's representation of these two fictive cowboys correlates with the residual Romanticism and discontent I attributed to the real nineteenth-century cowboy. But earlier I also noted that such cowboys had their social blind spots, among them the role of women, and in this novel, I can also agree that McMurtry "presents them as having human weaknesses," most centrally, an "inability to achieve sustained, reciprocal heterosexual love," although again, I think this applies far more to Call (Busby 1995, 182–183).

"Texas Is Hard on Women and Horses"

This suggestion that these men cannot achieve serious heterosexual love then returns us to the question of women in these novels. In the screenplay, and in most of *Lonesome Dove*, we meet them almost exclusively as prostitutes or much older women who are not central to the story, as "appendages to the male world" (Reilly 2000, 109). But again, Gus is a bit different. At one point, he admonishes Call because he cannot seem to bring himself to use personal names for women, preferring "her" or "she." "'I don't see that it matters,' Call said" (625). As the novel comes to its climax, and as if responding to Call's oblivious sexism, McMurtry begins to develop two women, the aforementioned Lorena Wood, and Clara Forsythe Allen, both of whom had their screenplay antecedents in Evangeline, Lorena Tyler, and Kate. We begin to sense that a distinct women's story is taking shape, and we will see this intertwined narrative duality again. I agree up to a point with Reilly that in this novel, "[A]ll of the women are portrayed sympathetically and allowed complexity that assures us that they are more than just whores, but it is Clara alone who furnishes a world for herself" (2000, 109). Of course, Clara was never a "whore," but among the "whores" a special place must be made for Lorena who will figure prominently in *Lonesome Dove* and even more so in its sequel. She is *not*, what in a rare miss, the leading scholar of Texas letters, my friend, the late Don Graham, called simply the "whining prostitute" in the novel (1989, 313).

We first meet Lorena, sometimes called Lorie, as the novel begins back in South Texas, where she is a prostitute in Lonesome Dove with a room above the Dry Bean saloon. The Dry Bean takes great pride in its piano which it generously shares with the church next door for Sunday services as we get another foreshadowing angle of vision on Lorena who would come "out on the backstairs of the saloon, practically undressed, and [listen] to the hymns" (McMurtry 1985, 31). Her cowboy clients fall in love with her as does Wanz, the saloon owner and piano player, for she is a beautiful woman, a "soiled dove," to use Busby's phrase (1995, 185). Anxious to get out of South Texas and prostitution, like Evangeline in the screenplay, she takes up with one such cowboy, Jake Spoon, and joins the cattle drive to Montana, hoping somehow to make it to San Francisco, the city of her dreams. Along the way, Jake leaves her alone to go gamble in Austin, and, straying from the camp, she will be abducted by Blue Duck, a renegade Indian and gang raped by other renegades. Jake then leaves the cattle drive altogether, so it falls to Gus to rescue her. In gratefulness but also mutual attraction, she and Gus will come to love each other. Lest further harm come to her, the two agree that she should stay with Clara Allen—Gus's former girlfriend from his younger days as a Texas Ranger, who is now living in Nebraska—as the party passes through that state.

Clara will be instrumental in Lorena's development. Clara was from a good family in Austin and said to be the prettiest girl in Texas. Gus had courted her in his younger days, but she married a Kentucky horse trader, Bob Allen, and moved to start a ranch in Nebraska, although the memory of Gus never leaves her. Toward the end of the novel, we find her in trial and tribulation in the Nebraska winters, bearing five children, losing three boys to pneumonia, and then raising two girls. She will also run the ranch and conduct horse trading almost by herself, after Bob is kicked by a horse, mentally incapacitated, and bedridden as was Martin Dean before in the screenplay. She will see him through to his death, but she does tell her girls about men: "A bond has to work two ways. If a man don't hold up his end, there comes a time to quit" (McMurtry 1985, 678). As the Hat Creek Outfit makes its way through Nebraska to leave Lorena, Gus describes Clara as a "formidable woman, perhaps too formidable" (684). In an extended penultimate section of the book, McMurtry creates a powerful moment of female support and solidarity as Clara, the elder, tutors Lorie in the difficulties but also the potentialities of life. Lorena is growing into an accomplished woman helping to care for the farm and the children but also learning to read, an emergence oddly overlooked by most of the novel's critics (Busby 1995, 194; Reilly 2000, 109; Frye 2017, 76–77).

The novel reaches a climactic moment as we return to the world of men and Gus and Call in particular. The party enters Montana, and while scouting ahead in Pea Eye's company, Gus decides to go chase buffalo again, but this time he pays a heavy price. He and Pea Eye are attacked by Indians and Gus is gravely wounded and eventually succumbs to his wounds. In a marvelous but somewhat surrealistic episode (unless, of course, you are a Texan), Call takes Gus's body back to Texas as he promised him he would shortly before Gus died.[19] In his last conversations with Gus and this ritualistic funereal movement back to Texas, Call seems to echo the song and its narrator-cowboy as another cowboy has died having done wrong, this time in a modernist flight of fancy after the buffalo. Thus, to paraphrase the old proverb about two birds and one stone, McMurtry addresses two issues with the death of one key cowboy. While reminding us of the song, he also removes from the scene the only consistent "left-wing" critic of modernity; its most dissident pro-indigenous and ecologically-minded outlier; its most resistive conscript, as if to signal that modernity will prevail, for better or worse; for there is a kind of "better," namely the productive conjunction between women and modernity.

Body in tow, Call stops to see Clara and Lorena in Nebraska to bring them letters from Gus. Clara insists that Gus be buried there on her ranch, presumably close to the two women he has loved, but Call means to keep his promise to his friend by completing the ritual to Texas. With Lorena watching, Clara then chastises Call:

> I'm sorry you and Gus McCrae ever met. All you two done was ruin one
> another, not to mention those close to you. Another reason I didn't marry him

was because I didn't want to fight you for him every day of my life. You men
and your promises: they're just excuses to do what you plan to do anyway,
which is leave. You think you've always done right—that's your ugly pride,
Mr. Call. But you never did right and it would be a sad woman that needed
anything from you.[20] You're a vain coward, for all your fighting. I despised
you then, and I despise you now, for what you're doing. (831)

One is wholly persuaded that "Lorena and the Allen females testify to the endurance of women, to the McMurtry conviction that women suffer deeply but
maintain deep optimism and resilience" but also, I would add, a lot of fight (Lich
1987, 56).

   After burying Gus by what was then the beautiful Guadalupe River in
Central Texas where Gus once picnicked with Clara, Call simply does not know
where to go, including Montana which is now "settled" territory, so he simply
continues south to Lonesome Dove where he began. Arriving, he learns that the
Dry Bean saloon has burned down. A man named Dillard tells Call that the
saloon owner, Xavier Wanz, deliberately did commit suicide in the bargain. "He
sat in her room a month and then he burnt it." Call has been gone a long time
and seems to have forgotten some things, so he asks: who is "her"? Given what
we now know about Lorena and the more we are about to learn, it is a choice
piece of dramatic irony that the final line in this novel is the reply: "'The woman,'
Dillard whispered. 'The woman. They say he missed that whore'" (843). We, of
course, know she is no longer a "whore," and in this, the final line of the novel,
McMurtry seems to be inviting us to see the new Lorena as the principal outcome of the novel and not for the last time. Indeed, we shall meet this woman
again and follow her to the streets of Laredo.

3:10 to Laredo

Lonesome Dove is certainly an extended continuation of McMurtry's fundamental questioning of gender roles, but his sequel, *Streets of Laredo* (1993) and its film
version (1995), fully complete that task. This ultimate revision is a surprising and
wholly transformative outcome that brings together McMurtry's abiding interest
in our ballad and in the fortunes of women within a modernizing Texas. Beyond
its obvious title, the novel also has this epigraph taken from the song.

   We beat the drum slowly and shook the spurs slowly,
   And bitterly wept as we bore him along;

For we all loved our comrade, so brave and so handsome,
We all loved our comrade, although he'd done wrong. . . .

Again, McMurtry offers no citation although he appends this note: "'Streets of Laredo,' ca. 1860" but with no explanation for this particular date. Along with the obvious title, this epigraph again alerts us to the probable importance of our song in this novel which is composed of two distinct but interrelated stories.

They begin almost as one, gradually become distinct and are then reunified. In the seemingly more dominant narrative, we find Woodrow Call now in his later years in the 1890s, no longer a Texas Ranger nor taking cattle drives to Montana. Those storied stories are no more in Texas. As a means of subsistence that also takes advantage of his Texas Ranger past, he is now a bounty hunter. The Hat Creek Outfit has dissolved—Gus McCrae is dead—although we immediately meet up again with two other key characters from *Lonesome Dove*: Pea Eye Parker and Lorena Wood who, surprisingly, are now married with children, and farming also in the Texas Panhandle around Amarillo. Call and this family will respectively generate our two distinct clearly gendered narratives that will also take on distinct geographical pathways.

McMurtry consistently inserts real historical figures into his novels, and a fictive Charles Goodnight has a special place in this novel based on the well-known historical ranching figure with great presence and influence in the Panhandle whom we met in chapter 1 (Busby 1995, 36; Reilly 2000, 92; Frye 2017, 75–76; Hagan 2007). From the beginning, he is a kind of mediator between the two stories. He partially supports the aging Call, who, between jobs, lives in a shack on Goodnight's land "not far from the north rim of the Palo Duro Canyon" (McMurtry 1993, 16). More significantly, perhaps, Lorena has now become a schoolteacher and is also supported by Goodnight "who wrote a check . . . sufficient to allow the community to construct a one-room schoolhouse" (27). McMurtry wants these people in the Texas Panhandle which, along with much of Texas, is becoming reasonably "settled" into modernity—Pea Eye is a farmer, after all, while she is a teacher—and of course there is Charles Goodnight's corporate ranching, and the railroads will soon make their appearance. As the fictive Goodnight muses, "the Panhandle was no longer the Wild West—not by a long shot" (341). Yet they are all still in some geographical proximity to what remains of that "West," and therein lies the plot that is about to unfold: the larger story, but the other story as well, the latter principally through the figure of Lorena.[21] I shall tack back and forth between the two until they are united and resolved in the end.

In the dominant narrative, Call has been hired to capture or kill one Joey Garza, a nineteen-year-old train robber but also a cold-blooded pathological killer. Within Call's assignment, capitalist modernity is immediately evident. Specifically, Call has been hired by one Colonel Terry, a Civil War veteran and New York City railroad tycoon, who also sends an accountant named Brookshire, identified as a "salaried man," by train to Amarillo to accompany Call and keep track of expenditures. The Brooklyn accountant will be useless as a manhunter, so Call tries to hire his loyal former cowboy, Pea Eye, against fierce resistance from Lorena who undoubtedly recalls Clara's scathing assessment of Call in Nebraska in *Lonesome Dove*. The guilt-ridden Pea Eye turns him down, and Call begins his hunt for Garza with only Brookshire in tow.

Charles David Grear

Figure 7

It is not at all clear where and how Call will find Garza who had been "stopping trains in remote areas of the Southwest . . . and killed eleven men so far . . . at random" (37). Early on, we do learn they will be taking a train from the Panhandle to San Antonio through Dallas/Fort Worth and Austin.[22] Since they are going through San Antonio, Call seems to be thinking broadly of northern-western Mexico and southwestern Texas with some possible predilection for Mexico; for, notwithstanding his strange very American nickname, "Joey," Garza is a Mexican national.

Call decides for Mexico although at this moment it is not entirely clear why. Call has also decided that Laredo is a good place to cross over into northern Mexico, so from San Antonio, he and Brookshire set out for my hometown. However, as we recall from chapter 1, the railroad was available from San Antonio to Laredo as well, but instead, after getting supplies, McMurtry puts them *on horseback* from San Antonio to Laredo. They could have taken the train in greater comfort and then acquired those horses and supplies in Laredo, so we can only surmise that McMurtry wants these men on horseback, perhaps in case they run into Garza between San Antonio and Laredo, but more likely as a reminder that we are still in some semblance of the Old West.

At this point in my first reading of this novel with *this* title, it was impossible *not* to think that they will encounter Joey in Laredo. In addition to a much-foreshortened novel, such a scene would have been a disappointment to be sure, because, after all, Joey is *not* our cowboy—not a cowboy at all—and it would be the very bad 1949 film all over again. A better, but still disappointing, ending would be to have Call, now an old cowboy, die in a kind of morbid reversal of the ballad accentuating the end of the Old West. Fortunately, neither will turn out not to be the case. As it happens, Call and Brookshire arrive safely in Laredo—there is no Joey—and make only a brief stopover to pick up telegrams from Colonel Terry and get supplies, but they also meet with the Laredo sheriff Bob Jekyll and his deputy Ted Plunkert. With only the mostly hapless Brookshire to help him, Call hires Plunkert for the hunt, much to his pregnant wife's consternation as the second story picks up a second female character. McMurtry devotes several pages to Doobie's lament in losing her husband to Call and to certain danger. All she wants is to have her husband with her and smell his saddle-soaped body at night, and her long- term dream is that "someday Sheriff Jekyll would move away and Ted would be sheriff of Laredo" (127).

The first narrative then returns as the now three bounty hunters continue their mission first into northern Mexico and toward Chihuahua (fig. 7, second red arrow). They pick up telegrams in Chihuahua City and learn that Garza is still doing very bad things. Then, seemingly out of the blue, Call recalls hearing that Garza was originally from a poor village just northwest of the also poor village of Boquillas on the Rio Grande and that would be Ojinaga (162). The manhunters will then cross back into Texas at Ojinaga (fig. 7). Indeed, Garza is from Ojinaga some 500 miles west by north from Laredo and also on the Rio Grande. Presidio, its American sister town, is just across the river. Garza's single mom, María, also lives there with two other small children, Rafael and Teresa, who is blind and very attached to her chickens. We learn that Joey hates his mother, thinking she is a whore because, after the death of his father, other men come and go. Indeed, he also hates his little siblings because "they were merely the products of her whoring" (334).

Later, we will also learn that Call seemed to know all along about Garza's home territory. When the group asks Call where they are going, he replies, "Presidio. . . . I think the Garza boy comes from around there" (209). In this narratively unanticipated recollection, we sense that McMurtry is up to something else for which Laredo, at least for now, has been only a crossing point. In opting for western Texas/northeastern Mexico for his climax, we can sense McMurtry grappling with a cultural geographical conundrum for his two stories. Simply put, he has put Call on a very roundabout way to get to Presidio, which is to say, through Laredo. If indeed, Call already knew about Garza and Ojinaga/Presidio, as he seemed to, he and Brookshire had two other possible shorter routes to get there from the very beginning: (a) on horseback directly from the Panhandle to the Ojinaga/Presidio area; or (b), after taking the train from the Panhandle, on horseback from San Antonio to Presidio, perhaps stopping in Del Rio for rest, supplies, and breakfast tacos. They could have skipped Laredo altogether. Even Ted Plunkert gets into this act. As they are about to leave Laredo into Mexico, he, a Laredo native, suggests they take a shorter route from Laredo along the Rio Grande and cross at Del Rio which would also keep them in Texas longer since as a *gringo* lawman, he is not popular with border Mexicans. Call rejects this proposal, saying he wants to avoid settlements in Texas from which Garza might be forewarned, as if there were no such settlements in northern Mexico, Garza's home country (157). In fact, very early on, via word of mouth, Garza learned that Call was coming (175–176). But, in rejecting Plunkert's idea, Call/McMurtry make a kind of narrative slip of the tongue: "Avoiding the river made sense to him. *Also, he had never traveled very deeply into Mexico, and he wanted to see it* [emphasis mine]" (198). We recall *Lonesome Dove* where Call supposedly wanted to make money in Montana but really just wanted to see it before modernity had its way. Here, and not for the first or last time, Mexico, with its presumed absence from modern history, beckons the American (and British) literary intellectual ... or the cowboy whose way of life is coming to an end in Texas.[23]

We are thus being taken from an expanding Texas modernity—the Panhandle and Laredo—to one of its peripheries, adding a "heart of darkness" drama to the hunt accentuated by a truly awful place called Crow Town where Garza also spends his time. Yet, we can appreciate that McMurtry has almost no other choice as a setting for violence on horseback in the Texas of the 1890s when Garza's particular border country was still very much a part of the mythic Old West, the last of the "bad lands," if you will. Even Cormac McCarthy's much later, dark "post-western" novel, *No Country for Old Men*, was set in this part of Texas and *in the 1990s* (N. Campbell 2013, 328–350).

Contrary to our initial expectations, Laredo will not—perhaps, cannot—be the site for the expected shoot-out with Garza. Perhaps that is all to the historical good, for it would be inconsistent with Laredo's emerging identity as a site of American modernity that we noted in chapter 1—a Laredo, by the way, at this point in the novel, on the eve of having its first citywide George Washington's Birthday celebration (Peña 2020). (McMurtry was probably unaware of this Laredo identity). Nevertheless, he still has to live up to his title. McMurtry has obviously foregrounded Laredo and our ballad in his title and yet not made it the central setting for the coming, assuredly violent, encounter. McMurtry is having it both ways: he wants the principal action to happen in the only place it could happen—in the 1890's western Texas heart of darkness, adding exotic Mexico for good measure, while still bringing Laredo into the story. But is Laredo only as a crossing point enough justification for his title and the promise of the ballad?

We will soon discover that he has other, even better, plans for Laredo within the second narrative led by Lorena, one ultimately driven by his siren song and his decision to finally respond to it in an extended treatment beyond mere epigraphs. This second, female narrative picks up two hundred pages later as Laredo reappears in a still relatively brief but more compelling fashion. The forlorn Doobie Plunkert decides to go to the sheriff's office to see if there is any news about her husband whereupon, alone with the sheriff, she resists his sexual advances, and Jekyll violently rapes her in a jail cell. With an intense sense of dishonor and shame, she commits suicide by taking poison that the local Mexicans use for rats (288–293).[24] With McMurtry's womanist tendencies, we sense that surely more will follow upon this awful narrative moment, but for the moment, he will have us wait.

Deep in the Dark Heart of Texas

The action quickly shifts back to West Texas as the bounty hunters cross into Presidio where they meet up with Pea Eye just arrived from the Panhandle. Wracked with guilt about having abandoned Call, he has changed his mind and, leaving Lorena in anguish, he sets out to find his Captain Call and his men. He, however, will get to them in the sensible cowboy fashion that Call and Brookshire might have followed. Foregoing railroads, he mounted his horse, Patches; he "made sure his rifle and scabbard were tight," and from the Panhandle, "turned himself south, toward Mexico, to go to the assistance of Captain Woodrow Call" (155). (See fig. 7.) Along the way, he reconnects with a wandering old Indian friend, Famous Shoes, who walks everywhere and is a renowned tracker who will help him find Call. Once in Presidio, the local and racist sheriff arrests Famous Shoes on a past and bogus charge of horse thievery and also Pea Eye for even being in his company. Call shows up and frees them in what is surely one of the most engaging scenes in the book and the film in which, with a rifle butt, Call beats the sheriff within an inch of his life, leaving the sheriff such a broken man that he will later take that inch and commit suicide. Ted Plunkert, the deputy, is no longer with them. He has learned of Doobie's death and is returning to Laredo although he will be killed by Mexican bandits along the way.

We will meet several other new characters along the way, especially one really evil bandit named Mox Mox who likes to burn people alive after he robs them. While not an official target like Garza, Call, the former Texas Ranger, decides to hunt him down as well. We also meet real-world historical figures like Judge Roy Bean, John Wesley Hardin, and Charles Goodnight again. Indeed, back on the farm in the Panhandle, we find Lorena one day reading a letter from Clara suggesting to her that as a schoolteacher, she should now learn Latin (215). She is considering this possibility when Goodnight pays a call. He has come to warn her that Mox Mox, the man-burner, is on the loose and close by, and Lorena remembers her capture by Blue Duck and Mox Mox in *Lonesome Dove*.[25] Her first thought is that Pea Eye is in even greater danger, and she is determined to find him to warn him but also hopefully to bring him back. She decides to send her children to Clara in Nebraska. Declining Goodnight's offer of a cowboy escort— "None of your cowboys married him," she says—but with his financial help and the loan of a pistol, she sets out on her mission and our second story continues to take shape (229). From Amarillo, she comes first to Laredo by train—the one Call and Brookshire could have taken—and has a two-day stopover.

When Women Walk the Streets of Laredo

After arriving in Laredo, Lorena witnesses Doobie's funeral as our second story comes to a climax. Because it is so, I quote at greater length, for it is also McMurtry at his best. By chance, she first meets a man for whom she worked as a prostitute in her early days in South Texas who tells her the details of Doobie's death. Since he knows of her past, he makes some sexual advances. She vehemently rejects him, and she decides to walk with the funeral procession for Doobie identifying with "the young woman who must have felt hopeless." She "began to walk along with the funeral" for "it seemed as if everyone in town was following the wagon that had the coffin in it," led by a "few churchwomen" and "six whores" all who are singing various hymns as they walk along and later at the gravesite. There, "one of the whores, the smallest, a slip of a girl with curly brown hair," who sang in "in a beautiful soprano voice," led the singing and "when she sang 'Amazing Grace,' her voice rose over all the other singers, the other five whores and the few churchwomen." After "Rock of Ages" and "Will the Circle Be Unbroken," "the women . . . looked around, wondering if they should sing more." Lorena thinks "three hymns at a funeral" already "unusual," and therefore found it "odd . . . that no one was hurrying away," and then "the young whore with the beautiful voice finally spoke to one of the churchwomen, and the women begin to sing "There's a Home Beyond the River'" (304). Until,

> one by one, the other whores and the churchwomen fell silent, and the beautiful voice of the whore with the curly hair soared on, in lonely lament for the lost life of a woman the young whore had not known, and perhaps had not even met. (304)

That night, in her hotel room, "Lorena's thoughts returned to the dead woman and the funeral" and the "young whore who could sing soprano, and a deep sadness came with memory." Lorena knew that this girl "with the beautiful voice was back being a whore. The churchwomen who had spoken to her at the funeral wouldn't allow themselves to speak to her in their day-to-day lives." She would be just a whore "as Lorena herself had been once" (305).

In his predominant representation of a world of male violence in the American West for which he is justly famous, why does McMurtry offer us this extended female and funereal ritual scene at this moment in this particular narrative? Why does he site Doobie's life and death and Lorena's timely arrival in Laredo when most of the novel's action is elsewhere? Clearly, he is indebted to the song that gives him his title which he must then justify in some manner, and I believe that is exactly what he is doing here. I propose that it is here—in an action literally occurring through the streets of Laredo—where he creatively transforms the song within a narrative rather than just as an epigraph, or the obvious and somewhat mechanical use of the song in the film scenario we saw earlier where he did not quite know how to manage it. In this novel and this scene, McMurtry has made great progress. We can chart the song's influence in this scene through its three creative major revisionary tropes: its principal actors, the funerary ritual, and the singing itself.

Like the dying cowboy in the song, Doobie Plunkert is one of only two major characters whom we can imagine walking the streets of this Laredo—to the sheriff's office, back to her home and then to the Rio Grande to die.[26] Let us recall that the song has a second cowboy who witnesses the events. He is identified by the dying cowboy: "I see by your outfit that you are a cowboy," for whom we find a parallel in Lorena herself who also walks the street of Laredo as witness to and narrator of the scene. In chapter 1, I argued that the conversation between the two cowboys has to be imaginary. In similar fashion we have a kind of imagined conversation between Lorena and Doobie, as Lorena recognizes a kindred woman, likely "wrapped in white linen," a woman who suffered like Lorena herself. Then, as in the song, we have a funerary ritual to bury the young protagonist, one in which we have a "few churchwomen," but also an explicitly numbered "six whores," and we are reminded of the "six jolly cowboys" and "six pretty maidens" of the song. Why does McMurtry turn to this particular number? Surely it cannot be random, and it is the key indicator of the ballad's presence in this scene.

The second trope is the funeral itself. As I suggested in chapter 1, the presence of cowboys as pall bearers who in their very presence offer a compensatory cowboy culture that affords us some large measure of redemption for the young cowboy's death within modernity after having "done wrong." Here, however, Doobie has certainly done no wrong; indeed, for these gathered women, no one has done wrong except Sheriff Bob Jekyll and the malevolent patriarchy he represents. In utopian fashion, we are offered a striking representation of female solidarity in a moment of what anthropologist Victor Turner called *communitas* "liberation of human capacities of cognition, affect, volition, creativity, etc., from the normative constraints incumbent upon occupying a sequence of social statuses," in this case against divisive male-sanctioned identities (1982, 44). While temporary—the prostitutes and the churchwomen will return to their respective

social roles—it nevertheless allows us to glimpse a moment of female emancipation from their assigned and segregated roles in the American West.

Then finally there is the singing itself. These women offer famous traditional
hymns in consolation, but in doing so, they effectively substitute themselves in
place of the singing cowboys who traditionally rendered "The Streets of Laredo,"
especially the curly-haired soprano, the lead cowboy, if you will. We are especially
made aware of this singing and its meaning through Lorena's sensibilities. Wife,
mother, teacher, reader of English literature, student of Latin, and full woman—she
now also becomes profound music critic. That night in her hotel room, she "remembered the young whore who could sing soprano, and a deep sadness came with
the memory." Lorena knew that "in a building not far away, the young whore with
the beautiful voice was back being a whore . . . as Lorena herself had been, once"
and . . .

> The only thing that was true in the four hymns the girl had sung was the
> music itself, Lorena thought. Neither the whore nor the dead woman over
> whose grave she'd sung had received any grace at all, to draw upon; nor did
> they have any rock to stand on; nor any circle to shelter or protect them.
> (305–306)

In noting "the music itself," Lorena seems to believe that the plight of women
in the American West at that moment is such that the religious images in these
songs can do little for them. Here, for Lorena, there is nothing equivalent to the
compensation of imagining themselves as gay and dashing in the saddle, only a
traditional Christianity. One suspects that neither the churchwomen, nor even the
"whores," would agree and perhaps not even Doobie, but it serves to mark yet
another aspect of Lorena's entrance into a secular modernity, namely that women
must also rely on themselves to address their condition as she has done. Yet, like the
ballad's lento tempo and cadences, the music was beautiful. We must then wonder,
however, what would she might have thought—what would the other women
think—of that other song of the American West that helped give rise to "The
Streets of Laredo," namely "The Bad Girl's Lament" about a dying prostitute that
according to Goldstein "was crowded out of the picture," by "The Streets of Laredo"
(1960, 1). It is not at all unreasonable that the six "whores" in this episode (although
perhaps not the church ladies) might well have known this song that offers a more
realistic appraisal of their own condition.

Gunfight at the Not-So-OK Corral

The hunt out west continues, but the effect of Lorena's convergence with our song in the streets of Laredo is such that there is almost an anticlimactic feeling to the end of the first story about the manhunt; as if the second one has taken over the novel's moral center of gravity. Garza has attacked a train near San Angelo, and Call takes after him by himself, leaving the rest of the group near Ojinaga in case Joey slips back into town. In his now solo search for Garza, Captain Call encounters Mox Mox and kills him, rescuing two kidnapped children that Mox Mox planned to burn. Back in Laredo, and after Doobie's funeral, Lorena learns of Woodrow Call's likely location from two Texas Rangers. Thinking her husband is with him, she takes yet another train to Fort Stockton not far from San Angelo and Presidio/Ojinaga (366).[27] (See fig. 7.) By chance, Call also shows up in Fort Stockton to leave the rescued children, and he and Lorena meet. She insists on leaving with him on his continuing hunt and hers for her husband. Because it involves her husband, and she is likely to go it alone, Call reluctantly agrees to take her along, especially since Joey Garza is still out there. Our two narratives finally intersect although Lorena takes center stage as if she has been empowered by the streets of Laredo.

She and Call finally encounter Garza, but rather than an Old West conclusion where the good guy finishes off the bad guy, we get a New West ending. Catching the aging Call uncharacteristically off guard, Joey badly wounds him in the leg with his German-made scope rifle as modernity makes yet another appearance. Lorena saves Call's life by cutting off his gangrenous leg with Call's Bowie knife whose edge she chips on a rock, making it into an improvised saw. In addition to her surgical skills, we also learn more about Lorena's intellect. Exhausted from this ordeal in this violent West, one evening she dreamily recalls how "she and Clara sometimes daydreamed of making a trip to England together to see civilization. They meant to visit Shakespeare's birthplace and to see a play. They had amused themselves . . . by imagining what they would say if they happened to meet Mr. Browning on the street, or Mr. Carlyle" (410–411).

While Messrs. Browning and Carlyle walked the streets of London, in the not-so-civilized western Texas, the violence continues and comes to an end when the other hunters that Call left behind encounter Joey Garza in Ojinaga. By this time, the pathological Joey has killed his own mother, María, leaving her other children, Teresa and Rafael, as orphans.[28] Garza is finally killed—not by the wounded Old West hero, Captain Woodrow Call, now minus one leg—but by an ignoble combination of Pea Eye, who is wounded in the encounter, and Gordo, an ordinary butcher for the community. Brookshire also dies in this encounter, but not before he has taken his own symbolic leave of modernity by also helping to kill Joey. With Call in her care, Lorena makes her way to Ojinaga to be reunited with her wounded husband.

The first story and the Old West thus come to an end. Our major critics have lent their principal attention to Call's narrative. For Steven Frye, the novel offers fundamental and final revisionism of the Old West, "a stark and unforgiving picture of life on a fading frontier" as "Call's decline mirrors the transformation of the western region and the lifestyle he has spent his life defending." Even as Call retains something of the Western hero in his mission and demeanor, he "finds himself weakened by time and by the brutal land he has always loved" (2017, 83). Reilly reads the novel as "a process of normalization" to capitalist modernity as "Call's pursuit of the bandit Garza is meant to protect the railroads that have become crucial to the workings of a national economy, which among other things, requires dependable transportation of beef from the West to the East" (2000, 98–99). As with much of McMurtry's previous work, Busby also sees this novel as "marked by a fundamental ambivalence about the legacies of the old world" (1995, 275–276). These critics are surely correct, but they say very little specifically about Lorena's narrative, our second story, which continues.

Lorena has also decided to adopt the late María's children, and everyone is more than ready to go home to the Panhandle as the second narrative has effectively taken over. In his revisionary transformation of Lorena, McMurtry puts her and her newly reconstituted family in Laredo one final time to take the train back to the Panhandle. As it happens, they meet up with Colonel Terry, the capitalist railroad tycoon who initiated this whole story when he hired Woodrow Call to hunt for Joey Garza. He has now come to Laredo, Texas, to complete the contract. He offers them all free transportation back to the Texas Panhandle, including Teresa's chickens, but he has also noted the very attractive Lorena. On the way back, Lorena is walking past his sleeping compartment on her way from the dining car carrying a plate of bread for Teresa's chickens. Colonel Terry emerged and

> grabbed Lorena's arm and tried to pull her into the compartment. Lorena dropped the plate, and it broke. . . . The Colonel was strong . . . but the next moment his hand was pouring blood. Lorena had picked up a piece of the broken plate and had slashed him with it across the top of his hand. . . . The

Colonel looked scared. Men usually did, if you hurt them a little. . . . "You're lucky it wasn't your throat," Lorena said. "One of these days, if I'm not left alone, I'm going to cut a man's throat, I expect." (520–521)

Lorena, and by metaphorical implication, all Texas women, then leave the streets of Laredo and ride the train of modernity to a new destination but now also understanding that modernity does not eliminate sexism and the abuse of women.

They finally all return to the Texas Panhandle now as one narrative. Call, minus his leg and his left arm, will live with Pea Eye and Lorena, their own children now joined by María's orphaned children, along with Teresa's chickens. Call will learn to sharpen tools to make ends meet in a final scene of everyday domesticity but one clearly now in the firm hands of a matriarch. With great theoretical acumen, Cordelia Barrera elaborates on this familial ending, seeing it as a "third space," beyond Old and New West, and articulated through Call's diminished body, resulting in a "more inclusive, bordered consciousness . . . that accommodates an often neglected Other voice." For Barrera, that other voice is principally that of women as she notes the woman-centered revisionism that we first saw clearly in *Lonesome Dove* but whose appearance in McMurtry's work goes even further back. She offers this assessment of Lorena but also the other Mexican females.

Lorena, whom we first met as a young prostitute in *Lonesome Dove* is now a schoolteacher, a mother of five, and Pea Eye's wife. In *Streets of Laredo*, she saves Call from death when she saws off his leg with a nicked knife blade in the wild, a symbolic act rife with "Freudian implications of castrating the man and the myth" (Nickell, 68). McMurtry in effect foregrounds the feminine in *Streets of Laredo*: Lorena, María, and Teresa (María's young daughter) all act as saviors, pushing the limits of inherited patriarchal codes. (2013, 238)

I mostly agree with this assessment although, "as saviors," I would give primacy to Lorena. In addition to her care of Captain Call, not to mention her own wounded husband, it is she who also willingly takes in Teresa and Rafael at the request of their dying mother. This reconstituted familial world of children, her husband, Pea Eye, and Call is effectively authored by this strong woman now a long way from the prostitute in *Lonesome Dove*.[29] Barrera's assessment also does not take any account of Lorena's time in the streets of Laredo, a vital phase in her progression as a woman in partnership with another white woman, Doobie Plunkert.[30]

In my concern for "The Streets of Laredo," I can be only very grateful to Larry McMurtry for finally taking up in an extended narrative what had obviously been his lifelong concern with it as well. In this fiction by that title, this leading figure of western American creative writing has also served me well in my overall thesis, namely in narrating in an engaging fictional form the life of the cowboy and his residual Romanticism against the pressures of modernity, principally through the character of Gus McCrae but shared by his other cowboys in varying degrees. It is Woodrow Call, however, who offers a greater sangfroid recognition of modernity's inevitability and therefore the more radical transformation of our ballad to women like Lorena in a greater amplification of their social status. If the cowboy must pass away so must his ballad in its original form. Modernity takes, but it can also give. We can now only recall our song in various forms, but Larry McMurtry has offered us its most engaging, historically instructive, and therefore efficacious recollection.

Women and Modernity in Texas

Whatever his other few historical lapses, McMurtry understood what Lorena might also symbolize for real women in Texas within the contradictions of modernity. Although a fictional creation, Lorena exemplifies historian Elizabeth Jameson's summation of women in the American West who,

> expected and found lives largely shaped by family responsibilities and hard work. If they understood their lives as parts of family endeavors[,] . . . they did not see themselves as passive civilizers or as uniquely oppressed, as wholly private or public. They understood that they performed valuable work for their families and their communities whose interests were intertwined. (1984, 7)

Within the constraints of a short introduction to a special issue of *Frontiers* on women in the American West, we do not expect Jameson to demonstrate the linkage between women's progress and capitalist modernity. Whatever its other consequences, late-nineteenth and early-twentieth centuries, modernity produced beneficial changes for women in Texas in a variety of spheres such as education, business, and the medical profession but also domestically, if only by way of modern appliances. As a recent volume on such changes demonstrates, they were, not surprisingly, tied to that most salient sign of capitalist modernity—urbanization (Turner, Cole, and Sharpless 2015). The town of Waco, Texas, located between Austin and Dallas, provides a very illustrative instance of such change. The male citizens of Waco wanted the town largely to "remain an important cattle stop on the way to the more metropolitan locales of Dallas, Fort Worth, Austin, and San Antonio," but "women entrepreneurs maintained a public economic presence in the city throughout the Reconstruction period, performing vital functions in the growing town of Waco: they provided capital, fostered competition, employed citizens, and created businesses." Such women "not only witnessed but also facilitated and aided the growth of cities through their own labor and capitalistic endeavors" (Sager 2015, 129).

In later-nineteenth-century Texas, such female-assisted urban activity was largely restricted to the Dallas–Austin–San Antonio—and Laredo—corridor, an urbanization also codependent with farming. While obviously fictional, Gus McCrae's earlier critical observations correlate with this urbanizing area as it started to infringe on the Chisholm Trail that the Hat Creek outfit probably used on their cattle drive through Texas and on to Montana. Historian Randolph Campbell confirms Gus's observation when he says, "During the 1870s Texas drovers begin to find farms in the way of the Chisholm trial" (2003, 298).

As we have seen in *Streets of Laredo*, by the 1890s, the railroad connecting this corridor brought Lorena and the others from the Panhandle to Laredo. But in the Panhandle itself, where this tale begins and ends, Lorena experienced modernity in a different way; not as a woman involved in "capitalistic endeavors," such as those women in Waco, but rather in her transition from prostitute to her modern professionalization as a teacher even while taking great responsibility for their farm and family. However, we do sense something else in McMurtry's crafting. She is also an emerging intellectual—recall Carlyle, Browning, and Latin—perhaps of the kind that McMurtry admired such as his good friend Susan Sontag (1999, 124–125). In the 1890s, Lorena would have been in her forties. McMurtry does not say exactly how she got to be a teacher, but had he taken his narrative into the twentieth century, I would like to imagine her getting fully credentialed in her late fifties by taking classes at the new West Texas State Normal College founded in 1910 in nearby Canyon, Texas, an institution that would later flourish into the present day as West Texas A&M University. Indeed, had she still attended in 1916, she might have met another formidable woman on campus, the newly hired head of their art department, Georgia O'Keeffe (Von Lintel 2020).

Yet, like other modernizing Texas citizens and institutions, including the University of Texas at Austin established in 1883, Lorena was also the consequence of a different kind of capitalism—corporate ranching, and later, oil—a capitalism in which Charles Goodnight had an important role as we noted toward the end of chapter 1. In *Streets of Laredo*, McMurtry amplified this distinctive male role. McMurtry's fictional Goodnight is "an evident representative of a cowboy ethic," but Goodnight was also clearly a figure of some economic substance not at all far from the historical reality in either capacity, a successful and good man, the gentleman cattle baron noted in chapter 1 (Reilly 2000, 92). Both attributes led him to support Woodrow Call in *Streets of Laredo*, but perhaps Lorena even more substantially in her role as a teacher and for her trip to Laredo to rescue her men. Lorena puts the matter well. When the now-older Goodnight thinks about going after Mox Mox himself, Lorena talks him out of it saying, "people here need you.... This whole part of the country needs you. You're the man who built the school, and I know you built others, too. You brought the doctor here. You paid for the courthouse. You're needed" (McMurtry 1993, 228). What Lorena probably does not know, which is also to say, what McMurtry does not make evident in this novel, is that this corporate development of ranching including Goodnight's, was also underwritten by British capital (R. Campbell 2003, 300–301).

This influence of British capital is perhaps an example of what Krista Comer has called "Global Wests" (2016). Such global influences do play out in "strategic locales" with differential permutations and longevities, or what earlier I referred to as "sites," in some instances geographical, in others, phenomenal such as agricultural modernity, more often, a melding of the two. In the story we have tried to tell in these pages, these obviously also include the demise of the cowboy and the cattle drive together with the emergence of the gentleman cattle baron such as Goodnight. Comer also marshals the idea of critical regionalism to foreground localized critical progressive responses to such a globalized modernity; for her, principally an overlooked archive of "women writers" and "women protagonists" in an otherwise male-gendered scholarship of the American West (2016, 3). In the present work, however, we find a male Larry McMurtry identifying an active Lorena as representative of a generation of women but also of an initiation of a long century of women's struggles within modernity in Texas that he also fictionally charted. This long century now also includes a very present moment centered around reproductive rights. Yet, I have also argued that the cowboy and his balladry, principally "The Streets of Laredo" were also such sites of a critical and creative regionalism, but that in McMurtry's hands, nevertheless and paradoxically, acknowledged its male-centered bias by transforming it into a women's sphere of musical presence.

Such a reversal should not come as a complete surprise. As McMurtry himself has said, "My interest in women characters has always been strong. One of my problems is finding men worth having in the same book with women. Women are always the most admirable characters in my novels" (Bennett 1980, 28). We must also note his sustained commentary on women in the history of the American West (1990, 35). McMurtry's affirmative relationship to women is a recurrent theme in the collection of literary eulogies that recently appeared after his passing, especially and not surprisingly from women authors who knew him (Getschow 2023). That he has joined this feminist perspective to his lifelong fascination with "The Streets of Laredo" in *Streets of Laredo* is, for me, the most revisionary and creative acknowledgement and response to the "most famous cowboy ballad" of the American West. His is a sanguine recognition of modernity in Texas, its discontents and its gains, most centrally the growing emancipation of women in Texas. And yet, for McMurtry, but also for John Lomax, and, one suspects, for many Texans, even in 2024, the cowboy maintains a certain pride of place in our psyche, which is also to say in our society and culture, one underscored by our ballad.

EPILOGUE: SE LE ACABÓ LA CANCÍON

The song and its cowboys seemed to fascinate and even haunt McMurtry with the specter of death—the sociocultural death of the cowboys, as we have seen, but also intertwined with his own cowboy father's death, literal and otherwise. As I am finishing this book, word arrives of McMurtry's own death from cardiac arrest on March 25, 2021, so perhaps we should even figure in his own extended account of his long and severe depression after quadruple-bypass heart surgery (1999, 140–151). I think he would not object. When it comes to this ballad and its creative uses, he will always have pride of place. Death generates its own folklore of which funeral rites are the most evident example, as we have seen in "The Streets of Laredo"—ballad and novel. As this study comes to an end, let us recall that, with their cattle and vaqueros, the Tejanos of South Texas first helped launch this entire story with a wee bit of help from the Texas Irish. "Among my people" in South Texas, when a person of merit died, especially someone of some estimable presence in the community, we used to say, "*se le acabó la canción*" (his or her song is over), a phrase certainly more elegant than "he kicked the can" and clearly suggesting the deceased's creative, productive life was now over, that indeed his or her life had been like a song.[31] In this study of why the song, "The Streets of Laredo," mattered in Anglo-American culture, McMurtry gets the last word, because it mattered most to him.

After the *Lonesome Dove* tetralogy, and in the final phase of his long and productive life, McMurtry turned more to the essay, principally his collections *Walter*

Benjamin at the Dairy Queen (1999) and *Paradise* (2011). Both provide the basis for some final words on our song's journey. In the first, McMurtry models himself on Walter Benjamin and his famous essay, "The Storyteller," about the Russian writer, Nikolay Leskov. At first, one thinks that he will be discussing the storytelling among the locals who gather at the Dairy Queen, one of the ubiquitous American fast-food places with indoor dining, this one in his hometown of Archer City, Texas (1999, 13). This will turn out not to be the case. As literary setting, the DQ quickly recedes, useful as it was for telling us that our well-traveled, erudite, cosmopolitan writer is after all "back home," from Washington, DC, if not Dodge City like his beloved cowboys. Rather, it is much less the DQ, and far more the high cultural Europeanist, Walter Benjamin, who serves as inspiration for what will turn out to be McMurtry's own nonfictional storytelling about his life growing up in Archer City; his time as a college student at Rice University; his avid reading of good books; and his life as a book scout/seller in Washington, DC, and later back in Archer City. He offers witty but smart commentary on great writers and filmmakers he has known; on heartache, figurative and literal; but also and more fundamentally, on his parents and the life of cowboys, both in these pages and later in those of *Paradise,* leading to a crisis that calls forth our song for one last performance.

As we have already seen, the life of the open range cowboy started coming to an end by the late 1880s, but for McMurtry personally, it extended at least in some quite limited but still affective measure until almost mid-twentieth century. McMurtry reports that as a youngster, he was "constantly and always frequently on horseback on the land" helping his father, Jeff McMurtry (1999: 195). While the critical romance of the open range was over, "its legacy of habit, costume, assumption, and to a reduced extent, practice formed the whole of the world I was born into in 1936," which is to say into his father's world, although his dad knew that the ranching tradition that he had inhabited from a very young age "was doomed" (50–51). Nevertheless, it was all his dad knew, "his devotion to it was deep," and "it was, for him, tragic that the work he loved most—the outdoor work with men and horses—was not going to last beyond his time" (51–52).

As young McMurty came of age, what most impressed him in "the cattlemen, my father most particularly, was the intensity of their desire to make it last. No Indian ever wanted to call back the buffalo more intensely than the cattle men wanted to call back the open range" (196). It is clear that what his father, Jeff, and other cattlemen wanted to last—the "it"—was not really the everyday business of ranching which, of course, they did want. The real "it" was the romantic desire that "the open range survives still, as Edenic fantasy of carefree nomadism in which cattle are allowed to follow grass wherever grass grows" because "such men, pantheistic by nature, resolutely reject anything that smacks of the modern world" (197). For McMurtry, even today, "cowboys, when questioned, will claim to envy no one—they don't believe that there is a more fulfilling life than the life of the range, a life that takes them outside every day to study the land, to work with horses" (198).

The open range and the cattle drive were long gone, replaced by a modern corporate ranching much better able to deal with drought, ice storms, falling cattle prices, available credit, sick cows, and other adversities. As we saw earlier, corporate ranching not only made its peace with the railroad, it took full advantage of it to get its cattle to market. A parallel devil's bargain was also struck with the competing economy of oil that McMurtry so vividly describes in *Horseman, Pass By* (1961). Yet, these economic pressures of modernity that brought his father's worldview to an end were an externalized centrifugal force. There was also a centripetal internalized pressure that was also part of the cowboy's identity and these two forces, of course, fed into each other. The nineteenth century "legacy of habit, costume, assumption, and to a reduced extent, practice" of the cowboy also included their relationship to women which even in 1930s Texas still reflected "prevailing Victorian attitudes about respectable women as innocent and in need of protection. The degree to which men could protect women, moreover, was a traditional marker of manhood" (Moore 2010, 141). We have also seen McMurtry's resolution of this contradiction.

Sadly, McMurtry's father was thwarted in such a patriarchally gendered claim as modernity also made its presence felt in this domestic, intrapsychic realm as well. His father, "was haunted all his life by the privations his mother endured as a frontier woman[;] . . . to the end of his days my father found it difficult to forgive women the ease of modern arrangements" (47). From here, McMurtry begins a narrative of what he calls the "mother dominance" of his widowed grandmother, Louisa Francis. In 1934, Jeff married Larry's mother, Hazel, and having no money in the midst of the Depression, they moved in with Louisa Francis, "who was not pleased to have a pretty young woman, my mother, under her roof." Louisa Francis had raised twelve children "on a naked frontier with a not always sober husband" and thus, Hazel, who only "wanted to make herself useful . . . had no chance" against this hardened mother-in-law. "One morning, annoyed by some domestic trifle," Louisa Francis slapped Hazel, and his parents "were, thus, sadly undone at the very outset of a long marriage." Even though Jeff moved them out into a small house on the mother's property that he built himself, "the damage was done." That slap "echoed through my parent's marriage until the marriage collapsed forty-four years later." As a grown man, when Larry would make attempts to stop his parent's continuous fighting, their arguing "would slide, within minutes, back through forty years of ragged incompatibility to the slap in the kitchen in 1935" (48). Yet, in this writing, McMurtry leaves unsaid intervening factors that likely also motivated that slap—no mere "domestic trifle"—which had great consequences, centrally the full undoing of Jeff's cowboy identity in regard to women and to which he returns in the second book, *Paradise*.

In addition to an account of his own great career, the *Benjamin* book was also a hymn to his father and the cowboy's way of life. *Paradise* is a sad, muted, and more introspective rumination in which almost all semblance of an Edenic cowboy paradise in Texas is now replaced by a more classical Eden *contra* modernity. In this travelogue, McMurtry takes us to Polynesia; to be perfectly historically legally correct, we should say *French* Polynesia. McMurtry is only too conscious that he is visiting one of modernity's colonial possessions, this one French, although not dedicated to slavery like Toussaint Louverture's Haiti. Whatever postcolonial merit his book may have, we shall discover that this place is really a setting for his ruminations on that other and failed paradise—Texas—and the continuing life of his parents.

To be sure, on the Polynesian side of things, we do get much about the multiple islands—flora and fauna in more or less equal measure—including the European touristic fauna for which he evinces disdain, despair, and only occasional delight. He disappoints us only by taking the predictable pose of so many artistic intellectuals, or what Renato Rosaldo called "imperialist nostalgia" (1989, 68–87). He chose to come to this place, he says, "because I wanted to spend a little time in a culture neither American, European, nor Asian" as he hoped "to escape for a bit from the culture of over achievers, and the Tahitians I am first among do not disappoint" for they "seem happy, competent, friendly, talkative." For this reason, he feels "indignant, on their behalf, that their beautiful sea-circled world is known to the rest of the planet because of the European overachievers who happened to stop off here: Captain Cook, Melville, Maugham, Michener, Gauguin" (2001, 19–20). In an odd lapse for this ardent bibliophile, Melville and Michener were, of course, not European, but following them, McMurtry, himself one of the most overachieving writers in American culture, now also shows up, and he adds well to the genre.

Almost necessarily, he must include French colonial modernity's most famous fugitive from itself, the painter, Paul Gauguin. Indeed, in a telling placement, Gauguin's famous painting, *Words of the Devil*, that seems to evoke his Polynesian mistress, Teha'amana, is on the front cover of *Paradise*. Thus, we are surprised, if not startled, when two pages into the book, we see an old photograph of McMurtry's parents, Jeff and Hazel, their visages, dress, and poses on their front porch, as American-Texan as it gets for that period of time circa the 1930s or '40s, or about the time of the infamous "slap" and its aftermath. For the purposes of the photo, they look happy enough.

This is the span of time and culture that McMurty proposes to cross in this extended essay which, a few pages later, is indeed given the subtitle: "My Parents and Polynesia." He sees a commonality between the two, more specifically between Teha'amana and his parents, an innocence of history for she "knew only her island; my parents, only their ranch and one small town" (19). The comparison is not—cannot be—sustained, if only because his parents were not innocent of history for even on the ranch or small town in Texas, they were deep within modernity and its pressures as we already saw in the Dairy Queen account and much more here, as we shall see. Teha'amana also experiences imperialist modernity's effects literally upon her body as its famous fugitive, Gauguin, "who, besides deserting his European family, coolly abandoned at least three mistresses while they were pregnant by him—including Teha'amana" (36). Yet, McMurtry insists that "my parents would have been scornful of Paul Gauguin," although, in even making this linkage, he seems to be suggesting a difference of degree but not of kind. When he is not exploring this paradise and its fascinating contradictions, McMurtry spends the rest of his time reflecting again on his parent's life. Whatever he might wish to say about Polynesia, it is really this hidden familial story that he wishes to tell, hidden from him until his later years, *and it ain't pretty*. We have already seen it at one level in the *Benjamin* book, but here we learn more in an extended narrative of some thirty pages.

At its beginning, he is going off to college, and he now recalls his mother telling him, for the first time, of her earlier marriage and a divorce not "respectable" in the Texas society of that time. His father is aware of this previous relationship, but yet he accepts her, like Lorena, as a "soiled dove," and since his grandmother also surely *knew*, we also begin to wonder if this is the barely subconscious motivation for the infamous "slap" (36). Midway into this story, we learn again that the couple had a difficult marriage, but now, we find out that, to quote Big Mama in William's

Cat on a Hot Tin Roof, "when a marriage goes on the rocks, the rocks are there, right there" as she gestures toward the bed. In another frank recitation to her now older son, after his father has passed, McMurtry learns of their sexually dysfunctional marriage where she did not know that she was supposed to have and enjoy orgasms. He also learns that his dad was anxious about being ten years older than she, but perhaps he was also anxious about the previous soiling of his dove. The final part of his mother's story speaks mostly of his mother's acute anxiety and restricted lifestyle, which, to this professionally untutored ear, sounds like classical clinical depression brought on by her upbringing, her marriage, and, of course, that unforgettable slap in the kitchen. The slap is recounted from the *Walter Benjamin at the Dairy Queen* book with a proper footnote, but *Paradise* adds this: "I can remember my parents screaming at one another[;] . . . most of the screaming was about something my grandmother had done," but more fundamentally, it had more to do with "my father's failure to adequately defend his wife against his mother's malice, or worst yet, his reluctance to attack his mother on behalf of his wife" (48–49). And in this centripetally centered failure, Jeff McMurtry yielded what remained of his cowboy identity after the centrifugal pressures; in both cases, modernity wreaking its havoc.

This narrative of domestic difficulty was occasioned by the slap, of course, but more fundamentally by his father's inaction as does not befit a real cowboy. As he is narrating it, McMurtry also fashions a distinctive and telling intra-narrative literally imbedded in the overall domestic tale and does so in two instances. In the first, he abruptly shifts back to Polynesia, if only for two short paragraphs, worth quoting in full:

> Today at lunch, in the pleasant open-air restaurant on the beach, while I ate my filet of shark, a petite gray Tahitian dove wandered around beneath the tables, pecking at crumbs of good French bread: the lonesome dove following me even to the South Seas.
>
> Were that not enough, the Muzak suddenly blared forth with a medley of country-western songs, in French, the first of which was "Streets of Laredo." Again and again, that young cowboy died. (38–39)

After this, the next sentence takes us back to his parents with this: "It is only after a parent is dead, or past recollection, that a child realizes how sketchy is his or her knowledge of the parent's emotional history" (39).

Then, later, we have another abrupt return to Polynesia with this:

"Streets of Laredo" was on the Muzak at the restaurant again this morning. As I was sitting on my porch watching fish, two small reef sharks came idling along, startling an old French couple who had been snorkeling nearby. The southern waters are said to be unusually warm this year, tempting sharks inside the reef. These two are about the size of gars. They make no attempt on the old French couple, who soon go back to their snorkeling. A long, skinny, almost transparent needle-nosed fish shows up, sporting a bright blue tail. (44)

From here, we just as abruptly return to the larger narrative about his parents.

While McMurtry did suggest a comparability between Gauguin/Teha'amana and his parents, here Polynesia has a different role. It is as if these two recollections of "The Streets of Laredo" are intended as a closing commentary on his parent's life. In the first instance of our song's reappearance, the memory of the cowboy life returns both by way of the lonesome dove but also, of course, in the very evocation of the ballad. Both remind us of his father's double-passing, "again and again"; his literal death picked up in the sentence that follows this seeming digression, but the other more important and first "again" is the complete death of the cowboy's way of life represented by his father's dwindling prospects as a rancher but also his failure to "act like a man" in his domestic affairs, the less-than-complete cowboy. There in paradise, eating his filet of shark in the pleasant restaurant and watching the dove, our very modern cosmopolitan author seems to have made his peace with this double-passing, but that is not entirely the case in the second instance. This second return of the song still reminds us of the cowboy, of course, but this time it seems secondary to our author's acute awareness of the old French couple and the threat of the live reef sharks, not yet filets. The threat passes, and this older couple returns to their shared vacationing pleasure, with the added visual gratification of the newly arrived bright blue-tailed fish, and what I am sure our author and we can only envision as a fruitful old age with lives well lived and their happiness deserved, one that Jeff and Hazel never really had. That cowboy just died.

In both cases, however, we cannot help but notice the status of the song itself which now may have gone beyond what Neil Campbell has called the "post-western" (2013). Our song may have had its critical moments in the creative and well-regarded forums that I have tried to address in this study. But what can we possibly continue to say about a song that the venerable Larry McMurtry now offers in Muzak, in French, and in a touristic colonial Polynesia; a song now fully comfortable among postmodernity's expressive furniture and probably exhausted as a critical resource for the twenty-first century? Again, and again—and now, yet again—the cowboy has died, but in all probability so has our song and any remaining legacy. In the coming twenty-first century, in culture and perhaps too literally, we are becoming "degraded prisoners / destined / to hunger until we eat filth," as William Carlos Williams put it, and, it is "only in isolate flecks that something is given off," such as our song, but, continues Williams, there may be "no one to witness" (1986, 217).

As a Texas literary intellectual, Larry McMurtry has provided more than flecks in his witnessing of "the Streets of Laredo." After the long ride up the trail from nineteenth-century South Texas and toward a remarkably uncertain future—which is to say, after McMurtry, and in the Texas and United States of today—there will probably no longer be such a ballad and its creative transformations about a dying cowboy and his ritually compensatory funeral to keep us going; no cowboy gay and dashing in the saddle; no maidens and roses; no young cowboy pall bearers; no green valley; no pipes playing lowly, nor banging of the drum slowly. *Se nos acabó la cancion* (now our song is over).

Coda

It is my hope that this book has shed some light on a complicated Texas history and an equally complicated history of this cowboy ballad, "The Streets of Laredo," such that the cowboy, this ballad, and its Texas legacy can now be interpretively approached in both a widely and deeply contextualized and textually focused way that has not been offered before for this or any other cowboy song, as far as I know. In doing so, I have tried to draw upon but also revise and add to the disciplinary legacies of the New Western history, the history of folkloristics, the literature of the American west, and, of course, the studies of the cowboy and his balladry. With this book, I also hope to respond to the most fundamental elision in current discussions about the American West as seen by Larry McMurtry in his more specific criticism of the New Western historians and their corresponding literary critics. He spoke of a "failure to do justice to the quality of imagination that constitutes part of the truth . . ." as they "simplify or ignore the emotions and imaginings" of westerners such as cowboys who, in their songs and in this particular ballad, offered perhaps a "fantasy" but as "part of the fiber that helped them survive the severities that the land put them to" (1990, 37). I would only add that the most pervasive and fundamental severity was the almost inevitable triumph of a modernity that ultimately usurped the moral and critical nourishment offered by the cowboy on horseback riding and working across that same open land. Finally, since I have also come to this topic from my own identity shaped in Texas, it might also be the case that a kind of personal exorcism is also at hand, which is that now, with a much greater and nuanced knowledge of the history of Texas and by way of this ballad, this book is a kind of recognition of the "other side"—not always as a *bête blanche*, but as ordinary men and women in Texas—fellow Texans—caught up in a not always beneficial social change which their fellow Texans known as Mexican Americans have always known.[1] It is my hope that this account of these central figures in Texas history—the ordinary cowboy, this ballad, but also figures like John Avery Lomax and Larry McMurtry—will prove illuminating as Texas (and the world) lives through its current and deeply conflicted moment, which is to say, a far more complicated continuation of modernity by another, as yet undecipherable name, for which simply adding "post" will no longer do and from which it is now impossible to imagine an alternative as the cowboy once did.

Notes

PREFACE

1. For all my geographical references to Texas both here and in my introduction, please see "Map of My Texas" at the end of these remarks and before my introduction.
2. A revised summation of this book appears as "The Texas Cowboy as 'Other': From the Streets of Laredo to 'The Streets of Laredo,'" in the *Journal of Folklore Research* at Indiana University—Bloomington.

INTRODUCTION

1. Our American identity was also attested to by US military service such as that of two of my Laredo uncles who simultaneously served in World War II: one in the Navy on the carrier *Lexington* in the Pacific, another with the army's 7th Infantry Division in the Aleutians/Philippines/Okinawa campaigns. The two *tios* made it back to Laredo. When the Lexington was sunk at the Coral Sea, Uncle Beto floated around in the Pacific for a bit and later recalled that it was almost as hot as Laredo in the summertime! Uncle Pedro was in combat at Attu and then in the Philippines campaign which, by the way, almost got me named "Douglas" when I was born in 1944. My mother had a strange "crush" on General Douglas MacArthur. I was saved from this fate only by my stern grandmother who said there was no such name equivalent in Spanish; also in that moment, there was an unstated requirement for baptism that the baby have a Catholic saint's name, and she was certain there was no Catholic saint named "Douglas" (or, as she pronounced it, "doooglas"). Notwithstanding my mother's pretentions, Grand-mother—my *abuelita*—won the argument. I have been so grateful to her all my life as was my uncle Pedro who despised MacArthur as did many enlisted men.
2. Yet, among teenagers, one must note the English-language space reserved for a newly emerging anglophone rock-n-roll popular culture, albeit in an English language

inflected with African American idioms and rhythms, à la Chuck Berry, little Richard, and even Elvis.

3. We must also note a distinctive sociocultural space for the several European, continental Middle Eastern, and within these, Jewish, immigrants in Laredo. More on this later.

4. Many other young people also attended then Texas A&I University in Kingsville, Texas (now Texas A&M University–Kingsville), some one hundred twenty miles away, and many of these did so in car caravans from Laredo leaving very early in the morning and returning late at night. Laredo also had and still has a Laredo Junior College which many attended first and then transferred to these other four-year institutions. In the 1970s, Laredo created Laredo State University which then later became the present Texas A&M International University at Laredo.

5. A well-known Texas-owned and -operated grocery store chain founded by Howard E. Butt, hence the acronym taken from his name. The business started in Corpus Christi.

6. This move was not absolute. In what now seems like an effort to maintain my Spanish language fluency as well as what one might call a "Laredo sensibility," my mother would ship me back to Laredo on a Greyhound bus to spend the summers with my grandmother, at least until I was in high school and started working in summer jobs in Corpus Christi.

7. More than ironical in a Gulf Coast port city whose bay was named in 1519 in Latin by the Spanish explorer, Alfonso Alvarez de Piñeda, in honor of its discovery on the Catholic Feast Day of Corpus Christi which means "Body of Christ." However, the small Jewish community in Corpus represent a distinctive story.

8. Bret Anthony Johnston, Director of the Michener Center for Writers at the University of Texas at Austin, has written a fine collection of short stories set in his hometown of Corpus Christi in the 1970s, indeed titled *Corpus Christi* (2004). Only one of his ten stories has significant Mexican American characters, accurately reflecting the continuing ethnoracial divide in the city at that moment.

9. For the most wonderfully poetic recollection of a Mexican American boy in Texas recalling such an encounter with such films at this same time, see Tino Villanueva's *Scene from the Movie* GIANT (1995).

10. As many may know, but some may not, *vaquero*, the term for an ethnic Mexican cowboy, is derived from *vaca*, the term for a cow.

11. In Texas, folks often simply say "Corpus" rather than the full "Corpus Christi," when referring to the city. I now take that liberty here.

12. As it happens, *chaparral* is the Spanish word for the heavy cactus and mesquite, South Texas "brush" in which cowboys and vaqueros had to work. The Spanish term, *chaparerras* for the leggings vaqueros wore to protect against thorns and such, then gives us the English term, "chaps."

13. The word *kineño* is a Hispanicization of the English word "King" for an ethnic Mexican, usually a *vaquero*, who worked on the King ranch. The ranch as a whole is often called *la kineña*, an interesting use of the feminine, when one would think it

would be *el kineño*. What I did not fully realize then was that many of the *kineños* were descendants of a Spanish expansion from central New Spain into what is now southern Texas beginning in the mid-eighteenth century—a population by then significantly *mestizo*—and one that developed cattle ranching as its primary livelihood.

14. The well-known Texas screen writer and co-founder of *Texas Monthly*, William Broyles Jr. has written the best short account of the *kineños* (1980).

15. At this very same moment, the distinguished Mexican American public intellectual, Richard Rodríguez, was having an identical experience in California at Stanford. Referencing Shakespeare, the very first words in his autobiography are: "I have taken Caliban's advice. I have stolen their books. I will have some run of this isle" (1981, 3). Most recently he offers this thought: "Real revolution in language is taking the stranger's tongue and using it better than he" (Segura 2019).

16. By the 1960s, among south and southwestern state universities, UT–Austin was beginning to have a special status so as to be able to hire Ivy League, eastern, and midwestern PhDs, many of them left-liberal, a trend markedly accelerated by Harry Ransom and John Silber who stepped into leadership roles at the university at that moment. Ransom, of course was principally responsible for initiating the wonderful archive of twentieth-century world literary culture that now bears his name as the Harry Ransom Center.

17. *La llorona* (the wailing woman) is a very well-known Mexican folk legend. *Corridos* are Mexican folk ballads, and *chistes* are narrated jokes.

18. As it happened, my meeting and tutelage with Professor Paredes coincided with the advent of the ethnonationalist Chicano Student Movement at UT–Austin and elsewhere as other students with a background in racial conflict such as mine began to organize on behalf of their exploited ancestral community, hence the discovery of *With His Pistol in His Hand* and its perpetual absence from the library shelves. By 1972, its publisher, the University of Texas Press, finally put out a less expensive paperback issue.

19. Over time Mr. Paredes himself became such a hero to many of us, "with his pen in his hand" (Limón 1993).

20. Yet even as Paredes extended this generous understanding to the Anglo Other, he seemed to have bypassed another and more personal opportunity to do so. A narrative has developed around the publication of With His Pistol in His Hand that has acquired the status of an historical accuracy, but that may now be somewhat in question. According to this story, the University of Texas Press and its editor, Frank Wardlaw were initially reluctant to publish the book because of its pungent criticisms of historian Walter Prescott Webb and the Texas Rangers, a story upheld by Paredes himself to the end of his days (Saldívar 2006, 113). However, a young scholar working with the Paredes Papers at the University of Texas at Austin has uncovered correspondence between Wardlow and Paredes that mitigates this controversy (Salinas 2005). Based on these letters, what Paredes might have also said later is that, in 1956, he became quite aware that Webb was the chair of the UT Press faculty review committee that approved his

manuscript with the strong support of Webb himself. According to Wardlow, Webb, in fact, acknowledged the deficiencies in his own work that Paredes had noted and said of Paredes' work that "a study and service like this was long overdue" (Salinas 2005, 23). It would appear that, as far as UT Press was concerned, Wardlow's expressed reservations about Paredes' book were his alone, and that Walter Prescott Webb had lent his support to Paredes and by implication to the Mexican American community.

21. Yet oddly enough, in a manner all too frequent in studies of the American West, White could not resist using two verses from a cowboy song as an epigraph at the beginning of his book: "Whoopee Ti Yi Yo, Git Along, Little Dogies" whose key line, "it's your misfortune and none of my own," gives his book its title. The "misfortune" that will befall the dogies as the cattle drive gets closer to market is seemingly metaphorically transferred to all those who will suffer under white capitalist supremacy in the American West. As it happens, his source is Lomax (1910).

22. This critical movement also seems to have spawned another distinctive revisionary moment that is even more evident in the present day which is a plethora of postmodernist readings of the presumed still-reigning symbols of the "Old West," either directly or through its representations circa mid-twentieth century, principally in film. Thus, for example, the University of Nebraska Press launched a Postwestern Horizons Series in which two of their principal authors, for example, track the "tracks" of the Old West, principally in twentieth-century filmic representations, into current films and unlikely places like contemporary Los Angeles (N. Campbell 2013; Mitchell 2018).

23. The decline in such attention from folklorists since then may, in itself, warrant critical analysis.

24. Knowlton's relatively recent *Cattle Kingdom: The Hidden History of the Cowboy West* is a good example of the popular that relies heavily on secondary academic sources and cowboy memoirs, most centrally Abbott's (2017). He places much emphasis on the cattle ranchers and the capitalization of the American West rather than the working cowboy, no doubt reflecting his own primary career as an investment banker. A more accessible and comprehensive survey of the ordinary cowboy is to be found in Lawrence Clayton's essay, "The Cowboy"; however, it is not restricted to the nineteenth century (Clayton 2001, 67–154).

CHAPTER 1

1. A summary version of chapter 1 was presented as a paper, "Where, Indeed, Are the Streets of Laredo?" at the 2022 annual Conference of the Western States Folklore Society at the University of Southern California in Los Angeles.

2. As I quote Hand's 1955 essay for the first time, I wish to note that it appeared originally in German as "Wo sind die Strassen von Laredo: Die Entwicklungsgeschichte einer amerikanischen Cowboy Ballade" in *Festschrift fiur Will-Erich Peuckert zum 60.* In keeping with the more "classical" humanities culture at that time, Hand seems to have assumed that everyone in the humanities read German and never bothered to

translate this essay. For example, no such translation exists in the Wayland Hand archive at Utah State University. His later 1958 essay in English also references 1955 in its original German as do Goldstein (1960) and Fife and Fife (1966a). Not finding an English-language version, I had it professionally translated by the late Elizabeth Schneewind of New York City based on an ad she posted in *The New York Review of Books*. I take responsibility for any inadvertent errors. However, since the German-language version is obviously what Wayland Hand wanted in the public scholarly realm, my page references are to this work, but I can make Ms. Schneewind's translation available to anyone by e-document at Jose.Limon.5@nd.edu. All that said, it still strikes me as odd that Professor Hand did not wish to make a more direct English-language intervention when all the rest of the scholarship on the ballad in that decade was in English, most of it in *Western Folklore*.

3. These are to be found in the Broadside Ballad Collection in the Bodleian Library, Oxford.

4. It must be noted, however, that Irish immigration was also continuous between and after these two major moments and there was some religious overlap between these two major groups (Griffin 2006, 245).

5. In my use of *Tejano* to name people of Mexican ancestry with long-term residence in Texas beginning in 1821, I follow the now common usage of professional historians of Texas as a regional referent largely of convenience interchangeable with the longer "Mexican-Texan" or "Texas-Mexican" (A. Alonzo 1998; Campbell 2003; Valerio-Jimenez 2013).

6. According to Barber, "by the 1760s, some of these "Spaniards" were actually refugees from Ireland. British suppression of Catholicism had increased in 1690 with the Battle of the Boyne, the Treaty of Limerick, and the implementation of the Penal Laws. Many Irishmen fled to France and Spain, where they could practice their religion and take advantage of military and governmental opportunities from which they were barred in their homeland. Some of those opportunities took Irishmen to New Spain. The first Hispanicised Irish inhabitant of Texas to be known by name, Hugo Oconór, entered northern New Spain in 1767, as interim governor of the province" (2010, 27).

7. Here Davis turns to the term "Hispanic" presumably so as to acknowledge the original Spanish presence in Texas.

8. One scholar of cowboy culture even suggests that the very term "cow-boy" first "appeared in Ireland about AD1000" (Dary 1989, 83).

9. Terry Jordan has offered a spirited argument that the southerners coming into Texas already knew cattle culture and therefore were largely not indebted to Tejanos (1981). His arguments have not persuaded historians such as Randolph B. Campbell or Graham Davis. As Davis notes, "Jordan's case also rests on the contention that the Hispanic ranching tradition more or less ceased with the decay of the Spanish missions at the end of the eighteenth century, thus making way for the new predominantly Anglo settlers to establish their own ranching culture in Texas in the 1820s

and 30s" (1991, 196). Jordan thus falls into the common error of treating missions as metonyms for the presence of a larger Spanish/Mexican culture. As historians from J. Frank Dobie to Armando C. Alonzo have amply demonstrated, throughout Texas history, Spanish-Mexican ranching was greatly evident in ranches with thousands of cattle to the present day and certainly in the 1820s and '30s. By contrast, "it is generally agreed" says Davis, "that Austin's colonists brought only 5 to 10 cattle per family and were more likely to introduce their southern planter economy based on cotton, than to concentrate on stock raising" (196). Finally, the most encompassing historian of the cowboy re-settled the matter in quite definitive terms: "The Anglo-American cowboy learned his trade from the vaquero. Spanish terminology, equipment, and technique spread from Texas . . . throughout the western United States" (Slatta, 1990, 11–12). This is a finding more recently underscored by Clayton (2001, 70–71).

10. The most successful of the Anglo newcomers, especially after the Civil War, was Richard King, the founder of the legendary King Ranch, covering a good part of southern Gulf Coast Texas. He is an anomaly of a kind, for he was not Scots-Irish. Representing that northern Irish potato famine immigration, King was "the son of poor Irish parents in New York City" who had made his way to Texas during the US–Mexico War (Campbell 2003, 192).

11. Ironically, perhaps, these famous cattle drives largely did not include Tejano ranchers who had originated this ranching culture. Laredo and the surrounding ranching area were *not* primary departure points for the big cattle drives north as Hand erroneously suggested. Tejano ranchers and *vaqueros* from this area and others along the lower Rio Grande intersected with these cattle drives only indirectly. The conflicted history recounted earlier probably accounts for this only indirect participation. The probability of "considerable prejudice" north of the Nueces "worked to keep ethnic Mexican cattle-men from organizing their own cattle drives north" and, "it was expensive and also dangerous. Instead, they sold their herds to Anglo middlemen or brokerage firms in San Antonio or in a South Texas substation for the cattle drives north. Alice was such a town; here Tejano vaqueros turned over their herds to Anglo cowboys for the drive north" (Montejano 1987, 56). Alice, Texas, on present day Texas Highway 44 was per-fectly positioned halfway between the Laredo area and the developing Gulf Coast Anglo ranches. None of this is to say that some individual Tejano vaqueros did not make the long cattle drives to Kansas and other places north and west of Texas. We know that some certainly did with the Irish long before the Civil War, and even after, "ample evidence exists that Mexican vaqueros often drove cattle to Kansas, Nebraska and Montana," but with Anglo outfits and with "their trail driving . . . sanctioned by the organization of the outfit: Mexican cattle drovers worked for Anglo ranchers and Anglo trail bosses, an acceptable arrangement in Texas" (56). As Montejano clearly implies, the great majority of cowboys on the cattle drives north were Anglos accompa-nied by some Tejanos and African Americans. As Moore also notes, "a typical outfit

included from eight to ten men and usually had at least one Hispanic or black worker, either as a cook, horse wrangler, or occasionally as a regular hand" (2010, 40). Without citing Montejano or Moore, De León has offered a more recent spirited argument for the presence or "agency" of Tejanos on these cattle drives from beginning to end (2014, 6). Nevertheless, he also acknowledges that their overall number came to about 15 percent, although it is unclear how this percentage was derived (19).

12. For Flores, and drawing on David Montejano, the "tragedy" was modernity's seeming deleterious impact on Tejanos in the much later nineteenth century and into the twentieth as South Texas experienced large-scale capitalist cash crop agriculture dominated by new farming Anglos principally from the Midwest. They were aided and abetted by the refrigerated rail car, mechanical irrigation, cheap land, and above all, cheap ethnic Mexican labor, a social totality Flores calls "the Texas Modern" (2002, 2–5). For Flores, such besieged and beleaguered workers were the direct result of "the displacement of Mexican skilled workers, landowners, and *vaqueros* in disproportionate numbers," which is to say the successful South Texas Tejano ranching society delineated earlier but including some Anglo ranchers as well (3). However, the process was probably more complicated than his brief assessment suggests. As Alonzo has shown us, the displacement of ranching *Tejanos* was by no means universal. More importantly, both Montejano and Flores tend to elide the massive effects of the Mexican Revolution in producing a very large and marginalized labor force that was displaced, not from South Texas *ranchos*, but rather *into* South Texas from nearby Mexico at this historical moment, yet another effect of the larger transnational impact of modernity. For native Tejanos, these Mexican nationals were the *fuereños* (foreigners) in Américo Paredes' phrase (1958, 13). Flores seems to use this phrase to refer to both Anglo midwesterners and Mexican nationals coming to the Lower Rio Grande Valley, whereas Paredes means only Mexican immigrant nationals (Flores 2002, 3). We must also note that the nineteenth-century Laredo I have described was also severely impacted by this twentieth-century Mexican immigration that introduced a large underclass into Laredo society that heavily contributed to Laredo's mid-twentieth-century reputation as one of the poorest cities in the United States.

13. The entire volume in which Foster's work appears is a comprehensive statement of these "alternatives, alterities, anthropologies" in the name of a pluralized, nuanced modernity (Knauft, 2002).

14. Here Foster cites Tomlinson (1999, 61) who in turn draws this quote from Marshall Berman (1982).

15. His analysis of that complexity, those conditions and those effects, is offered as an alternative to what he terms "anti-colonialist narratives" derived from the 1950s and 1960s anticolonial struggles which posit colonized societies rising in redemptive struggle against their colonial oppressors. Such a view continues even among so-called postcolonial theorists who continue "to be concerned with exposing the negative

structure of colonialism's power and with demonstrating the colonized agency in resisting or overcoming these conditions" (6). As such, they continue to lend themselves, in Hayden White's terms, to narrative emplotments of romance, i.e. heroic resistance against formidable oppressors (1973, 8).

16. In sharp contrast, Wright analyzes the same process drawing principally on Marxist social theory, but with little empirical data and focusing on what he calls the "mythical cowboy," an assortment of stereotypes drawn from films and dime novels, with little to no reference to any reality of cowboy life (2001).

17. The JA was one of other such large ranches, such as the even larger XIT also in the Panhandle, but also, noted earlier, the King Ranch in South Texas. The latter inspired the 1956 blockbuster film, *Giant*, directed by George Steven based on the 1952 Edna Ferber novel by that same title (Graham, 2018). One suspects that the film in turn reinforced an emergent popular image of such large Texas ranches as the product of enterprising, ambitious but fundamentally good and "gentlemanly" American men such as Goodnight although such an image was also being fostered even in their own time (Moore 2010, 110–16). In the late nineteenth century, they became the ranching equivalents of those other quintessential American capitalists, Henry Ford, Andrew Mellon, and J. D. Rockefeller. Later, along with *Giant*, American popular culture fostered the image of the gentlemen cattle baron in television series such as *Bonanza* and *High Chaparral*. Along with the "lawman," such as Matt Dillon in the TV series *Gunsmoke*, such figures offered the final if symbolic displacement of the ordinary cowboy in the popular imagination. Only our ballad remained to tell us of our young cowboy gay and dashing in the saddle.

18. To be sure there was some overt resistance. "Angry at this treatment, in 1883, a group of cowboys demanded higher wages and went on strike against five ranches"—a strike that failed "because the ranchers had no trouble hiring replacements" (Campbell, 303; Chapman 2011; Lause, 2017). That other great writer of Texas and UT-Austin alum, Elmer Kelton, also wrote a memorable fictional account of this strike (2008).

CHAPTER 2

1. In effect, Williams asks us to consider vintage stores, hiking trails, environmental vacations, etc., in the modern world as "a leisure function of the dominant order itself," to which one might also add the way in which any corporate attorney in Dallas longs to acquire a piece of land in West Texas (1977, 122).

2. For a marvelous elaboration of this idea, see Sennett's *The Craftsman*.

3. Monica Muñoz Martínez has documented some of the history of Anglo anti-Mexican violence in Texas. Surprisingly, she has little to say about the nineteenth century or cowboys in particular as paradoxically, by her account, most such violence seemed to have occurred in the early twentieth century within Flores's Texas Modern and often

by Texas Rangers or vigilantes (2018). A working cowboy and also a Texas Ranger, John Young, offered this candid and balanced assessment:

> Among the cowboys, true enough, there were "bad" men, vicious men; but the great majority of them were honest and truthful and were against outlawry and viciousness. They were hard and diligent workers, and men who worked hard out in the open generally led straight lives. (Dobie [1929] 1981, 100)

4. At the considerable risk of fictional dramatization, I cannot help but think of the "kid" coming to Texas in the 1840s in Cormac McCarthy's *Blood Meridian*.
5. In the aforementioned Tejano ballad, "El Corrido de Kiansis," the composer has this opening verse, translated by Américo Paredes, about a loved one back in South Texas:

> When we left for Kansas on a big cattle drive, my *caporal* [foreman] shouted, "Take good care of my beloved." Another caporal replied, "Have no fear, she has no other loves; for if a woman is virtuous, no matter if she lives among men." (Paredes 1976, 55)

6. Does this also explain the double pleasure of an Anglo-American imperial victory in the US-Mexico War then articulated in the naming of Palo Alto, California; Cerro Gordo, Iowa; and Buena Vista, Georgia, after key battles in that war?

CHAPTER 3

1. Since we are dealing with the histories of folkloristics, I met Professor Hand in 1979 when he was already in retirement, and I was a successful candidate for an assistant professor appointment at UCLA in anthropology and folklore. With decidedly mixed feelings, I chose instead to accept an offer from the University of Texas at Austin where I had just received the PhD in folklore under another esteemed folklorist, Américo Paredes. Paredes was Hand's good friend and through him, I was already familiar with Hand's work, particularly on legend, including his editing of the very influential *America Folk Legend: A Symposium*, in which Paredes also participated. Only much later did I come to know of Hand's work on "the Streets of Laredo" when I began work on the present study.
2. This twentieth-century constellation was heavily male dominated, a condition fundamentally changed over time to a woman-centered folklore discipline, a change that merits its own research project.
3. In his e-journal article, Winick reproduces two Thoms articles published in *Athenæum* both entitled "Folk-Lore." The term "folk-lore" is first used and defined in the first, published on August 24, 1846, and the more extended statement that I quote appears in the second published on August 29, 1846. Winick does not provide page numbers for the *Athenæum*.

4. Cowboys were sometimes referred to as "cowpunchers," probably in reference not to the cowboy on the open range but rather to cowboys loading cattle unto railroad cars in places like Kansas using "metal pointed poles" to prod the animals (Dary 1989, 275).

5. I have much debated placing this and the other several song texts that will follow in an appendix rather than imbedded within my narrative. I have opted for the latter thinking that the reader might prefer a ready access to these various ballad versions rather than having to go to the back of the book each time.

6. Callison's book offers no biographical information on himself or Jones whatsoever, and I have been unable to find any other information. The total first-person narration of the adventures might even suggest that Callison was a pen name for Jones, or that Jones is a fictive stand-in for Callison.

7. We also cannot rule out that only Wister actually learned of the song from oral tradition, wrote it into his novel, and Callison, the seemingly later writer, then appropriated the verses and the funerary revision from the very well-known Wister and joined them to his version of Maynard's "Tom Sherman's saloon."

8. As it happens, in their introduction to Thorp's book, the Fifes also cited and generally narrated Callison's story about the dog's accidental shooting in Dodge City. With minimal attribution and no explanation, the Fifes made several arbitrary changes in Callison's narrative such as giving the dog a name, Flora (Fife and Fife 1966b, 148–150). We can only surmise that mid-twentieth-century disciplinary coherence varied from folklorist to folklorist.

9. Indeed, the Fife volume is a study in incoherence, often rambling, with confusing details and references, and at times moralistic Christianity. In keeping with their faulty editing, the Fifes reprinted and imbedded the Thorp booklet toward the end of their own commentary rather than at the very end as an appendix. Moreover, they included it within their page enumeration even while also preserving Thorp's own original enumeration. In the Fife's enumeration, Thorp's text occupies approximately pages 258–303 while Thorp's own enumeration covers pages 9–50 plus title and prefatory pages. For the sake of clarity and consistency, I cite Thorp's own page numbers when referring to his text in this nevertheless more accessible volume. The Fifes also wrote an introduction to the volume along with "Variants, Commentary, Notes and Lexicon," the latter appearing separately with each song. I enter these in the bibliography under their own names and page numbers.

10. The controversy has continued by way of travel writing and more popular essays about cowboys and the West (Gioia 2005; Moon 2014).

11. Here Hand means Lomax's *Cowboy Songs and Other Frontier Ballads* (1910).

12. Hand says "1885" in "Wisner, Wisconsin," while Thorp has it in "1886" in "Wisner, Nebraska."

13. At this juncture, to simplify matters, I will refer to the different versions using only their publication date.

14. Why Hand could not access 1908 is also a bit of a mystery.

15. Hale makes a brief reappearance in Thorp's autobiography in a humorous anecdote about wives and gambling but with no mention of the ballad (1945, 209–211).

16. While they include Hand's 1955 German-language essay in their bibliography, they make almost no use of it in their assessment of "The Cowboy's Lament," including his error in crediting Thorp with Lomax's production. Again, there is no English translation, and the Fifes likely did not read German.

17. Such a *mea culpa* in English would have had long-term consequences such as in Tatum's 1994 aforementioned analysis of what appears to be Lomax's text, thinking it to be Thorp's (67–69). "The song" that he is discussing, says Tatum, "appears in Thorp's 1908 edition, as well as—though bowdlerized—in Lomax's 1910 edition" (67). He then proceeds to the analysis of "the song," but, like Hand, he clearly is not examining Thorp's 1908; otherwise, he would not ask the reader to "consider the song's opening stanza, in which the dying cowboy lying on the streets of Laredo notes a passing stranger's 'get-up,' or outfit identifying him as a fellow cowboy" (67). That is not Thorp's 1908 first stanza at all. Here it is that first stanza again:

    > 'Twas once in my saddle I used to be happy
    > 'Twas once in my saddle I used to be gay
    > But I first took to drinking, then to gambling
    > A shot from a six-shooter took my life away.

    However, it is the *third* stanza in Thorp's *1921* edition which, of course, as we have seen, Thorp "borrowed" from Lomax like Pap Finn "borrowed" chickens. Tatum's citation is also curious because he is also using the Fife edition of Thorp's 1908 booklet, and, as noted earlier, it is the Fifes who twice make us aware that Thorp used Lomax's 1910 text in his 1921 version and claimed it as his own (1966b, 151n25).

18. This collection is the John Avery Lomax Family Papers housed in the Dolph Briscoe Center for American History at the University of Texas at Austin in 1948.

19. Even into my undergraduate years at UT-Austin in the 1960s, I noticed among men this kind of informal conversational reference to "Smith," "Jones," or "González," even though they were all friends.

20. Roy Bedichek became a well-known naturalist writer and folklorist and joined J. Frank Dobie and Walter Prescott Webb as a then very well-known Texas triumvirate of liberal writers associated with the University of Texas at Austin in the 1930s and 1940s. A statue of all three may be seen at Austin's Barton Springs, its famous spring-fed artesian water swimming area in Zilker Park, where these gentlemen liked to swim and talk (Owen 1969). Unless, of course, the new "Austin" has shut it down and sold it for "development."

21. The manuscript is undated but begins by quoting J. Frank Dobie's 1941 book, *The Longhorns,* and we also find the following note in the file: "JAL, Sr. manuscript as submitted to Stith Thompson (1947?) not published to my knowledge." It was signed by one of his two sons, "John Lomax, Jr. March 30, 1961." Stith Thompson was yet another

elder within the mid-twentieth-century folklorist cohort, he at the University of Indiana, and arguably the most famous of them. His focused dedication to the classification of folktales using a motif indexing approach represents, perhaps, the utmost disciplinary coherence. He had met Lomax at the beginning of his career at the University of Texas–Austin in 1918 when he rented a bedroom in the Lomax household (Porterfield 1996, 185). Although, he was "never exactly a Lomax partisan" (400). So, it is somewhat surprising that when, in the mid-1940s, he was preparing a series of volumes on regional folklore, he asked Lomax to contribute something "on the subject of the cattle range[,] . . . a more personal account of cowboys than had surfaced in *Cowboy Songs*" in 1910 (474). Being near eighty and in poor health may certainly account for why Lomax never published this work before his death in 1948. According to his son, it was submitted, but the inevitable editorial process likely could not be completed, or perhaps Thompson did not accept it.

22. And, as noted much earlier, E. C. Abbott, the former nineteenth-century cowboy also known as Teddy Blue, also recalls the singing of "The Streets of Laredo" in 1876 (1939, 222–223). However, his recollection of this moment in the late 1930s as an older man makes one take pause since it allows for the possibility that he may be retrofitting the popularity of the ballad in the 1930s, ironically, as a result of Lomax's work.

23. Paredes's essay was published only in Spanish. The translations are my own.

24. I am very grateful to Joanna Ray Zattierro for this reference to The Cowboy's Lament in the Cheyenne Transporter (2020, 105).

25. According to Porterfield, this project was initially begun in 1944 exclusively by the elder Lomax by way of another title, "The Ninety-Nine Best Ballads." Again, by the time of its publication in 1947, the elder Lomax was likely too ill to see it through editing and publication, and his other son, Alan, took over the editorship and thus also took coediting credit (474). It is also possible that, for Lomax, this project also took precedence over that in footnote 21, also accounting for that project's nonpublication.

26. Oring is quite clear that he is offering this concept only as a hypothesis that could be empirically tested into a true law.

27. Again, Paredes first published this work in Spanish in 1972, my first reference date. Thereafter, I cite his much more accessible 1972 English translation.

28. In all of this we also cannot ignore that Lomax was, in his youth, a poet *manqué* (Porterfield 1996, 59).

29. But also Américo Paredes at the University of Texas-Austin. We often overlook the manner in which chapter 2 of *With His Pistol in Hand* called "The Legend" offers Paredes' own crafted composite of the various legends about Gregorio Cortez (1958, 33–54).

30. In his account of the early beginnings of folklore study at the University of Texas–Austin, Bauman notes the founding of the Texas Folklore Society in 1909 by Professor Leonidas Payne of the UT Department of English (2020, 121). He does not mention Lomax at all, including that in 1913, Lomax offered a "course called 'Folklore and Balladry' as a tentative step toward an extended program in folklore at the

University," also in the hope that it would "further the aims of the Texas Folklore Society" of which he also served as president (Porterfield 1996, 163, 426).

31. Within this debate in folkloristics, we must also note that Lomax was twice elected president of the American Folklore Society (Porterfield 1996, 172, 176). By 1937, however, "elitists within the AFS . . . now declared him unacceptable as a folklorist because he lacked a PhD" as disciplinary coherence began to take shape (407).

32. Davis's chapter, "The Austin Liberals" (2009, 124–130) is a very stimulating beginning for a full intellectual history of Texas liberal thought and politics not always based in Austin—to which Davis has already also contributed a wonderful assessment of Texas "outlaw" writers at mid-twentieth century (2004). In a nuanced assessment of Lomax, Porterfield notes that he had a comfortable fit within this liberal tradition stretching back to Sam Houston who read Alexander Pope, defended Indians, and refused to lead Texas into the Confederacy. Within such a history, he includes Bill Moyers, Barbara Jordan, and J. Frank Dobie (1996, 2–3), and I would add Alonso Perales, Henry B. González, and, of course, Américo Paredes. This liberal trajectory continues with contemporary writers who have voiced a discontent with modernity as witness only three recent titles (Christensen 2001; Bass and Christensen 2004; L. Wright 2018).

33. His opposition to FDR and the New Deal did not stop Lomax from taking advantage of the New Deal's Works Progress Administration (WPA) and its financed sponsorship of his work with African Americans in the South, as the "mass of contradictions" continued (S. Davis 2004, 87).

34. For those not familiar with the Kalevala, it is the national epic of Finland collected in part and in parts from oral tradition but refashioned in the nineteenth century by more contemporary folklorist poets, principally Elias Lönnrot.

35. Oddly enough, in his own 1960 edition of North American folksongs, Alan Lomax chose not to use the 1947 "The Streets of Laredo," but opted instead for a version he calls "The Dying Cowboy" with an opening line, "As I rode out by Tom Sherman's bar-room" recalling Frank Maynard although without crediting him (1960, 384–85).

36. Johnny Cash and Marty Robbins, "Streets of Laredo," 1969, *The Johnny Cash Show*, Full Episode, Episode 7.

37. For his collection, Goldstein collected this professorial parody as sung by none other than Roger Abrahams, presumably on the Penn campus while he was still a graduate student (1960, 8).

38. The singular exception may have been the television series *Rawhide* of the early 1960s with the young Clint Eastwood as Rowdy Yates.

39. Other well-know examples might include John O'Hara on politics (*Ten North Frederick*, 1955); Mickey Spillane (the Mike Hammer detective series from 1947 until well into the later twentieth century); Allen Drury on Washington, DC, political intrigue (*Advise and Consent*, 1959), Harper Lee's southern fiction, *To Kill a Mockingbird* (1960, but also Norman Mailer's quasi-fictional 1968 *Armies of the Night*, on 1960s radical

politics; and, later, John Grisham's many fictions of the legal system. Closer to a high modernism but still straddling this boundary, we might also consider the work of, again, Norman Mailer, on the public culture of World War II in his 1948 *The Naked and the Dead* but also Joseph Heller's 1961 *Catch 22*.

40. Of course, Ives then went on to have an even larger career on stage, television, and film, most memorably his role as "Big Daddy" in the 1958 film Cat on a Hot Tin Roof.

41. By way of Simon & Schuster's online contact information, I queried Mr. Irving on this question by written communication, but, unfortunately, I received no response.

42. In other works in progress, I examine a wide range of this legacy beyond Texas in an essay, "Being and Nothingness: 'The Streets of Laredo,' Mark Harris, and John Irving," and in a book-length project, Return to the Source: "The Streets of Laredo" and Twentieth Century Anglo-Irish Literature and Culture where I treat the Anglo-Irish poet, Louis MacNeice; the also Anglo-Irish short story writer, Sam Keery; and the English poet, Peter Riley, and musicians Elton John and Bernie Taupin, but also the particularly Irish use of the song in the American film The Ballad of Buster Scruggs.

CHAPTER 4

1. Although written later, the other two novels in the tetralogy are chronologically set before *Lonesome Dove* and take us back to the time when the central protagonists were not exactly cowboys but rather Texas Rangers "pacifying" the Texas frontier against all manner of exaggerated evil doers. These are sprawling unfortunate works clearly intended to boil the *Lonesome Dove/Streets of Laredo* pot a bit more. One also has the sense of a failed McMurtry response to Cormac McCarthy's 1985 masterpiece, *Blood Meridian*. For all these reasons, they are irrelevant to my present argument.

2. I have also chosen not to treat the film and television versions of these works since they follow closely upon the written texts, especially since McMurtry was closely involved in their production.

3. *Horseman, Pass By* was made into the film, *Hud* (1963). *The Last Picture Show* also became a film with the same title (1971).

4. Since he provides no citation, it is unclear what versions attracted McMurtry. The first song, "The Dying Cowboy," matches the well-known version in the 1947 collection by Lomax and Lomax, but "The Cowboy's Lament" does not match their version, nor is it that of Frank Maynard by that same title (1947, 264–265; 2010, 155–156).

5. As it happens, *Urban Cowboy* was set and filmed in Houston.

6. The two versions of the screenplay are to be found respectively in the Witfliff Collections at Texas State University and in the McMurtry Archive in Special Collections at the University of Houston. I am very grateful to both institutions.

7. Here undoubtedly, McMurtry is knowingly evoking a famous name closely associated with the Texas cattle drives, Jesse L. Driskill (1824–1890), whose other claim to fame is building the well-known Driskill Hotel in Austin, Texas. https://www.tshaonline.org/handbook/entries/driskill-jesse-lincoln

8. Surely it cannot be the case that with Hoot Crane, "Hart Crane" was on McMurtry's playful mind!

9. According to Laura June Davis, this evocative sentimental song was a "particular favorite among the Rebels, many of whom named their daughters Lorena" (2012, 1). It has also appeared in several "Western" films, most notably in John Ford's 1956, *The Searchers* (Cumbow 2009; McConnell 2017).

10. In this episode, we also see McMurtry's unfortunate indulgence in an American literary and popular tradition of "Mexican" stereotypes concerning sexuality, violence, and emotionalism (Limón 1998, 135–139). On the other hand, it is interesting that McMurtry acknowledges that this encounter with Mexico is set in motion by Anglo-Texan thievery of such horses. He does, however, displace such thievery into Mexico whereas livestock was more often stolen from Mexican-owned ranches in South Texas and often the ranches themselves were taken (A. Alonzo 1998, 146–148). I more fully review McMurtry's representational relationship with Mexican-origin peoples in another book manuscript in progress entitled *Neither Friends, Nor Strangers: Anglos and Mexicans in the Literary Making of Texas*.

11. Historical anthropologist, Richard R. Flores, reports that the Alamo did not start becoming a site of public culture as we now know it until the late 1890s (2002, 61–92).

12. Here McMurtry is referencing what has been called the "second battle of Adobe Walls" which "occurred on June 27, 1874, when a buffalo hunters' camp, built in the spring of that year in what is now Hutchinson County, about a mile from the adobe ruins known as Adobe Walls, was attacked by a party of about seven hundred Plains Indians, mostly Cheyennes, Comanches, and Kiowas, under the leadership of Quanah Parker and Isa-tai." The first Adobe Walls was built in the 1840s and abandoned in 1848 after the first battle with Indians. https://tshaonline.org/handbook/online/articles/bta0.

13. It would appear that McMurtry and Bogdanovich are being playful again in the choice of "Martin Dean" as a name. Dean Martin, a "crooner," and mostly comic actor, had roles in a number of "Western" movies at this time including the 1966, *Texas Across the River*.

14. It is possible that McMurtry is alluding to a violent political conflict that did occur in Laredo although much later in 1886, since the number "62" is not that far off from the actual casualties that resulted. This involved organized groups and might actually speak to the high level of political consciousness in Laredo at that time and not to a mindless "Mexican" violence that McMurtry's character seems to imply (Thompson 2017, 279–310). Such organized, politically conscious violence was not unknown in the United States as witness the Haymarket Affair in Chicago in that same year of 1886.

15. In 2009, McMurtry offered this interesting elaboration on why it was turned down: "The three actors . . . saw no reason for the Old West to end, and if for some reason it did *end*, they wanted the last adventure to be a wild success, not a dim moral victory of the kind we had planned for them (McMurtry 2009, 94).

16. Maureen Orth is an accomplished journalist and close friend of McMurtry's. It is interesting that he chose this woman from among his many and probably predominantly male friends for this dedication.

17. Perhaps a stand-in for Richard King (1824–1885), founder of the King Ranch, which is geographically congruent with the Lonesome Dove village.

18. Although McMurtry is habitually sparse with dates, early in the novel, we learn that Lorena Wood is twenty-four years old as the cattle drive begins and that her parents brought her to Texas when she was twelve when they left Mobile, Alabama, fleeing the Federal attack on the city in 1864–65, thus twelve years before this cattle drive begins (36).

19. Here McMurtry is drawing on the story about the famous cattleman Charles Goodnight discussed at the end of chapter 1. With permissible elaboration, he is tracking on real historical occurrence. Goodnight accompanied the body of his close friend and business partner, Oliver Loving, back to Texas after Loving was killed by Indians in New Mexico. https://www.tshaonline.org/handbook/entries/loving-oliver

20. Rather, like the ballad's cowboy, Call has "done wrong."

21. Conceivably, McMurtry could have placed these folks in South Texas, perhaps at the old Lonesome Dove ranch, but farming was not yet underway in that part of the state although commercial cash crop farming would take off in the early twentieth century in the Lower Rio Grande Valley. Also, the railroads had not fully been developed in this region yet. One imagines that the King Ranch and Richard Kleberg might have substituted for Charles Goodnight, but the latter was clearly a hero for McMurtry in ways that Kleberg was not.

22. My placement of these locales on the map is closely proximate. I wanted their names to be as prominent as space allowed.

23. For many literary intellectuals and artists, Laredo, Texas, has historically been the gateway to exotic Mexico, among them the other José Limón, the greatest modern dancer of the twentieth century, a Mexican American, who traveled through Laredo from New York City in 1956 in an effort to reconnect with his ancestral Mexico (Limón 2004). Then there is the 1969 film, *The Wild Bunch*, where some aging Anglo bad men feel the need for one last shoot-out in Mexico. In Cormac McCarthy's *All the Pretty Horses*, the young cowboys, John Grady Cole, Lacey Rawlins, and Jimmy Blevins also traversed through this same western territory on their way to Mexico in 1950.

24. This the only extended reference to this ethnic group that almost wholly defined the historical Laredo as we saw in chapter 1. What McMurtry offers in this instance is the following:

> Laredo was overrun with . . . giant brown pack rats that lived under houses and also under the giant piles of prickly pear. Sometimes the Mexicans stuffed the ratholes and set the piles of prickly pear afire. Once the fire burned down, they dug out the rats and ate them" (291).

This gratuitous comment offered by McMurtry is as nasty, racist, and non-historical as it is unnecessary for the plot or characters.

25. Here McMurtry is engaged in an interesting narrative sleight of hand. In *Streets of Laredo*, when Lorena is recalling Blue Duck to Goodnight, she tells him of "the day Blue Duck . . . handed her over" to the other renegades. "But not Mox Mox. He hadn't been there then. Then Mox Mox arrived . . . and wanted to burn me. . . . Blue Duck wouldn't let him burn me. Blue Duck wanted me for bait . . . to catch Gus McCrae." Lorena then tells Goodnight that both Blue Duck and Mox Mox left before Gus showed up and killed the other Indian renegades, rescuing Lorena. As it happens, Mox Mox is not at all mentioned in *Lonesome Dove*, but McMurtry has Lorena explain that she "never told nobody this" about Mox Mox and the threatened burning, including Gus, which is supposed to explain why we are learning about it only now some twenty years later (221–222). (Occasionally the now educated teacher Lorena slips into double negatives).

26. I am deeply grateful to my wife, Teresa McKenna (Professor of English Emeritus at USC), for first pointing out to me Doobie's walk in the streets of Laredo that then led to my recognition that it is several women who ritually walk the streets of Laredo and sing and that Lorena narrates this scene.

27. Since McMurtry cannot have a woman—even this woman—riding horseback from Laredo to Fort Stockton all by herself, he conveniently overlooks the fact that there was no such rail service until well into the twentieth century.

28. In her recollection of her life with McMurtry, Diana Ossana takes some credit for writing the characters of María and her two children. She showed him "the five pages I had rewritten and asked him to read what I felt would give his María the strength she needed to carry on for her two damaged children." She reports that "the only changes" McMurtry made "were in the first sentence; everything else was exactly as I had written it" (2023, 153–154).

29. In an updated analysis of this final moment, Barrera also recognizes that this familial situation within modernity necessarily means that that "no longer is Call bound to a vanishing mythology or the vast unsettled spaces of the frontier; instead, he will live out his days in the shelter of a secure domestic space[,] . . . not a home of his own, but a start" (2022, 83). I would only add that, in all likelihood, the old cowboy will remain, in Barrera's own major critical trope, positively "haunted" by his past as a working cowboy on the cattle drives, a reality and not a mythology.

30. As with other critics, also absent in her fine feminist assessment is any reference at all to the city of Laredo and to our song other than as an epigraph. Indeed, all scholarly commentary on McMurtry's work gives only the most minimal and passing attention to the song and his affinity to it, an absence especially evident in the critical work on this novel that carries its name. Why this song title and how is it effected in the novel? I ask this question because in his other books the relationship between title and contents is utterly evident, in some cases only slightly metaphorical—*The Last Picture*

Show—in others much too literal—*Duane's Depressed*—or even *Lonesome Dove*. For *Streets of Laredo*, for example, neither Reilly nor Frye have a word to say about this relationship. Barrera does use a stanza of the song as an epigraph to her article but does not address it at all in her discussion, as if it is meant only to vaguely evoke the West. Mark Busby does take some minimal account of the song only to note the possible "ambiguous references," to both Call and Joey Garza, who had both "done wrong" (1995, 264). I find this unpersuasive simply because Call does not die in the novel, and Joey is hardly a young cowboy, "dashing and gay in the saddle," and, it's not that he hasn't done wrong; he is *wrong* incarnate. He cannot fall from grace because he has never been there. On the other hand, McMurtry himself may have encouraged this inattention because, at first glance, he appears to have selected this title simply as a loose evocation of the American West, much as he has used stanzas of the song in his other writings. In similar fashion, none of these critics even mentions the town of Laredo in their discussions. It needs to be said, however, that Barrera has offered a marvelous account of her own native Laredo in her more recent work (2022).

31. I borrow the phrase, "among my people" from my fellow South Texan *mexicana*, Jovita González, and her essay "Among My People" (1932).

CODA

1. As with so much else in my academic life, the—I think—felicitous phrase *bête blanche* must also be first credited to Américo Paredes (1977, 1).

Works Cited

Abbott, E.C., and Helena Huntington Smith. 1939. *We Pointed Them North: Recollections of a Cowpuncher*. Norman: University of Oklahoma Press.

Abrahams, Roger D. 1972. "Folklore and Literature as Performance." *Journal of the Folklore Institute* 9 (2/3): 75–94.

———. 2000. "Mr. Lomax Meets Professor Kittredge." *Journal of Folklore Research* 37 (2/3): 99–118.

Adams, John A., Jr. 2008. *Conflict and Commerce on the Rio Grande: Laredo, 1755–1955*. College Station: Texas A&M University Press.

Allen, Esther. 2020. "Fiction and Responsibility." *New York Review of Books* 38 (12): 22–25.

Allmendinger, Blake. 1992. *The Cowboy: Representations of Labor in an American Work Culture*. New York: Oxford University Press.

Alonzo, Armando C. 1998. *Tejano Legacy: Rancheros and Settlers in South Texas, 1734–1900*. University of New Mexico Press.

Anttonen, Pertti J. 2005. *Tradition through Modernity: Postmodernism and the Nation-State in Folklore Scholarship*. Helsinki: Studia Fennica.

Armitage, Susan. 1989. "'The Legacy of Conquest' by Patricia Limerick: A Panel of Appraisal." *Western Historical Quarterly* 20 (3): 306–309.

Aron, Stephen. 2016. "The History of the American West Gets a Much-Needed Rewrite." *Smithsonian Magazine*, August 16, 2016. https://www.smithsonianmag.com/history/history-american-west-gets-much-needed-rewrite-180960149/.

Arreola, Daniel D. 2002. *Tejano South Texas: A Mexican American Cultural Province*. Austin: University of Texas Press.

Barber, Marian Jean. 2010. "How the Irish, Germans, and Czechs Became Anglo: Race and Identity in the Texas-Mexico Borderlands." Unpublished PhD diss., University of Texas at Austin.

Barrera, Cordelia E. 2013. "Written on the Body: A Third Space Reading of Larry McMurtry's *Streets of Laredo*." *Western American Literature* 48 (3): 232–252.

———. 2022. *The Haunted Southwest: Toward an Ethics of Place in Borderlands Literature*. Lubbock: Texas Tech University Press.

———. 2023. "Reader's Review of the ms. 'The Streets of Laredo: Texas, Modernity, and Discontent." Available upon request.

Barry, Phillips. 1911. "Irish Folk-Song." *Journal of American Folklore* 24 (93): 332–343.

———. 1912. "Some Aspects of Folk-Song." *Journal of American Folklore* 24 (97): 274–283.

Barsness, John. 1967. "The Dying Cowboy Song." *Western American Literature* 2 (1): 50–77.

Bass, Rick, and Paul Christensen. 2004. *Falling from Grace in Texas: A Literary Response to the Demise of Paradise*. San Antonio: Wings Press.

Bauman, Richard. 1975. "Verbal Art as Performance." *American Anthropologist* 77: 290–311.

———. 2020. "The Texas School." In *Folklore in the United States and Canada: An Institutional History*, edited by Patricia Sawin and Rosemary Lévy Zumwalt, 129–141. Bloomington: Indiana University Press.

Ben-Amos, Dan. 2020. *Folklore Concepts: Histories and Critiques*. Edited by Henry Glassie and Elliot Oring. Bloomington: Indiana University Press.

Bendix, Regina. 1997. *In Search of Authenticity: The Formation of Folklore Studies*. Madison: University of Wisconsin Press.

Bennett, Patrick. 1980. *Talking with Texas Writers: Twelve Interviews*. College Station: Texas A&M University Press.

Berman, Marshall. 1982. *All That is Solid Melts into Air: The Experience of Modernity*. New York: Simon & Schuster.

Bowman, Timothy P. 2016. *Blood Oranges: Colonialism and Agriculture in the South Texas Borderlands*. College Station: Texas A&M University Press.

Breen, Richard. 2016. "Documenting and Displaying the Folklore Process," Unpublished MA thesis. Maynooth, County Kildare, Ireland: National University of Ireland.

Bronner, Simon. 1986. *American Folklore Studies: An Intellectual History*. Lawrence: University Press of Kansas.

———. 2002. *Folk Nation: Folklore in the Creation of American Tradition*. Wilmington, DE: Scholarly Resources

Broyles, William, Jr. 1980. "All the King's Men." *Texas Monthly*, October, 1980. https://www.texasmonthly.com/travel/all-the-kings-men-3/

Busby, Mark. 1995. *Larry McMurtry and the West: An Ambivalent Relationship*. University of North Texas Press.

Callison, John J. 1914. *Bill Jones of Paradise Valley, Oklahoma*. Chicago: M.A. Donahue.

Campbell, Neil. 2013. *Post-Westerns: Cinema, Region, West*. Lincoln: University of Nebraska Press.

Campbell, Randolph B. 2003. *Gone to Texas: A History of the Lone Star State*. New York: Oxford University Press.

Cantú, Norma Elia. 2019. *Cabañuelas. A Novel*. Albuquerque: University of New Mexico Press.

————. 2023. *Fiestas in Laredo: Matachines, Quinceñeras, and George Washington's Birthday*. College Station: Texas A&M University Press.

Cantwell, Robert. 1996. *When We Were Good: The Folk Revival*. Cambridge: Harvard University Press.

Cash, Johnny, and Marty Robbins. 1969. "Streets of Laredo." *The Johnny Cash Show*. Season 1, episode 7. Aired July 26, 1969.

Cavazos, Lauro. 2008. *A Kineño Remembers: From the King Ranch to the White House*. College Station: Texas A&M University Press.

Chapman, Art. 2011. "Cowboy Strike of 1883." *Encyclopedia of the Great Plains*, edited by David J. Wishart. http://plainshumanities.unl.edu/encyclopedia/doc/egp.pd.015

Christensen, Paul. 2001. *West of the American Dream: An Encounter with Texas*. College Station: Texas A&M University Press.

Clayton, Lawrence. 2001. "The Cowboy." In *Vaqueros, Cowboys, and Buckaroos*, edited by Lawrence Clayton, Jim Hoy, and Jerald Underwood, 67–154. Austin: University of Texas Press.

Clifford, Craig, and Tom Pilkington, eds. 1989. *Range Wars*. Dallas: Southern Methodist University Press.

Coen, Joel, and Ethan Coen, directors. 2018a. *The Ballad of Buster Scruggs*. Annapurna Pictures. 2 hr., 13 min.

Coen, Joel, and Ethan Coen. 2018b. "Filmmakers Joel and Ethan Coen on Singing Cowboys and Working with Oxen." Interview by Terry Gross. *Fresh Air*, NPR, November 19, 2018. Audio. https://www.npr.org/2018/11/19/669204732/filmmakers-joel-and -ethan-coen-on-singing-cowboys-and-working-with-oxen.

Coffin, Tristam P. 1957. "'Mary Hamilton' and the Anglo-American Ballad as an Art Form." *Journal of American Folklore* 70 (277): 208–214.

Cohen, Norm. 2005. *Folk Music: A Regional Exploration*. Westport, CT: Greenwood Press.

Cohen, Ronald D. 2002. *Rainbow Quest: The Folk Music Revival and American Society, 1940–1970*. Amherst: University of Massachusetts.

Comer, Krista. 1997. "Literature, Gender Studies, and the New Western History." In *The New Western History: The Territory Ahead*, edited by Forrest G. Robinson, 99–134. Tucson: University of Arizona Press.

————. 2016. "Thinking Otherwise Across Global Wests: Issue of Mobility and Feminist Critical Regionalism." *Occasion: Interdisciplinary Studies in the Humanities* 10 (1): 1–18.

Cox, John Harrington. 1925. *Folk-Songs of the South*. Cambridge: Harvard University Press.

Cumbow, Robert C. 2009. "'Somebody's Fiddle': Traditional Music in 'The Searchers.'" *Parallax View*, December 14, 2009. https://parallax-view.org/2009/12/14/somebodys-fiddle-traditional-music-in-the-searchers/.

Daniels, William R. 1985. *The American 45 and 78 RPM Record Dating Guide, 1940–1959.* Westport, CT: Greenwood Press.

Danker, Frederick E. 1975. "Johnny Cash." In *Stars of Country Music: Uncle Dave Macon to Johnny Rodríguez*, edited by Bill C. Malone and Judith McCulloh, 289–308. Champaign: University of Illinois Press.

Dary, David. 1989. *Cowboy Culture.* Lawrence: University Press of Kansas.

———. 1995. *Seeking Pleasure in the Old West.* Lawrence: University Press of Kansas.

Daugherty, Tracy. 2023. *Larry McMurtry: A Life.* New York: St. Martin's Press. Kindle.

Davis, Graham. 1991. *The Irish in Britain, 1815–1914.* London: Gill & Macmillan.

———. 2002. *Land!: Irish Pioneers in Mexican and Revolutionary Texas.* College Station: Texas A&M University Press.

Davis, Laura June. 2012. "Lorena." *The Civil War Monitor*, May 21, 2012. https://www.civilwarmonitor.com/blogs/lorena.

Davis, Steven L. 2004. *Texas Literary Outlaws: Six Writers in the Sixties and Beyond.* Fort Worth: Texas Christian University Press.

———. 2009. *J. Frank Dobie: A Liberated Mind.* Austin: University of Texas Press.

Dawson, Melanie, and Meredith L. Goldsmith. 2018. *American Literary History and the Turn to Modernity.* Gainesville: University Press of Florida.

De Caro, Frank, and Rosan Augusta Jordan. 2004. *Re-Situating Folklore: Folk Contexts in 20th-Century Literature and Art.* Knoxville: University of Tennessee Press.

De León, Arnoldo. 1983. *They Called Them Greasers: Anglo Attitudes Toward Mexicans in Texas, 1821–1900.* Austin: University of Texas Press.

———. 2014. "'Vamos pa' Kiansis': Tejanos in the Nineteenth-Century Cattle Drives." *Journal of South Texas* 27 (2): 6–21.

Diekman, Diane. 2012. *Twentieth Century Drifter: The Life of Marty Robbins.* Champaign: University of Illinois Press.

Dobie, J. Frank. 1929. *A Vaquero of the Brush Country.* Austin: University of Texas Press.

———. 1941. *The Longhorns.* New York: Grosett and Dunlap.

Domino, Anna, vocalist. 1999. "Laredo." Track 5 on Snakefarm, *Songs from My Funeral.* LTMCD 2539, compact disc.

———. 2005. "Naomi Wise, 1807." In *The Rose and the Briar: Death, Love and Liberty in the American Ballad*, edited by Sean Wilentz and Greil Marcus, 69–80, 361–362. New York: W. W. Norton.

Dundes, Alan. 1965. "The Study of Folklore in Literature and Culture: Identification and Interpretation." *Journal of American Folklore* 78 (2): 136–142.

Dyer, Geoff. 2020. "Ranging Across Texas: On First Looking into Larry McMurtry's *Lonesome Dove.*" *Times Literary Supplement*, July 17, 2020. https://www.the-tls.co.uk/articles/geoff-dyer-lonesome-dove-essay/.

Emmons, David M. 2010. *Beyond the Pale: The Irish in the West, 1845–1910*. University of Oklahoma Press, 2010.

Farley, Tom. 2005. "Canyons, Cowboys, and Cash: Walt Whitman's American West." *Mickle Street Review: An Electronic Journal of Whitman and American Studies*. http://msr -archives.rutgers.edu/archives/Issue%201718/pages/Scholarship/Farley.htm.

Felski, Rita. 2021. "Recognizing Class." *New Literary History* 52 (1): 95–117.

Fenster, Mark. 1989. "Preparing the Audience, Informing the Performers: John A. Lomax and Cowboys Songs and Other Frontier Ballads." *American Music* 7 (3): 260–277.

Fife, Austin E., and Alta S. Fife. 1966a. "Introduction." In *Songs of the Cowboys*, edited by Austin E. Fife and Alta S. Fife, 3–10. New York: Clarkson N. Potter.

———. 1966b. "Variants, Commentary, Notes and Lexicon." In *Songs of the Cowboys*, edited by Austin E. Fife and Alta S. Fife, various pages. New York: Clarkson N. Potter.

Filene, Benjamim. 1991. "'Our Singing Country': John and Alan Lomax, Leadbelly, and the Construction of an American Past." *American Quarterly* 43 (4): 602–624.

Flores, Richard. 2002. *Remembering the Alamo: Memory, Modernity, and the Master Symbol.* Austin: University of Texas Press.

Foster, Robert J. 2002. "Bargains with Modernity in Papua New Guinea and Elsewhere." In *Critically Modern: Alternatives, Alterities, Anthropologies*, edited by Bruce M. Knauft, 57–81. Bloomington: Indiana University Press.

Frantz, Joe B. 1967. "Cowboy Philosophy." In *The Frontier Re-examined*, edited by John Francis McDermott, 162–185. Urbana: University of Illinois Press.

Frye, Steven. 2017. *Understanding Larry McMurtry*. University of South Carolina Press.

Gard, Wayne. 1954. *The Chisholm Trail*. University of Oklahoma Press.

Gardner, Mark L. 2005. "Introduction: A Tribute to Jack Thorp." In *Songs of the Cowboys*, edited by Mark L. Gardner, 11–24. Santa Fe: Museum of New Mexico Press.

Getschow, George. 2023. *Pastures of the Empty Page: Fellow Writers on the Life and Legacy of Larry McMurtry*. Austin: University of Texas Press.

Giddens, Anthony. 1990. *The Consequences of Modernity*. Stanford: Stanford University Press.

Giddens, Anthony, and Christopher Pierson. 1998. *Conversations with Anthony Giddens: Making Sense of Modernity*. Stanford: Stanford University Press.

Gioia Ted. 2005. "The Big Roundup: John Lomax Roamed the West, Collecting Classic Songs from the Cowboy Era." *American Scholar* 74 (2): 101–111.

Goldstein, Kenneth S. 1959. "Still More of 'The Unfortunate Rake' and His Family." *Western Folklore* 18 (3): 35–38.

———, ed. 1960. "The Unfortunate Rake: A Study in the Evolution of a Ballad." Folkway Records, Album FS 3805. Liner notes: 1–8.

Gómez-Quiñones, Juan. 1973. *Fifth and Grande Vista*. New York: Coleción Mensaje.

González, Jovita. 1927. "The Folklore of the Texas-Mexican Vaquero." In *Texas and Southwestern Lore*, edited by J. Frank Dobie, 7–22. No. 7 of *Publications of the Texas Folklore Society*. Dallas: Southern Methodist University Press.

———. 1932. "Among My People." In *Tone the Bell* Easy, edited by J. Frank Dobie, 99–108. No. 10 of *Publications of the Texas Folklore Society*. Dallas: Southern Methodist University Press.

González, Jovita, and Eve Raleigh. 1996. *Caballero: A Historical Novel*. College Station: Texas A&M University Press.

———. 1989. "Lonesome Dove: Butch and Sundance go on a Cattle Drive." In *Taking Stock: A Larry McMurtry Casebook*, edited by Clay Reynolds, 311–317. Dallas: Southern Methodist University Press.

Graham, Don. 2002. *Kings of Texas: The 150-Year Saga of an American Ranching Empire*. New York: Wiley.

———. 2018. *Giant: Elizabeth Taylor, Rock Hudson, James Dean, Edna Ferber, and the Making of a Legendary American Film*. New York: St. Martin's Press.

Graham, Don, James W. Lee, and William T. Pilkington, eds. 1983. *The Texas Literary Tradition: Fiction, Folklore, History*. Austin: College of Liberal Arts, University of Texas at Austin.

Gray, Richard. 2000. *Southern Aberrations: Writers of the American South and the Problems of Regionalism*. Louisiana State University Press.

Green, Douglas B. 2002. *Singing in the Saddle: The History of the Singing Cowboy*. Nashville: Vanderbilt University Press.

Griffin, Patrick. 2006. "The Two Migrations Myth, the Scotch-Irish, and Irish-American Experience." In *Re-Imagining Ireland*, edited by A.H. Wyndham, 244–248. Charlottesville: University of Virginia Press.

Gummere, Francis Barton, 1901. *The Beginnings of Poetry*. New York: Macmillan.

Hagan, William T. 2007. *Charles Goodnight: Father of the Texas Panhandle*. Norman: University of Oklahoma Press.

Hand, Wayland. 1955. "Where are 'The Streets of Laredo'?: The Developmental History of an American Cowboy Ballad." Translated by Elizabeth Schneewind. Appeared originally as "Wo sind die Strassen von Laredo: Die Entwicklungsgeschichte einer amerikanischen Cowboy Ballade" In *Festschrift für Will-Erich Peuckert*, edited by Helmut Dölker, 144–161. Berlin: Erich Schmidt Verlag.

———. 1958. "The Cowboy's Lament." *Western Folklore* 17 (3): 200–205.

Harris, Mark. (1956) 1984a. *Bang the Drum Slowly*. Lincoln: University of Nebraska Press.

Hinojosa, Gilberto M. 1983. *Borderlands Town in Transition: Laredo, 1755–1870*. College Station: Texas A&M University Press.

Hinojosa, Rolando. 1978. *Korean Love Songs*. Berkeley: Editorial Justa Publications.

Hirsch, Jerrold. 1992. "Modernity, Nostalgia, and Southern Folklore Studies: The Case of John Lomax." *The Journal of American Folklore* 105:183–207.

———. 1998. "Review of Nolan Porterfield, *The Last Cavalier: The Life and Times of John A. Lomax, 1867–1948*." *Western Historical Quarterly* 29: 530–531.

Hoig, Stan. 2005. *The Sand Creek Massacre*. Norman: University of Oklahoma Press.

Hoy, Jim. 2010. "Maynard's Poetry." In *Cowboy's Lament: A Life on the Open Range*, by Frank Maynard. Edited by Jim Hoy, 135–137. Lubbock: Texas Tech University Press.

Hudson Wilson M. 1976. "Bedichek, Roy (1878–1959)." *Handbook of Texas*. https://www .tshaonline.org/handbook/entries/bedichek-roy

Irving, John. 2015. *Avenue of Mysteries*. New York: Simon & Schuster.

Iverson, Peter. 1994. *When Indians Became Cowboys: Native Peoples and Cattle Ranching in the American West*. Norman: University of Oklahoma Press.

Ives, Burl. 1941. "Streets of Laredo." YouTube video, 2:18, https://www.youtube.com/watch ?v=-poDnGAYRhE.

———. 1948. *The Wayfaring Stranger*. New York: Whittlesey House.

Jameson, Elizabeth. 1984. "Women as Workers, Women as Civilizers: True Womanhood in the American West." *Frontiers: A Journal of Women Studies*. Special issue, *Women on the Western Frontier* 7: 1–8.

Jameson, Fredric. 1984. "Postmodernism, Or the Cultural Logic of Late Capitalism." *New Left Review* 146: 59–92.

———. 2013. *A Singular Modernity: Essays on the Ontology of the Present*. New York: Verso.

Jenkins, Richard. 2019. "The Unfortunate Rake's Progress: A Case Study of the Construction of Folklore by Collectors and Scholars." *Folklore* 130 (2): 111–132.

Johnston, Bret Anthony. 2004. *Corpus Christi*. New York: Random House.

Jordan, Terry. 1981. *Trails to Texas: Southern Roots of Western Cattle Ranching*. Lincoln: University of Nebraska Press.

Joyce, P.W. 1909. *Old Irish Folk-Music and Songs*. London: Longmans, Green and Co.

Kermode, Frank. 1967. *The Sense of an Ending: Studies in the Theory of Fiction*. New York: Oxford University Press.

Knauft, Bruce M., ed. 2002. *Critically Modern: Alternatives, Alterities, Anthropologies*. Indiana University Press.

Knowlton, Christopher. 2017. *Cattle Kingdom: The Hidden History of the Cowboy West*. New York: Houghton-Mifflin.

Lambert, Neal. 1970. "Owen Wister's *Lin McLean:* The Failure of the Vernacular Hero." *Western American Literature* 5 (3): 219–232.

Lause, Mark A. 2017. *The Great Cowboy Strike: Bullets, Ballots, and Class Conflict in the American West*. London: Verso.

Leslie, John Kenneth. 1957. "Un Romance español en Mexico y dos canciones de los vaqueros norteamericanos: la influencia del tema 'no me entierren en sagrado.'" *Revista de Dialectología y Tradiciones Populares* 13 (3): 286–298.

Lich, Lera Patrick Tyler. 1987. *Larry McMurtry's Texas: Evolution of a Myth*. Austin: Eakin Press.

Limerick, Patricia Nelson, Clyde A. Milner, and Charles A. Rankin. 1991. Eds. *Trails: Toward a New Western History*. Lawrence: University Press of Kansas.

Limón, José E. 1981. "Américo Paredes: A Man from the Border." *Revista Chicano-Riquena* 8: 1–5.

———. 1983. "A 'Southern Renaissance' for Texas Letters." *The Texas Observer* (October 28, 1983): 20–23. A somewhat different version of this essay also appears in *The Texas Literary Tradition: Fiction, Folklore History*, edited by Don Graham, James W. Lee, and William T. Pilkington. Austin: College of Liberal Arts, University of Texas at Austin, (1983): 145–151. Reprinted in *Range Wars*, edited by Craig Clifford and Tom Pilkington. Dallas: SMU Press (1989), 59–68.

———. 1991. "Representation, Ethnicity, and the Precursory Ethnography: Notes of a Native Anthropologist" In *Recapturing Anthropology: Working in the Present*, edited by Richard Fox, 115–135. Santa Fe: School of American Research.

———. 1992. *Mexican Ballads, Chicano Poems: History and Influence in Mexican America Social Poetry*. Oakland: University of California Press.

———. 1993. "Américo Paredes and the Mexican Ballad: The Creative Anthropological Text as Social Critique." In *Creativity: Self and Society*, edited by Renato Rosaldo, Kirin Narayan, and Smadar Lavie, 184–210. Ithaca: Cornell University Press.

———. 1994. *Dancing with the Devil: Society and Cultural Poetics in Mexican-American South Texas*. Madison: University of Wisconsin Press.

———. 1998. *American Encounters: Greater Mexico, the United States, and the Erotics of Culture*. Boston: Beacon Press.

———. 2004. "Greater Mexico, Modernism and New York: Miguel Covarrubias and José Limón." In *The Covarrubias Circle: Nickolas Muray's Collection of Twentieth-Century Mexican Art*, edited by Kurt Heinzleman, 83–102. Austin: University of Texas Press.

———. 2012. *Américo Paredes: Culture and Critique*. Austin: University of Texas Press.

———. 2020. "From the Streets of Laredo to the Palo Duro Canyon and Other Texas Stories." Facebook, October 29, 2020. https://www.facebook.com/watch/?v=584043092341899.

———. 2022a. "Gone to Texas: Laura Krey, the Southern Renaissance, and Greater Mexico." *Journal of the American Studies Association of Texas* 51: 8–24.

———. 2022b. "Where, Indeed, Are the Streets of Laredo?" Paper presented at the Annual Conference of the Western States Folklore Society, April 8, 2022. Los Angeles: University of Southern California.

Limón, José E., and Mary Jane Young. 1986. "Frontiers, Settlements and Development in Folklore Studies." *Annual Reviews in Anthropology* 15: 437–460.

Livingston, Jay, and Ray Evans. 1949. "The Streets of Laredo (A New Original Song)." New York: Famous Music Corp.

Lodewick, Kenneth. 1955. "'The Unfortunate Rake' and His Descendants." *Western Folklore* 14 (2): 98–109.

Logsdon, Guy. 1989. *"The Whorehouse Bells Were Ringing" and Other Cowboys Songs*. Urbana: University of Illinois Press.

Lomax, Alan. 1960. *The Folk Songs of North America*. New York: Doubleday and Co.

Lomax, John A., ed. 1910. *Cowboy Songs and Other Frontier Ballads*. New York: Sturgis & Walton Co.

———. 1947. *Adventures of a Ballad Hunter*. New York: Macmillan.

———. 1948. *Lomax, John Avery, family papers*. Briscoe Center for American History. University of Texas at Austin.

Lomax, John A., and Alan Lomax, eds. 1966 (1947). *Folk Song U.S.A.* New York: The New American Library.

Löwy, Michael, and Robert Sayre. 2002 *Romanticism Against the Tide of Modernity*. Translated by Catherine Porter. Durham: Duke University Press.

Maffett, George West, and Lafe Merritt. 1886. "The Cowboy's Lament." *Cheyenne Transporter* 7 (21): 1.

Major, Mabel. 1932. "British Ballads of Texas." In *Tone the Bell Easy*, edited by J. Frank Dobie, 131–168. No. 10 of *Publications of the Texas Folklore Society*. Dallas: Southern Methodist University Press.

Marcus, Greil. 2005. "Envoi." In *The Rose and the Briar: Death, Love and Liberty in the American Ballad*, edited by Sean Wilentz and Greil Marcus, 349–354. New York: W. W. Norton & Co.

Martínez, Monica Muñoz. 2018. *The Injustice Never Leaves You: Anti-Mexican Violence in Texas*. Cambridge: Harvard University Press.

Maynard, Frank. 2010. *Cowboy's Lament: A Life on the Open Range*, edited by Jim Hoy. Lubbock: Texas Tech University Press.

McConnell, Scott A. 2017. "100 Seconds of Greatness: Analyzing the First Scene of John Ford's *The Searchers*."MovieMaker, https://www.moviemaker.com/archives/moviemaking/the-searchers-scene-analysis-video/

McGuane, Thomas. 1999. *Some Horses*. Guilford, CT: Lyons Press.

McMurtry, Larry. 1961. *Horseman, Pass By*. New York: Simon & Schuster.

———. 1963. *Leaving Cheyenne*. New York: Simon & Schuster.

———. 1966. *The Last Picture Show*. New York: Dial Press.

———. 1968. *In a Narrow Grave*. Austin: Encino Press.

———. 1970. *Moving On*. New York: Simon & Schuster.

———. 1972. *All My Friends are Going to be Strangers*. New York: Simon & Schuster.

———. 1975. *Terms of Endearment*. New York: Simon & Schuster.

———. 1977. "Unfinished Women." *Texas Monthly* 5 (106): 160–166.

———. 1978. *Somebody's Darling*. New York: Simon & Schuster.

———.1981. "Ever a Bridegroom: Reflections of the Failure of Texas Literature." *The Texas Observer* (October): 12–15.

———. 1982. *Cadillac Jack*. New York: Simon & Schuster.

———. 1983. *Desert Rose*. New York: Simon & Schuster.

———. 1985. *Lonesome Dove*. New York: Simon & Schuster.

———. 1987. *Film Flam: Essays on Hollywood*. New York: Simon & Schuster.

———. 1990. "How the West Was Won or Lost." *The New Republic*, October 22, 1990, 32–38.

——— .1993. *Streets of Laredo*. New York: Simon & Schuster.

——— .1995. *Dead Man's Walk*. New York: Simon & Schuster.

——— .1997. *Comanche Moon*. New York: Simon & Schuster, 1997.

——— .1999. *Walter Benjamin at the Dairy Queen: Reflections at Sixty and Beyond*. New York: Simon & Schuster, 1999.

———. 2001. *Paradise*. New York: Simon & Schuster.

———. 2009. *Literary Life: A Second Memoir*. Simon & Schuster.

McMurtry, Larry, and Peter Bogdonavich. 1972a. *The Streets of Laredo: A Scenario*. Unpublished.

———. 1972b. *The Streets of Laredo: Original Screenplay*. Unpublished.

Mendoza, Louis Gerard. 2001. *Historia: The Literary Making of Chicana & Chicano History*. College Station: Texas A&M University Press.

Miller, Kerby A. 1985. *Emigrants and Exiles: Ireland and the Irish Exodus to North America*. New York: Oxford University Press.

Mills, C. Wright. 1951. *White Collar: The American Middle Class*. New York: Oxford University Press.

Mintz, Sidney W. 1985. *Sweetness and Power: The Place of Sugar in Modern History*. New York: Penguin Books.

Mitchell, Lee Clark. 2018. *Late Westerns: The Persistence of a Genre*. Lincoln: University of Nebraska Press.

Montejano, David. 1987. *Anglos and Mexicans in the Making of Texas, 1836–1986*. University of Texas Press.

———. 2012. "Mexican Merchants and Teamsters on the Texas Cotton Road." In *Mexico and Mexicans in the Making of the United States*, edited by John Tutino, 141–170. Austin: University of Texas Press.

Moon, Freda. 2014. "In New Mexico, on the Cowboy Trail of Jack Thorp." *New York Times*, September 28, 2014. https://www.nytimes.com/2014/09/28/travel/in-new-mexico-on -the-cowboy-trail-of-jack-thorp.html.

Moore, Jacqueline M. 2010. *Cowboys and Cattlemen: Class and Masculinities on the Texas Frontier*. New York University Press.

Narváez, Peter, and Martin Laba. 1986. *Media Sense: The Folklore-Popular Culture Continuum*. Bowling Green: Bowling Green State University Press.

Nickell, Pat Smith. 1999. "Postmodern Aspects in Larry McMurtry's *Lonesome Dove*, *Streets of Laredo*, *Dead Man's Walk*, and *Comanche Moon*." PhD diss., Texas Tech University.

O'Connor, Alan. 1989. *Raymond Williams: Writing, Culture, Politics*. New York: Basil Blackwell.

Oklahoma Historical Society. 1886. "Cheyenne Transporter." *The Gateway to Oklahoma History*. https://gateway.okhistory.org/explore/collections/DARLIN/.

Oring, Elliot. 2022. "Four Laws of Folklore." *Western Folklore* 81 (1): 51–73.

Ossana, Diana. 2023. "Stirring the Memories." In *Pastures of the Empty Page: Fellow Writers on the Life and Legacy of Larry McMurtry*. Edited by George Getschow, 147–161. Austin: University of Texas Press.

Owen, William A. 1969. *Three Friends: Roy Bedichek, J. Frank Dobie, Walter Prescott Webb*. Garden City, NY: Doubleday Publishers

Paredes, Américo. 1958. *"With His Pistol in His Hand": A Border Ballad and its Hero*. Austin: University of Texas Press.

———. 1963. "El cowboy norteamericano en el folklore y la literatura." *Cuadernos Del Instituto Nacional de Antropologia* 4: 227–240.

———. 1972. "El Concepto de la 'Medula Emotiva' Aplicado al Corrido Mexicano." *Folklore Americano* 17: 139–176. Reprinted in English translation as Paredes, 1993.

———. 1976. *A Texas-Mexican Cancionero: Folksongs of the Lower Border*. Champaign: University of Illinois Press.

———. 1977. "On Ethnographic Work among Minority Groups." *New Scholar* 6: 1–32. Reprinted in *Folklore and Culture on the Texas-Mexican Border*, edited by Richard Bauman (1993), 73–112. Austin: University of Texas at Austin, Center for Mexican American Studies.

———. 1978. "The Problem of Identity in a Changing Culture: Popular Expressions of Culture Conflict along the Lower Rio Grande Border." In *Views across the Border: The United States and Mexico*. Edited by Stanley Ross, 68–94. Albuquerque: University of New Mexico Press.

———. 1993. "The Concept of the Emotional Core Applied to the Mexican *Corrido* 'Benjamín Agumedo'" in *Folklore and Culture on the Texas-Mexican Border*, edited by Richard Bauman, 143–176. Austin: University of Texas at Austin, Center for Mexican American Studies. English translation of Paredes, 1972.

Peart, Andrew. 2015. "'The Abstract Pathos of Song': Carl Sandburg, John Lomax, and the Modernist Revival of Folksong." *New Literary History* 46 (4): 691–714.

Peña, Elaine A. 2020. *¡Viva George: Celebrating Washington's Birthday at the US-Mexico Border*. Austin: University of Texas Press.

Perritt, Henry H. Jr. 2019. "Rise and Fall of the Cowboy: Technology, Law, and Creative Destruction in the Industrialization of the Food Industry." *North Dakota Law Review* 94 (2): 361–427.

Piñón, Fernando. 2015. *Searching for America in the Streets of Laredo: The Mexican American Experience in the Anglo American Narrative*. Mexico, D.F.: Centro de Estudios Sociales Antonio Gramsci A.C.

Porterfield, Nolan. 1996. *The Last Cavalier: The Life and Times of John A. Lomax, 1867–1948*. Urbana: University of Illinois Press.

Reilly, John M. 2000. *Larry McMurtry: A Critical Companion*. Westport, CT: Greenwood Press.

Reynolds, Clay. 1989. "Come Home, Larry: All is Forgiven. A Native Son's Search for Identity." In *Taking Stock: A Larry McMurtry Casebook*, edited by Clay Reynolds. 280–288. Dallas: Southern Methodist University Press.

Robinson, Forrest G. 1997a. "Clio Bereft of Calliope: Literature and the New Western History." *The New Western History: The Territory Ahead*, edited by Forrest G. Robinson, 61–98. University of Arizona Press.

———, ed. 1997b. *The New Western History: The Territory Ahead*. University of Arizona Press.

Rodríguez, Richard. 1981. *Hunger of Memory: The Education of Richard Rodríguez*. Boston: David R. Godine.

Rodríguez, Nestor. 2023. *Capitalism and Migration: The Rise of Hegemony in the World-System*. Berlin: Springer Nature.

Rosaldo, Renato. 1989. *Culture and Truth: The Remaking of Social Analysis*. Boston: Beacon Press.

Rosenberg, Neil V. 1986. "Big Fish, Small Pond: Country Musicians and Their Markets." *Media Sense: The Folklore-Popular Culture Continuum*, edited by Peter Narváez and Martin Laba, 149–166. Bowling Green: Bowling Green State University Press.

Sager, Robin C. 2015. "Capitalist Women in Central Texas, 1865–1880: 'A Ready Market.'" In *Texas Women: Their Histories, Their Lives*, edited by Elizabeth Turner Hayes, Stephanie Cole, and Rebecca Sharpless, 128–145. Athens, GA: University of Georgia Press.

Saldívar, Ramon. 2006. *The Borderlands of Culture: Américo Paredes and the Transnational Imaginary*. Durham: Duke University Press.

Salinas, Sonia. 2005. "Américo Paredes: Uncovering the Multi-Faceted Life of the Scholar." MA thesis. University of Texas-Rio Grande Valley.

Sawin, Patricia, and Rosemary Lévy Zumwalt, eds. 2020. *Folklore in the United States and Canada: An Institutional History*. Bloomington: Indiana University Press.

Scott, David. 2004. *Conscripts of Modernity: The Tragedy of Colonial Enlightenment*. Durham: Duke University Press.

Segura, Olga. 2019. "Why the Writer, Richard Rodríguez, Refuses to be put into a Box." *American Magazine*, January 25, 2019. https://www.americamagazine.org/arts-culture /2019/01/25/why-writer-richard-rodriguez-refuses-be-put-box.

Sennett, Richard. 2008. *The Craftsman*. New Haven: Yale University Press.

Sharp, Cecil J. 1932. *English Folk Songs from the Southern Appalachians*. Edited by Maud Karpekes. London: Oxford University Press.

Slatta, Richard W. 1990. *Cowboys of the Americas: The Realties of Cowboy Life*. New Haven: Yale University Press.

Slowik, Michael. 2012. "Capturing the American Past: The Cowboy Song and the Archive." *The Journal of American Popular Culture*. 35 (3): 207–218.

Standage, Tom. 2007. *The Victorian Internet: The Remarkable Story of the Telegraph and the Nineteenth Century's On-Line Pioneers*. New York: Walker.

Stanley, David, and Elaine Thatcher, eds. 2000. *Cowboy Poets & Cowboy Poetry*. Urbana: University of Illinois Press.

Stevens, Wallace. 1954. "An Ordinary Evening in New Haven." In *The Collected Poems of Wallace Stevens*. New York: Alfred A. Knopf.

Stoeltje, Beverly J. 2012. "Paredes and the Hero: The North American Cowboy Revisited." *Journal of American Folklore* 125 (495): 45–68.

Tatum, Stephen. 1994. "The Heart of the Wise is in the House of Mourning." In *Eye on the Future: Popular Culture Scholarship into the Twenty-First Century*, edited by Marilyn F. Motz, John G. Nachbar, Michael T. Marsden, and Ronald J. Ambrosetti, 57–72. Bowling Green: Bowling Green State University Press.

———.1997. "The Problem of the 'Popular' on the New Western History." In *The New Western History: The Territory Ahead*, edited by Forrest G. Robinson, 153–190. Tucson: University of Arizona Press.

Texas State Library and Archives Commission. 2023. "The Railroads come to Texas." https://www.tsl.texas.gov/exhibits/railroad/beginnings/page2.html

Thompson, E. P. 1971. "The Moral Economy of the English Crowd in the Eighteenth Century." *Past and Present* 50: 76–136.

Thompson, Jerry. 2017. *Tejano Tiger: José de los Santos Benavides and the Texas-Mexico Borderlands, 1823–1891*. Fort Worth: Texas Christian University Press.

Thorp, N. Howard (Jack). 1908. *Songs of the Cowboys*. Albuquerque: New Print Shop.

———. 1921. *Songs of the Cowboys*. New York: Houghton- Mifflin.

———. 1945. *Pardner of the Wind*. The Claxton Printers.

———. 1966a. *Songs of the Cowboys*. Edited by Austin E. Fife and Alta S. Fife. New York: Clarkson N. Potter.

———. 1966b. "Banjo in the Cow Camps." In *Songs of the Cowboys*, edited by Austin E. Fife and Alta S. Fife, 11–27. New York: Clarkson N. Potter. Originally appeared in 1940 in *Atlantic Monthly* 167 (2): 195–203.

———. 2005. *Songs of the Cowboys*, edited by Mark L. Gardner. Santa Fe: Museum of New Mexico Press.

Tinsley, Jim Bob. 2007. *He Was Singin' This Song*. Anaheim, CA: Centerstream Publishers.

Tomlinson, John. 1999. *Globalization and Culture*. Chicago: University of Chicago Press.

Trachtenberg, Alan. 1982. *The Incorporation of America: Culture and Society in the Gilded Age*. New York: Hill and Wang.

Trouillot, Michel-Rolph. 1991. "Anthropology and the Savage Slot: The Poetics and Politics of Otherness." In *Recapturing Anthropology: Working in the Present*, edited by Richard G. Fox, 17–44. N.p.: School of American Research Press.

———. 2002. "The Otherwise Modern: Caribbean Lessons from the Savage Slot." In *Critically Modern: Alternatives, Alterities, Anthropologies*, edited by Bruce M. Knauft, 220–24. Bloomington: Indiana University Press.

Turner, Elizabeth Hayes, Stephanie Cole, and Rebecca Sharpless, eds. 2015. *Texas Women: Their Histories, Their Lives*. Athens: U of Georgia Press.

Turner, Victor. 1982. *From Ritual to Theater: The Human Seriousness of Play.* New York: PAJ Publications.

Valerio-Jiménez, Omar S. 2013. *River of Hope: Forging Identity and Nation in the Rio Grande Borderlands.* Durham: Duke University.

Villanueva, Tino. 1995. *Scene from the Movie* GIANT. CT. Willimantic, CT.: Curbstone Press.

Von Lintel, Amy. 2020. *Georgia O'Keeffe's Wartime Texas Letters.* College Station: Texas A&M University Press.

Wallerstein, Immanuel. 1980. *The Modern World System.* Vol.1. New York: Academic Press.

Webb, Walter Prescott. 1935. *The Texas Rangers: A Century of Frontier Defense.* Austin: University of Texas Press.

Welch, Robert, and Bruce Stewart, eds. 1996. "Stage Irishman." In *Oxford Companion to Irish Literature*, 534–535. Oxford: Oxford University Press.

West, John O. 1967. "Jack Thorp and John Lomax: Oral or Written Transmission?" *Western Folklore* 26 (2): 113–118.

Whipp. Leslie T. 1990. "Owen Wister: Wyoming's Influential Realist and Craftsman." *Great Plains Quarterly* 10 (4): 245–259.

White, Hayden. 1973. *Metahistory: The Historical Imagination in Nineteenth-Century Europe.* Baltimore: Johns Hopkins University Press.

White, John I. 1989. *Git Along Little Dogies: Songs and Songmakers of the American West.* Urbana: University of Illinois Press.

White, Richard. 1991. *"It's Your Misfortune and None of my Own": A New History of the American West.* Norman: University of Oklahoma Press.

———. 2011. *The Transcontinentals and the Making of Modern America.* New York: W.W. Norton.

Whitman, Walt. 2023. *Specimen Days.* Oxford: Oxford University Press.

Wilgus, D. K. 1959. *Anglo-American Folklore Scholarship Since 1898.* New Brunswick, NJ. Rutgers University Press.

———. 1985. "The Aisling and the Cowboy: Some Unnoticed Influences of Irish Vision Poetry on Anglo-American Balladry." *Western Folklore* 44 (4): 255–300.

Williams, Raymond. 1977. *Marxism and Literature.* New York: Oxford University Press.

Williams, William Carlos. 1986. *The Collected Poems of William Carlos Williams: Volume 1 (1909–1939).* New York: New Directions.

Winick, Stephen. 2014. "The Two First 'Folk-Lore' Columns." *Folklife Today.* https://blogs.loc.gov/folklife/2014/08/the-two-first-folk-lore-columns/?loclr=blogflt

Wister, Owen. 1897. *Lin McLean.* New York: A.L. Burt.

Wright, Lawrence. 2018. *God Save Texas: A Journey into the Soul of the Lone Star State.* New York: Vintage.

Wright, Will. 2001. *The Wild West: The Mythic Cowboy and Social Theory.* London: Sage Publications.

Yellow Bird, Michael. 2004. "Cowboys and Indians: Toys of Genocide, Icons of American Colonialism." *Wicazo Sa Review* 19 (2): 33–48.

Zattiero, Joanna Ray. 2020. "Early Cowboy Songs and Musical Culture in the American West, 1870–1920." PhD Dissertation. Austin: University of Texas.

Zumwalt, Rosemary Lévy. 1988. *American Folklore Scholarship: A Dialogue of Dissent.* Bloomington: Indiana University Press.

———. 2020. "The 'Great Team' of American Folklorists: Characters Large in Life and Grand in Plans." In *Folklore in the United States and Canada: An Institutional History*, edited by Patricia Sawin and Rosemary Lévy Zumwalt, 61–75. Bloomington: Indiana University Press.

Index

Page numbers in italics refer to illustrations.

Abbott, E. C. "Teddy Blue," 15–16
Abernathy, R. B., 13
Abilene, Kansas, 18, 68, 73
Abrahams, Roger D., 21, 104, 105, 110–11, 113
Adams, John A., 35, 44–45, 46
Adobe Walls, Texas, 132, 135, 181n12
African Americans: cowboys, 64–65; folksong, 114–15
agriculture: agrarian societies, 115–16; agribusiness, 41, 43; agricultural modernity, 18, 41–42; cash crop farming, 9; Southern Agrarians, 21, 114–15, 116; white agricultural workers, 53–54. *See also* cattle ranching
Alamo, Texas, 35, 49, 132, 181n11
alcohol use: and masculinity, 60; saloons, 69–70, 72
alienation in modernity, 57–58, 65, 66
Allen, Esther, 124
Allen, Rex, 120
Allmendinger, Blake, 16, 61

Alonzo, Armando C., 47, 66
American Folklore Society, 114
American West. *See* New Western history
Anglo identities, 8–9; early settlers, 34; in Republic of Texas, 35–36; and violence, 64–65
Anglo-Mexican inter-racial relationships, 9
Appalachian South, 30, 37
Archer City, Texas, 125, 158
Athenæum (journal), 78
Austin, Stephen F., 32
author's experiences, 5–11; academic education and career, 10–11; family ethnic background, xiii, 167n1
author's methodology, 5, 16–23, 165–66
Autry, Gene, 120
Avenue of the Mysteries (Irving), 122

"Bad Girl's Lament, The," 25–26, 29–30, 37–38, 79–80, 150
Baez, Joan, 2, 21, 121
Ballad of Buster Scruggs, The (film), 1

balladry, 13; as poetic form, 78–79; rhyme
    schemes and meters, 71; Spanish, 60;
    traditional ballads, 37–39
Bang the Drum Slowly (Harris), 122
"Banjo in the Cowcamps" (Thorp), 93
Barrera, Cordelia, xv, 153
Barry, Phillips, 27, 28, 29
Barsness, John, 68
Bauman, Richard, 111
Bean, Judge Roy, 147
Bedichek, Roy, *100,* 101, 106, 177n20
Bee, Hamilton, 43
Ben-Amos, Dan, 76–77
Benavides, Basilio, 43
Benavides, José de los Santos, 43–44, 46
Benavides, Refugio, 44
Bendix, Regina, 77, 89, 111, 113
Benjamin, Walter, 158
Bennett, Patrick, 129, 135–36
Bill Jones of Paradise Valley, Oklahoma
    (Callison), 94
Black Americans. *See* African Americans
Bogdanovich, Peter, 22–23, 129–30
Bowman, Eric, xiii–xiv
Bowman, Timothy, 50
"Bury Me Not on the Lone Prairie," 101
Busby, Mark, 124, 128, 129, 138, 139, 152
Butte, Montana, 29

Cabañuelas (Cantú), 7
Cadillac Jack (McMurtry), 128–29
Callison, John J., 79, 83–84, 94, 105
Campbell, Neil, 163
Campbell, Randolph B., 34, 35–36, 40, 53,
    54, 61, 62, 155
Cantú, Norma Elia, 6–7
capitalism: capitalist modernity, 40, 41,
    45, 72, 78, 152, 154–55; corporate
    ranching, 47–48, 49–50, 155–56, 159;
    white capitalist oppression and slavery,
    15, 52–53

Caribbean slavery, 53
Cash, Johnny, 2, 22, 118
Catholic Irish immigrants, 36–37, 39. *See
    also* Irish immigrants
Cat on a Hot Tin Roof (Williams), 162
cattle drives, 48, 50, 52, 55, 68, 70,
    172–73n11. *See also Lonesome Dove*
    (McMurtry)
cattle ranching, 9, 38; cattle economy
    (1865–1890), 47–48; cattle trails, *48;*
    corporate ranching, 47–48, 49–50,
    155–56, 159; Irish immigrants, 34–35;
    ranches as family structures, 66
Cattle Trail, The (Lomax), 105
Cavazos, Lauro, 9
Cheyenne Transporter, The (newspaper),
    106–7
Chisholm Trail, 10, 48, 104–5, 155
Christianity: Catholic immigrants, 36–37,
    39; Protestant values, 70, 72
Clayton, Lawrence, 70–71
Coen brothers, 1
Coffin, Tristam, 110
Colquitt, O. B., 13
Comer, Krista, 156
communitas, 149
Confederate States of America, 18,
    43–44, 130
Corpus Christi, Texas, 7
Cortez, Gregorio, 11–13
cotton production/trade, 43–44, 61
cowboys: Anglo cowboys, 8–9, 38,
    46, 174–75n3; clothing, 70–71; as
    "conscripts of modernity," 55; cowboy
    culture, 56–57; cultural views of,
    62, 66–68; horses, skill with, 60–63;
    masculinity, 60–61; Mexico, appeal of,
    145–46; music and traditional ballads,
    37–39, 68; in popular culture, 15–16,
    174n17; Romanticism/idealized
    views, 12, 19, 57–58, 59, 138;

Romanticism vs. modernity, 13–14, 51–55, 63–66, 108–9, 115–16, 154; Tejano influence, 38; as tragic figures, 127; vaqueros, 8–9

Cowboys and Cattlemen (Moore), 60

"Cow Boys Lament" (Fife 1908), 85–86

"Cowboy's Lament, The": chronology of varying versions, 94–95; in dime novel (Callison 1914), 83–84; Lomax (1910), 87–89, 93–94, 96–103, *98–99, 100*; McMurtry's use of, 127; musical score, 101–2, *102*; Nebraska version, 90, 92–93; poem (1886), 107–9; Thorp's 1908 version vs. Lomax's 1910 version, 89–90, 177n17; Thorp version, 90–93. *See also* "Streets of Laredo" (ballad)

Cowboy Songs and Other Frontier Ballads (Lomax), 87, 95, 114, 115

craftsman, concept of, 63

Darlington, Indian Territory/Oklahoma, 106–7

Darlington Indian Agency, 106

Dary, David, 16, 56, 61–62, 68

Davis, Graham, 30, 34, 36, 38–39

Dawson, Melanie, 115

death as theme, 72, 136, 157, 163

De Caro, Frank, 112

de la Garza, Cayetano, 46

Delory, Michel, 118

Desert Rose, The (McMurtry), 128

Díaz, Porfirio, xvi

"disembedding," 51, 52, 54

"distanciation," 51, 52

Dobie, J. Frank, 21, 58, 64, 112, 116

Dodge City, Kansas, 73, 82, 83

Domino, Anna, 118

Dorson, Richard M., 77

Dundes, Alan, 68–69

"Dying Cowboy, The," 80–82

"Dying Girl's Lament, The," 79

Emerson, Ralph Waldo, 57, 58

Emmons, David M., 30

Eribon, Didier, 67

Farley, Tom, 59

Felski, Rita, 67

feminist perspectives: and balladry, 118; *communitas,* 149; McMurtry's work, 23, 125–29, 131, 134, 138–41, 153, 155–57. *See also* gender roles

Fenster, Mark, 120

Fenton, Leslie, 119, 126

Fife, Alta, 85, 93, 94, 105, 176n9

Fife, Austin, 85, 93, 94, 105, 176n9

Filene, Benjamin, 114

Flores, Richard, 49–50

folklore, 67–68; as academic discipline, 11, 16, 20, 77; authenticity, issues of, 103–6, 111; and folkloristics, 76–77; literary merit of, 68–69; "performance" folklore, 111–12; and poetry, 78–79; "politics of culture," 113; school of "disciplinary coherence," 77, 89, 97, 105, 109–10, 111–12; in tension with modernity, 78; "Texas School," 111

folk music revival (twentieth century), 117

Folksong U.S.A. (Lomax), 109–10

Fonda, Henry, 129, 135

Foster, Robert J., 51, 52

Fraga, Luis, xvi

Frankfurt School, 67

French Polynesia, 160–61

Frontiers (open access publisher), 154

Frye, Steven, 136, 152

funerals: funeral traditions, 157; symbolism of, 149–50

gambling, 60, 69–70, 72, 73, 83

Gard, Wayne, 79

Gardner, Mark L., 94

Gauguin, Paul, 161

gender roles: in British ballads, 26–27; in
    cowboy culture, 64; masculinity, 60–61,
    66, 159; patriarchal structures, 64, 66,
    149, 153, 159; women's roles, 154–57.
    See also feminist perspectives
"ghost dance," 52
Giant (film), 174n17
Giddens, Anthony, 41, 52
G. I. Jive (radio show), 121
"Gilded Age, The," 41
Goldsmith, Meredith L., 115
Goldstein, Kenneth S., 26–28, 30, 79, 150
Gómez-Quiñones, Juan, xvii–xviii
González, Jovita, 66
Goodnight, Charles, 35, 54, 142, 147,
    155–56
Goodnight-Loving Trail, 54
Graham, Don, 139
Green, Douglas B., 120
Grey, Zane, 15
Griffin, Patrick, 30
Grimm brothers, 78
guitars, 3, 74, 118
Gunfighter Ballads and Trail Songs
    (album), 118

Haitian Revolution, 52–53
Hale, Troy, 90, 92, 94, 105
Hand, Wayland: on ballad traditions, 27,
    28, 29, 39; on folklore as discipline, 16,
    20, 77, 89, 111, 116, 119; on Laredo
    as setting, 46, 48; on Maynard's
    composition, 83; on "The Streets of
    Laredo," 1; study published in German,
    95, 170–71n2; on twentieth-century
    ballad versions, 90, 92–93, 94, 105
Hardin, John Wesley, 147
Harris, Mark, 120–23
Hewston, James, 33
Hinojosa, Gilberto, 43
Hinojosa, Rolando, xvii–xviii

Hirsch, Jerrold, 114
Holden, William, 119, 126
Honneth, Axel, 67
Horseman, Pass By (McMurtry), 125–26,
    159
horses, skill with, 60–63
Houston, Texas, 128
Hoy, Jim, 82
Hunt, Alex, xv
Hurston, Zora Neale, 112
hymns and sacred music, 148, 150

In a Narrow Grave (McMurtry), 126–128
Ireland: emigration to North America,
    27–28; folksong roots of "Streets of
    Laredo," 25–27; Irish balladry, 29; Irish
    migration within England, 29
Irish immigrants, 33–34, 171n6; anti-
    Catholic threats to, 36–37; Catholic
    heritage, 39; cattle ranching, 34–35,
    38–39, 79; conflict with Anglos, 36;
    Irish folklore, 39; Irish poetry, 74–75;
    in McMurtry's work, 130–31, 134–35;
    migration within U.S., 30. *See also*
    Scots-Irish immigrants
Irving, John, 120–23
Ives, Burl, 2, 21, 121

Jameson, Elizabeth, 154
Jameson, Fredric, 41
Jefferson, Thomas, 52
Jenkins, Richard, 28, 39
Jordan, Rosan Augusta, 112
Jordan, Terry, 171–72n9
Joyce, P. W., 28

Kermode, Frank, 122–23
kineños, 9, 168–69n13. *See also* vaqueros
King, Richard, 34, 47, 49, 172n10
King Ranch, 40, 48, 174n17
kinship relationships, 8, 66, 71–72

Knauft, Bruce M., 51
Krey, Laura, 115, 116

Laredo, Texas, 72–73; and agricultural
modernity, 41–42; author's childhood
experiences, 6–7; and Chisholm trail,
30; commercial development/
expansion post-Civil War, 42–49;
history of, 30–37; map, *143*; "new
elites," 42; as site of modernity, 146
Last Picture Show, The (film), 129
Last Picture Show, The (McMurtry novel),
125–26
Lead Belly (Huddie William Ledbetter),
115
Leaving Cheyenne (McMurtry), 125–26
Leskov, Nikolay, 158
Limerick, Patricia, 14, 15
liminal spaces, 62–63
Limón, José (dancer), 182n23
Lin McLean (Wister), 84, 94
Logsdon, Guy, 85, 89–90, 114
Lomax, Alan, 2, 68, 109–10
Lomax, John Avery, 2, 3, 5, 20–21, 68, 79,
86–89; and African Americans, 115;
authenticity of, 103–6, 110; *Cowboy
Songs and Other Frontier Ballads*, 87,
95, 114, 115; disciplinary coherence
and authenticity, 112–13; *Folksong
U.S.A.*, 109–10; methodology, 89–90,
96–98, 103; popularity of, 115, 117.
See also "The Cowboy's Lament"
Lonesome Dove (McMurtry): cattle drives,
137–38; gender roles, 140–41;
overview as novel, 22–23, 135–38;
portrayals of women, 129, 136,
138–41; *Streets of Laredo* (film script),
129–35
Lonesome Dove tetralogy (McMurtry),
122–23, 124
L'Overture, Toussaint, 52–53

Loving, Oliver, 54
Lowell, James Russell, 78–79
Löwy, Michael, 57
Lutenski, Emily, xiv, xv

Maffet, George West, 107
Major, Mabel, 37
Maldonado, Idalia, xvi
Matagorda Bay, Texas, 79
Marcus, Greil, 118
Martin, Raymond, 43
Martinez, Ramón, 46
masculinity, 60–61, 66, 159. *See also*
gender roles
Maynard, Frank, 20, 65, 79–84, 94
McCarthy, Cormac, 146
McGloin, James, 33
McKenna, José Luz, xvii
McKenna, William, xvi–xvii
McMullen, John, 33
McMurtry, Hazel, 159–60, 161–62
McMurtry, Jeff, 158, 159–60, 161–62
McMurtry, Larry, 5, 22–23, 120–23; as
essayist, 157–58; Houston novels, 128;
In a Narrow Grave, 126–28; sexism,
146; Thalia novels, 125–26; women,
portrayals of, 125, 126, 128–29, 131,
134, 153, 155–57; youth/family
background, 158–62. *See also Lonesome
Dove* (McMurtry)
McMurtry, Louisa Francis, 159–60
Melville, Herman, 160
Mendoza, Louis Gerard, 121
Merritt, Lafe, 107
Mexican American identities, 5–6
Mexican American Studies, xiv
Mexican stereotypes, 181n10
Michener, James, 160
Midnight Cowboy (film), 128
Miller, Kerby A., 27, 30
Mills, C. Wright, 63

miners, 44, 61
modernity: agricultural, 41–42; and
    alienation, 57–58, 65, 66; alternative
    modernities, 51; capitalism, 40, 41,
    45, 72, 78, 152, 154–55; corporate
    ranching, 47–48, 49–50, 155–56, 159;
    and cowboy culture, 51–55, 69–71;
    in tension with folklore, 78; women's
    roles, 154–57. *See also* postmodernism
Montejano, David, 40, 42, 43, 45, 54
Moore, Jacqueline M., 16–17, 50, 60–61,
    62, 64, 65, 66, 68
music: guitars, 3, 74, 118; hymns and
    sacred music, 148, 150; singing
    cowboys, 68. *See also* balladry

Native Americans, 64; Darlington Indian
    Agency, 106; ghost dances, 52
Nelson-Cisneros, Victor, xviii
New Deal policies, 115, 116
New Western history, 14–17, 151, 153,
    165
New Western History, The (Robinson), 15
No Country for Old Men (McCarthy), 146
novels, 120–23. *See also Lonesome Dove*
    (McMurtry)

O'Connor, Thomas, 34–35
oil industry, 116, 125, 159
O'Keeffe, Georgia, 155
Old West, 152, 170n22
Oring, Elliot, 110
Orth, Maureen, 136
Othering, 8, 10

Palmito Ranch battle, 44
Palo Duro Canyon, Texas, xv
Paradise (McMurtry), 158, 160, 161–62
Paredes, Américo, 1, 10, 11–14, 36, 38, 60,
    65, 105–6, 109–10
Paredes Ybarra, Leonardo, 36

patriarchal structures, 64, 66, 149, 153,
    159. *See also* gender roles
Peart, Andrew, 74, 115
Perritt, Henry H., Jr., 54
Pierson, Christopher, 41
Piñón, Fernando, 7, 8
"plain folk," 61. *See also* "poor whites";
    "white trash"
"politics of culture," 111, 113
Polynesia, 160–61, 162–63
"poor whites," 34, 61
Porterfield, Nolan, 115
postmodernism, 122, 129; "post-western,"
    163–64, 170n22. *See also* modernity
Power, James, 33, 34
prostitution, 27, 64, 70, 138–39, 149–50,
    153
Protestant values, 70, 72

race: inter-racial relationships, 9; racial
    issues, 64–65
racism: anti-Mexican, 181n10, 182–83n24;
    in Corpus Christi, Texas, 7–10; "white
    trash," 53–54
railroads, 44, 47–48, 54, 155
Ransom, John Crowe, 115
Refugio, Texas, 33–34, 36
Reilly, John M., 125–26, 137, 139, 152
Republic of Mexico, 32
Returning to Rheims (Eribon), 67
Reynolds, Clay, 129
Rhymes of the Range and Trail (Maynard),
    80
Riders of the Purple Sage (Grey), 15
Robbins, Marty, 2, 9, 22, 74, 118, 121,
    126
rodeos, 120
Rodríguez, Maribel, xvi
Rodríguez, Nestor, 27
Rogers, Roy, 120
romances, Spanish-language, 60

Romanticism, 57–58, 59; in "The Streets of Laredo," 69. *See also* cowboys

Roos, Bonnie, xv

Roosevelt, Franklin D., 115, 116

Roosevelt, Theodore, 115

Rosaldo, Renato, 160

Rosenberg, Neil V., 118

Saldívar, Rámon, 36

Salois, Sherry, xv

Sánchez, Nicolás, 46

Sandburg, Carl, 74

San Patricio, Texas, 34, 36

Sayre, Robert, 57

Scots-Irish immigrants, 29, 30, 32, 35, 39. *See also* Irish immigrants

Scott, David, 18, 52–53

Scott, Zachary, 46

Searching for America in the Streets of Laredo (Piñón), 7

Seeger, Charles, 3, 102

Seeger, Pete, 3

Seeger, Ruth, 3, 102

Sharp, Cecil J., 37

Singular Modernity, A (Jameson), 41

Siringo, Charles A., 62

slavery, 34, 52–53, 65, 160

Slowik, Michael, 103–4, 113

Snakefarm, 118

Songs from My Funeral (album), 118

Songs of the Cowboys (Thorp), 84–85, 95

Sontag, Susan, 155

Southern Agrarians, 21, 115, 116. *See also* agriculture

Spanish place names, 73–74

Specimen Days (Whitman), 59–60

Stevens, Wallace, 117

Stewart, James, 129, 135

Stoeltje, Beverly, 120

"Storyteller, The" (Benjamin), 158

Streets of Laredo (1949 film), 119, 122

Streets of Laredo (McMurtry film script), 22–23, 129–35

Streets of Laredo (McMurtry, novel), 22–23, 122, 135–36, 141–54; "Lorena" character, 142, 147–48, 150, 151–53, 155–56; women in, 148–49

Streets of Laredo (TV mini series 1995), 141

"Streets of Laredo, The" (ballad): antecedents, 24–30; contemporary renditions, 117–20; Laredo, choice of, 72–74; lento tempo, 3, 19–20, 70, 71, 74, 150; literary analysis of, 68–72; Lomax 1947 version, 69, 75, 110, 116–20; lyrics, 2–3; McMurtry's interest in, 124–25, 127; McMurtry's use of, 141–42, 148–49, 157; musical score, 4; overview and history, 1–5; spread and popularity, 68. *See also* "The Cowboy's Lament":

"structure of feeling," 58–59

Such, H. P., 29

sugar plantations, 52–53

Tate, Allen, 115

Tatum, Stephen, 15–16, 72, 75, 110

Tejanos, 171n5; conflict with Anglo populations, 35–36; and Mexican ranches, 45–46; migration toward border, 40; Texas War for Independence, 35; vaqueros and modernity, 65–66, 173n12

Terms of Endearment (McMurtry), 128

Texas: Anglos contrasted with *Tejanos*, 32–33; capitalist modernity, 49–50; ethnic identities, xiv; European settlement, 30–32, *31*; independence movement, 35; Irish immigrants, 33–34; liberal thought within, 179n32; map, *xx*; and modernity, 115–16; "peace structure" after statehood, 39–41, 42; statehood and subsequent

Texas (cont.)
   growth, 39–41; twentieth-century
   history, 123
Texas Rangers, 12, 130, 136, 151,
   174–75n3, 180n1
Texas War for Independence, 35
Thalia novels, McMurtry, 125–26. *See also*
   McMurtry, Larry
Thompson, E. P., 59
Thompson, Jerry, 43
Thoms, William, 78
Thorp, N. Howard "Jack," 20, 56–57, 58,
   73, 79, 84–86, 89, 90–94, 95–96
Tinsley, Jim Bob, 45–46, 82
Trachtenberg, Alan, 41
trail drives. *See* cattle drives
transcendentalism, 57, 58
Travolta, John, 128
Trouillot, Michel-Rolph, 73
Turner, Victor, 149

"Unfortunate Rake, The," 25, 27–29, 37–38
University of Indiana, 77
Urban Cowboy (film), 128
urbanization, 155
US–Mexico War, 35

vaqueros, 8–9, 34; open market and wages,
   49–50
Villarreal, Florencio, 42

Waco, Texas, 154–55
Wallerstein, Immanuel, 53

Walter Benjamin at the Dairy Queen
   (McMurtry), 157–58, 161–62
Wayfaring Stranger, The (album), 121
Wayne, John, 129, 135
Webb, Walter Prescott, 12–13
Webb County, Texas, 46
Weinert, F. C., 13
West, John O., 89, 93
Western American Literature (journal),
   xiv, xv
Western Folklore (periodical), 94
Western history. *See* New Western history
Western Literature Association, xiv
White, John I., 84
White, Richard, 54, 64–65, 70
"white trash," 53–54
Whitman, Walt, 59–60
Wichita, Kansas, 73
Wilgus, D. K., 74–75, 89, 93, 97, 114
Williams, Raymond, 58–59
Williams, Tennessee, 161–62
Williams, William Carlos, 164
Wister, Owen, 20–21, 79, 84–85, 94, 105
With His Pistol in His Hand (Paredes),
   11–14, 169–70n20, 169n18
Words of the Devil (Gauguin), 161

Young, John, 64
Young but Not Afraid (Bowman painting),
   xiii–xiv

Zamora, Emilio, xviii
Zattiero, Joanna Ray, 67–68